Different Strokes

Different Strokes

The Lives and Teachings of the Game's Wisest Women

— Mona Vold —

Adams Media Corporation
Holbrook, Massachusetts

Published by
Adams Media Corporation, 2001
260 Center Street, Holbrook, MA 02343. U.S.A.
www.adamsmedia.com
by arrangement with Simon & Schuster

ISBN: 1-58062-474-X

Printed in Canada.

J I H G F E D C B A

Library of Congress Cataloging-in-Publication Data
is available from the publisher.

This publication is designed to provide accurate and authoritative information with
regard to the subject matter covered. It is sold with the understanding that the publisher
is not engaged in rendering legal, accounting, or other professional advice. If legal advice
or other expert assistance is required, the services of a competent professional person
should be sought.
— From a *Declaration of Principles* jointly adopted by a Committee of the
American Bar Association and a Committee of Publishers and Associations

Cover design by Janet Perr.

Cover illustration by Chris Spollen.

This book is available at quantity discounts for bulk purchases.
For information, call 1-800-872-5627.

Acknowledgments

*T*O ALL THE WOMEN HERE—and to the greater number who are not here in ink but certainly are in spirit—those who gave me countless hours and their goodness, and often shelter and refuge, thank you.

To my agent, Malaga Baldi, and my editor, Jeff Neuman, who gave me this chance, I offer my gratitude. Without Jeff Neuman this would have been a blind shot over the bay and through the trees. His eye and thoughtful guidance under extreme conditions brought this home. To him and his assistant, Frank Scatoni, I'm very grateful.

Charley Josef, with great caring, gave me what he had though he needed it himself. I won't forget it.

My friend Laurie Blakeney, though seldom immediately present, has been with me from the beginning in every task and adventure and this one was no different. I count on her. AT&T knows it. Likewise, some years ago, to my good fortune, the Powers-That-Be put Joyce Engelson, one of the rarest of editors, in my path. She generously not only guides my work but often, with great patience, my life—my endless thanks.

The following helped one way or another and though there is much to say about each, for brevity I will only name them: Mary Beth Nienhaus (for asking the question that led to everything); Sharon Lehtinen; Norman Keifetz; Jane Gottesman; Jane Hieb; Linda Graves; Linda Gruber; Kim Westerman; Sharon Jermstad; Gordie and Harriet Hong; Stewart and Mary North; Peter and

Sarah Kuhn; Rick Witscher and Katrina Ferrebee at Airlie; Carla Sieg; Shari Inderbo; my brother, Steven (for his love, his clubs, and his children); Ron Johnson (who with tremendous skill now oversees Thistledown); the Shivas Irons Society; the USGA, the LPGA, Liz Kahn and Rhonda Glenn (whose books helped me in my research); the crew at the post office; Deb Pete; John Leadholm; Brian and Linda Anderson; my parents and family (who give me everything); Stephen Luke and Matt Vold (the Mutta Man) and Matt's cousins Tubman, Hodd, Wisdom, and John Lester; Mark Head (for taking me to the fair when it was absolutely necessary); and, of course, Leah, and my kids and my team at Thistledown. Thank you.

Goldie Bateson, Betty Hicks, Maureen Orcutt, and Dorothy Gerrard (recounting Joanne Winter) gave me a presence that traveled with me. I'll always remember.

To him who has kindly named himself my "new best friend," thank you.

To Dot Germain for pointing me in the right direction . . . to Jane Miller for glee . . . to Divine Bess for her vigil . . . to Gentle Thunder—Namaste—what could be better? To Evelyn C. White for eons, Caz, and onward . . . to Rita Speicher who at the Writer's Center in 1976 taught me the true meaning of teacher . . . to Doc and the spirit of Owen Lux . . . and to my own teacher, Matia—La Que Saba . . . thank you.

To my parents, ESTER and LESTER VOLD

Contents

Great is the mystery, not only
of Godliness, but of Golf.

—ARNOLD HAULTAIN
The Mystery of Golf, 1908

Thistledown

*I*T HAD BEEN YEARS since I'd thought of her. Owen Lux was the most beautiful woman in the world. Sunlight always played in her hair. Her eyes glistened the whole day through. Her perfume was sweet, sweet lilac. She laughed quietly, easily, often, and long. My guess is that she was then thirty-five, forty years old; my friends and I were eleven and twelve. Owen Lux could hit the ball a mile. She putted like a whiz, craved birdie and eagle above all else, and reminded us at least once or twice an hour that any-thing, everything, was possible.

I needed Owen Lux. It was the early sixties and I was wander-ing a far-flung, nine-hole course, most often alone. I came to the game when I was seven—dropped off to join ten boys and two other girls for "lessons" at the local club. I bolted from the car that day toting a makeshift bag my mother had sewn from heavy curtains. My clubs were the usual motley assortment—a cut-down Walter Hagen spoon and a burn-stained Spalding 7-iron my brother had found in the dump. My putter, a rusty Wilson "driller," was one I'd admired and gained in trade for a well-used pitchfork. I was far from country club material. In a county known for having many more cows than people, my parents sold tractors and farm equipment by day and farmed at night.

But the local course was itself far from fancy. A modest public venture, it had been laid out on 110 flat, sandy acres. A bubbling creek ran through two holes; soybeans and cornfields lined the outlying fairways, and grass waged a constant battle with burrs, fireweed, and thistle. Members affectionately called it "Thistle-down."

My teacher, "Doc," a middle-aged man, was neither a real doctor nor a club or teaching pro but someone who consistently shot par locally and had twice made a respectable run at state-amateur champion. The boys, he spent a lot of time with; the girls, he put our hands on our clubs and said only, "Reach for the stars; shoot for the moon." I did, ardently. I was strong and wild, already in love with pinball and pocketknives, and, because of the age difference between me and my brother, adept at wheeling and dealing and constantly tussling with boys even ten years older.

Though I tore at the ball with a wide, flat swing and early wrist cock, by some miracle it flew higher and farther and straighter than anyone imagined. Still, "Thattagirl!" was all Doc had for me. Thattagirl.

The next year, though, he entered the ten boys and me in a nine-hole tournament at a private club thirty miles from Thistle-down. I showed up—worn jeans, tangled hair, same bag, same clubs. But barefoot. In my excitement at getting out of town, I'd forgotten shoes. In order that I not be disqualified, one of the mothers who'd driven us loaned me hers, and, thankfully, with the laces pulled tight, I walked without tripping.

In the girls' ten-and-under division, I shot good enough for second. The host club's ten-year-old star, Courtney Montgomery, shot 54, three better. She hadn't played in my group, but I studied her afterward; everyone did. She was a lesson in grace and elegance. But for me, the day went deeper. I knew I'd been whispered about, pointed at, made fun of, and finally dubbed "Satchel" for my makeshift bag. I went home and bargained with my brother. Two weeks earlier, I'd caught him naked with his girlfriend on my parents' sofa. I'd kept quiet, but now I had my price: not owner-ship, but full use of the matched set of Spaldings and the hand-some brown bag he'd bought with his gas-station earnings.

Though I struggled in carrying them, and Doc made no refer-ence to my acquisition, I was certain I'd moved up in the golf world. Somehow wielding their excessive length, I managed the few remaining seconds that year to Courtney's firsts; the next year, she passed into an older division and I cruised. But despite the ribbons and the trophies, my brother and his friends let me know I was nothing more than small-time. At matches I walked fast after any out-of-town, honest-to-goodness teaching pro or seemingly knowledgeable parent, hopeful for counsel, but the most any of them said was, "Hi." I'm sure I had the air of a nuisance; or maybe they thought that with a flat, reckless swing like mine, once youth gave way to nervousness and fear set in I'd be finished; maybe I was just too shabby. Whatever the reason, "Thattagirl!" was what I had to drive me.

Until Owen Lux. The other girls and I wanted a girls' teacher, someone to talk to *us*. We'd wished and waited and waited, two seasons, until finally, when she didn't come, I made her up. If Doc said something down the line to Willie or Dan or Pete that I couldn't hear, Owen said it better. If Doc found a new club for Mark or Steve or Ron, Owen shined Beth's and Julie's and mine all up. Par, bogey, double, triple, whatever the score, Owen moved us on. But in my thirteenth summer, mid-season, Doc died. He'd had a Hollywood-style heart attack and was buried with his putter three days later. "Come back," I said to him in his casket, but it wasn't any use. All out-of-town trips came to a halt. Beth and Julie blended in with the kids at the soda shop; more of the boys drifted to baseball. Me, I went round and round the same nine holes, from early light on into dusk—just me and Owen Lux. Round and round and round, until late season, in Thistledown's own tournament (the last Doc had scheduled), I knew the lies so well I shot 76, many strokes clear of second. That day Courtney's father spoke to me (she'd carded 79 in her division). They were moving soon to Florida. Naples. Naples was the place to be. "Good-bye," he said. "Congratulations."

The next summer, I played only once between swimming and odd jobs—the next year, not at all. Owen Lux dwindled. The clubs were eventually sold by mistake at a yard sale.

Not until twenty-four years later did I return to it. I'd been thirteen years on the East Coast after college and had settled back in the Midwest on a two-year project when a friend sent me Michael Murphy's *Golf in the Kingdom*. Like its many readers, I was awakened. I started walking the course again where Doc had first led me. Though the grounds were much improved, fireweed and nettle having now given way to manicured fairways, it was still a rural muni track, worlds away from the championship tests of a Mission Hills or Pine Valley. With every spare moment devoted to practice, I neared scratch quickly, and I read everything— golf history, psychology, biography, philosophy, Nicklaus, Palmer, Floyd, Armour, Norman, Couples, Snead, Pelz, Penick, Jones, Hagen. The night Mayo doctors worked to save my brother from an aortal hemorrhage, it was Hogan's *Power Golf* that calmed me.

I was thrilled, sustained. I'd returned to a game I loved. All within me marveled. Yet, despite the score, I realized I knew nothing. I wanted keener eyes, better balance, top equipment, and an earthbound version of *Golf in the Kingdom*'s pro, Shivas Irons—a whimsical, wise, larger than life magical master.

In early spring, I heard of her—or at least a hint of her— through something as unlikely as a long-lost friend serving coffee and doughnuts in a church kitchen. I tell this friend I'm working to apply for LPGA teaching-pro certification and that summer am starting a program at Thistledown for juniors and women. As for my own game—I demonstrate for her, there, in front of unsuspecting devout parishioners, the place in my swing that needs serious attention. I tell her that despite shooting par, I know too little.

She says there's a woman three hours east—an old master who teaches no two people the same, an odd sort of bona fide original. "Matia Lund. Go, and tell me what you think of her."

I say I'm going to, but then I don't, and then later I do, in July.

The clerk in the pro shop stops counting change when I ask for her. "You someone she knows?" he asks, giving me a good look over.

"Not exactly."

"Well, the world's funny. Hasn't been in for 'round a month. But she's here today. Over there, the bench, below the tree." As I glance quickly where he's pointed out the window, then turn for the door, he says loudly, "But she doesn't take now but one or two lessons. And doesn't go in much for chatter."

Outside, I gather my clubs over my shoulder, rehearsing an introduction, but as I near her, my breath shortens. Time scatters, then stops. She looks at me. And I can see clearly, in just that moment, she is the very embodiment of excellence—way beyond all I ever dreamed in those years of straining to overhear Doc's wisdom. Her sun-browned hands never slow, deftly braiding the rope of a heavy canvas safari bonnet. Her long, white hair glistens; her face is a treasure map of the world. Deep eyes shining, she nods, I nod, she nods, as if we'd just parted yesterday and nothing need be said in greeting.

I sit down slowly, barely on the edge of the bench, and there we are with the birds, one loud, triumphant cry from somewhere down a fairway, and my own heart beating. Quietly I start my story. When I've finished, she dons the bonnet and walks to the range.

"You can use that swing," she says after I've hit only two 7-irons, "it's here and here you suffer." She gestures first to her forehead, then her solar plexus. "You have a bad case of the 'If onlys'—the old 'If I had wheels, I'd be a wagon.' " She looks straight at me. "Whether by neglect or intent, your man Doc did you a favor. 'Reach for the stars; shoot for the moon'? In it he gave you the thing most valuable—freedom."

She takes my 7-iron and returns it to my bag. "More," she says, walking from me as I'm thinking that we've only just gotten started, "he left you hungry. You might thank him."

When I've grabbed my clubs and run to catch up with her, "You're like a thirsty fish," she says. But beside an old station wagon, in the parking lot where I've followed, she brings out a flat, black book, finds a page, and scratches my name in.

The three hours there, three hours back—I drive it the next week, the week after, the week after that, and again until deep on into fall; the winds come, acorns clutter the greens, then sleet, then snow—she's gone with the season.

But in a month a letter comes from Michigan, and when I write to tell her I'm doing the book I've wanted—golf wisdom for women from women—a note arrives again in answer. In script uncharacteristically clear and large, Matia tells me I must not forget that "Goodness is at the heart of wisdom. The good will find you." She tells me to be led by word of mouth, to respect the unknown as well as the lauded, to listen carefully to the names repeated. Above all be mindful of Mark Twain: "I do not wish to hear about the moon from someone who has not been there." Go, she says, be bold.

I set out east, west, south, and am greeted repeatedly with generosity and kindness. "You learn so much being asked a question," the great amateur and now seventy-nine-year-old pro Betty Jameson tells me. "Everyone needs a listener—something more than a seashell. We aren't just Proettes. Our days, our swings, our games, our minds are full. We have things to tell . . ."

Poolside at opulent country clubs, distant ranges; a small apartment in Oakland, Las Cruces, Durham, Philadelphia; a Denny's in Carlsbad; the magnificent dining room at Pine Needles; a bungalow in Cupertino; a farm in North Carolina; an equipment shed in Texas; a grand house in DeLand; on and on—women who have lived and loved the game, each one. In the eyes, most often pride; sometimes sadness, sometimes longing, joy, bravery, mischief. When I leave, I am given everything, anything, at hand— photos, clippings, a prized club, a ball, shoes, a money clip, books, a trophy, clothing, an apple, a bag of tangerines, a roll of tape. None of it, I know, is really meant for me. From these women (the pioneers especially), well-respected but sought and heard from so little, the physical mementos are the mere underpinnings of more—a willingness and a goodness meant for those whom they know now they will reach.

Home, with the stacks and stacks of tapes and tapes, and books, and notes, and photocopies from archives, there's another letter from Michigan. It's a response to my having written somewhere along the way that I can tell that with the many varied voices in this collection, I must strive to make it something more than a hodgepodge. Matia doesn't bother with a greeting, right off the top she starts: "Why fear hodgepodge? Women know hodgepodge. Think of the old quilts—stitched lovingly from hodgepodge—always warm, always useful." Forget preconceived ideas.

And forget the tapes and books and notes. They're only for later, for accuracy. For now, she says, I must rely on stillness. "Sit. And pay attention to what fights its way back to you; it's that that is right and true."

As for her, she's heading farther south to a place she hasn't seen, courses she hasn't walked. "You. You must work. Make something women can count on, go back to." Don't be too technical. Remember Mrs. Castle in Podunk, Anne Crawley in Westchester, Mildred Hegg in Sauk City, Kim Sightling at River Crest, Frieda Kane in South Dakota. "Make it human. Keep it short. Easy. When you least know it, I'll be with you. May the gods speed."

And so went the journey to what follows. A book unwittingly and longingly begun those days with Doc, then furthered and guided, simply and sparingly, by a teacher finally found.

The Road
to Ellen Griffin

As a kid, when winter came to Wisconsin I was never ready. Coat and mittens—it didn't matter, I still wanted to play golf. And I worried. I wondered if those precious, fragile grasses, lost now under hard layers of brittle ice and snow, would return—or, if weakened, in spring would give way further to weeds and thistles, and, like the club I had heard about some miles up the road, Thistledown would fold.

In school I could not sit still. Nothing contained the energy I had used up and down the fairway, thicket to trees, bunker to green. Fourth grade was especially long. The teacher had long before been dubbed "The Mad Beast." Her patience was practically nil. She seemed to like to grab the back of my neck, march me to the door, and toss me into the stash of coats and hangers that lined the hall. There among the jackets of wool and soft fluff of hoods and sleeves and high, damp, rubber boots, I passed the hours. If I'd known there was a St. Andrews, imagined there was a place called Bullybunion, or a Pebble Beach or an Augusta, I might have made the mental journey. If Mary, Queen of Scots (that pinched face with strangely curled hair in the book of dead kings and generals)—if I'd had even an inkling that she'd once strode with caddies on the best links of Scotland, as crazy as me for a game that would eventually help convict her of treason, I'd have shaken her loose and taken her on. If, in those moments, I'd known that a grand band of women—the likes of Patty Berg, Betty Jameson, Mickey Wright, Peggy Kirk Bell, Louise Suggs—rode the warm Southern circuit, some of them whistling through the skies in their own planes, stop to stop, I might have wandered off. If I'd known there was an Ellen Griffin who traveled to clubs and colleges coast to coast teaching teachers to teach, I would have begged Doc to get her for us. I might even have struggled with a letter myself. But that's not the way it was. Not until thirty-some years later did I hear of Ellen Griffin.

It was during my second lesson with Matia, the teacher I'd finally found. "Who you grew to imagine, does exist," she said. "You weren't wrong to want. Ellen Griffin, I met her once." She did not tell me that I was too late, that Griffin had died at age sixty-seven in 1985, maybe because we moved so surely that day on to something else. Maybe because in understanding the legacy of Ellen Griffin, no one sees her as gone. In the letter in which Matia said, "Go. Be bold," she didn't say I should start first with Griffin, that in LPGA circles Griffin was an icon. I guess she knew I'd discover that soon enough myself.

In 1944, Ellen Griffin, with Hope Seignous and Betty Hicks, formed the Women's Professional Golf Association, the first organization of any kind for women professional golfers. They made it a point in their charter that unlike most associations in the game, this organization was open to members of any race and economic background. In 1950, when the newly formed LPGA usurped the financially struggling WPGA, Griffin held no hard feelings; she joined and was instrumental in forming the LPGA Teaching and Club Professional Division.

"I met her once," were Matia's words, but she did not paint a physical picture. She did not speak of time or place, or why or how long. She didn't mention what all others would: a small woman in a floppy hat and mismatched clothes—a deeply weathered face, a mind as big as the sun. Instead, in her letter in among a few other names (full, proper ones), Matia scribbled, "FOR GRIFFIN—Marge Burns, Greensboro, North Carolina. Ask about Farm." And, I expect, to spur me on, in handwriting barely legible, Wendell Berry: " 'It may be that when we no longer know what to do, we have come to our real work, and when we no longer know which way to go, we have begun our real journey. The mind that is not baffled is not employed. The impeded stream is the one that sings.' I think it was like this for Griffin."

With that, I read all I could, tracked down a number for Marge Burns, and headed to Greensboro.

After twenty-two hours of driving, few of them given to sleep, I'm at her door. It's early evening, she's been dozing, she says, in front of the Golf Channel. I've been told by many that Marge Burns is a fine teacher in her own right. At seventy-three, she's an LPGA Master Life Professional. She does testing of teachers at all levels, apprentice through regular Masters. In 1986, she won the LPGA Teacher of the Year award. Tall and fit, she's gentle but serious, and to the point. As a remedy for driving, she suggests a walk and I hurry to match her brisk pace. The stately old neighborhood at that hour is lazy, lovely, a soft wind tossing around late fall's leaves. "With me," she says, "what you see is what you get. I'm tee to green, tee to green. Golf is my life. That's it."

Her house is a large colonial that was passed on to her from her parents. She lives alone with two cats who a while back had charmed their way in from the neighbor's. It's a very pleasant and solitary place, with more silver than I've ever seen—bowls, trophies, platters, cups from countless amateur victories. Golf books, photos, knockers, clubs, pillows, throws, trinkets—golf everything, all tasteful and in perfect order. On this wall Patty Berg, there Ernest Jones, Vare, Whitworth. Here George Zaharias, the Babe, Peggy Kirk Bell, Betty Dodd—the whole gang.

When I assure Marge I've eaten along the way, I plop down in a soft leather chair. That quick, in my lap, is a loose stack of photos, eight-by-ten snapshots of more of the old greats. I go back to one in particular, not for the subject—full-bodied Patty Berg in a straight wool skirt, long-sleeved sweater, and cap, feet rolled, arms posed holding her finish, her own sort of solid ballerina—though that itself is a treat. But it's the background that has me. A gallery of women, all in neat woolen coats, kerchiefs tied at the chin. Each clutches a purse. Their necks are craned, eyes rolled heavenward, searching for the ball that's soared out of sight. "Look at them— fresh out of their houses. Look at that zeal," I say.

I'm comfortable now, glad to be staying the night. Two nights. There's another photo I want, and I ask if we can make a copy. It's a *New York Times* print from the North-South Championship, a much younger version of Burns standing to the back of a green holding a putter, umbrella furled, towel draped around her neck. Her competitor is in the foreground putting, hair totally dripping from the pouring rain. "I always forget you played in skirts," I say. Burns bends to look at the photo herself. "And in the rain it became a much harder task," she says. "Those skirts got so heavy at the bottom, like weights. But that was good. Extreme elements, that's what makes a player."

Watching her look at herself there, I ask, "Were you a mudder?" I've always liked this term linking a player to horses and the track.

"I was a mudder," she says, pleased.

As it becomes night she tells me of a round with Maureen Orcutt and Ernestine Page. She says that as great as the women pros are today, they still need to work more on their putting and short game. I hear for the first time then what I will hear from so many: If only today's players had seen those close-game artists—Betsy Rawls, Patty Berg, Jameson, Ruthie Jessen, the Babe, Louise Suggs, Wiffi Smith.

This is the first time I've sat with someone who played with the greats, and I realize suddenly I'm bent so far forward I'm only inches from her face. I lean back and she moves slowly into the day she was grouped with Berg and Mickey Wright:

"I was usually a mudder, but one year in Tampa I played with Mickey and Patty in the first round because I had been low amateur the year before, Mickey was the defending champion, and Patty, they put Patty there because Patty was Patty. It was the coldest, messiest day you ever saw. The wind was blowing and it was sprinkling rain, just an awful day in Florida. Well, Patty used to put her putter in front of the ball and then behind it, and the wind was blowing so hard that twice it blew the ball into her putter so she had those penalty strokes. Mickey got around to the twelfth or thirteenth hole and found out she had fifteen clubs in her bag—and that was when you got penalized for every hole you played—so she was certainly out of the money. And I got in, and Patty had been keeping my score and I didn't even look at it. I just signed my name on it and went over to the clubhouse, came back and found out she had given me a four where I had five, so I was disqualified. So there we were, what most people would imagine a dream round, me playing with both of them at the same time. Well, Mickey had a hundred and something, I was disqualified, and Patty had at least four penalty strokes tacked on. It always kind of tickles, me that 'dream round.' "

She reminds me that there are players and there are teachers. Rare times, there are players who've become teachers. I must recognize the big difference: A player knows what she knows, a teacher knows how to teach.

She's laid the LPGA guide in my lap and is tapping her finger against it, so I read: " 'The Ellen Griffin award was instituted by the LPGA Teaching and Club Professional Division in 1989 and was created in honor of Ellen Griffin, the best-known golf teacher in American history. . . .' "

"It's given only to the best of the best," she says.

"What made her so good?" I ask.

"Patience, heart, imagination. And she always had a story, and a question. She always answered a question with a question; you'll hear that again and again. I'll take you to The Farm tomorrow unless you're sick."

"Sick?" I say and wonder as quickly as my brain works if I look poorly, if Burns is aware of something I'm not. "I'm fine, I think. I'm usually fine."

"We just can't bring any colds or flu. Dot Germain, the woman Ellen left The Farm to is feeling ill. Her resistance is low. But she'll open up the Tee House tomorrow so you can see it, provided we're both okay."

"Well, I'm good," I say. But when I go to the kitchen later to pour myself some juice between reminiscences, I sneeze, not once but twice and, despite my efforts, loud enough for Burns to hear.

"Was that a sneeze?" she calls from the other room.

"Yeah, but—"

"We'll see tomorrow."

When she shows me to my room, we start talking swing. An hour later, we're still talking, her in pajamas and robe, me brushing my teeth—heel pad, right elbow, left arm, shoulders, hands, feet, hitting versus sweeping, spin, laws, principles, preferences, rhythm, balance, tempo. I dig out something from *The Mystery of Golf,* first published in 1908: "Every stroke," it says, "must be played by the mind—gravely, quietly, deliberately." I page ahead to the passage that resolves the unending debate over whether the stroke is a swing or a hit: "It is in fact a subtle combination of a swing and a hit; the 'hit' portion being deftly incorporated into the 'swing' portion just as the head of the club reaches the ball, yet without disturbing the regular rhythm of the motion." We go on with this, saying good night four, five times as we do, then start again. Finally, when my head has hit the pillow and I've shut out the light, in a few minutes I hear her from the door, her voice quiet through the dark, "We can talk and talk swing," she says. "Nine out of ten times it's in the guts. I've seen some bad swings beat people." I raise up to my elbows to join in, but she is gone. It's 1:06, and we sleep.

The next morning, we drive in her large, comfortable car, an Oldsmobile or a Buick, and I wish for a minute we'd taken my old Saab—not because the sound system's been doctored to supreme, certainly not for the air-conditioning, which is totally out of sync. Mostly because it seems I've been everywhere of importance in that car—white with its deep, custom exhaust and deep violet interior, tiny ding in the door, 104,000 miles and just breaking in— and I'd like to drive myself these last miles to a place that once meant so much to so many in the game. But it's the Buick or Oldsmobile as we turn left off US-220 into the country. Depending on Dot's energy, Burns has said, we might end up staying only five minutes and for me not to even think tape recorder. It's lucky that Dot is up even for this.

Not knowing exactly what to expect, I've left my usual interview clothes behind and dressed as I would for any farm—jeans, worn fleece jacket, aviator sunglasses, faded Ping cap. At a leafless clearing barely wide enough for a buggy, Burns slows. "Back in there is where Dot lives. A quarter mile up is The Farm."

"Could we go even slower when we get there, just to see everything?"

"There's not much now," she says. "A vague outline—the tee house, a peacock or two, her old cart. That's about it. Griffin herself was the farm."

As we roll along the gravel path, I open the car window. The place feels neither inhabited nor abandoned. The air is not phos-phorescent, and on first take there's not a shadow of anything that links it to the game until I see the tiny hand-painted sign, TEE HOUSE, hanging on a small clapboard dwelling. For a quick in-stant I imagine the whole place is smiling, showing its old but very white, friendly teeth.

Burns is out of the car and I follow her inside. Dot holds the door wide open. I judge instantly that she will be a friend: I guess she's in her mid-forties, dressed much as me, minus the aviators (which I now miraculously for once remember to remove indoors). She's tall, thin, no-frills fair, and striking. Not shy. But quiet, very quiet.

The Tee House seems to be mostly one large room and my eyes scan it as fast as they can without me seeming a thief. (Dot and I laugh later about how through that whole two and a half hours, I never ceased thinking we'd have to leave in five minutes.)

Dot lights the old oil burner. The fall day is successfully driv-ing a biting freshness along the eaves and windows. This place is exactly right, I think, filled neither with life nor absence but simple everyday remnants, mostly in the corners—a frayed driving net and battered shag bags in one; stray clubs, shoes, balls, loop film, an ancient camera on a shelf in another. I'd be horribly poor at boxing up a life I'd respected and loved; I'm glad Dot hasn't made a clear sweep. A small picture frame calls me to one side, the words traced in a heavy hand: "Here, at whatever hour you come, you will find light, and help, and human kindness . . ." Albert Schweitzer.

The burner has caught and we each sit in a straight chair near it to get the heat. This, I learn, is where Griffin had touring pros sit when they came for guidance. At small school desks all in a semi-circle Griffin sat the best in the game there among eight- and ten-year-olds, next to housewives, seniors, anyone working to get better. Here a mechanic, there a surgeon, a baker, all students of the game, none above the other—but Griffin in front, unmistak-ably, as teacher.

"We'd come to The Farm straight off the tour," Debbie Massey, two-time British Open Champion, likes to tell. "We'd be there with the rawest of beginners. We sat where she put us because that was Ellen. She was remarkable, and you couldn't help but know it.

"I'd arrive, The Farm is busy and noisy. I'd think, Where am I? What am I doing here with the cows, the guinea hens? I'd look over where Ellen was teaching outdoors and one of the barn cats would be getting too close to a lesson. Ellen, not really noticing, would just reach out with her seven-iron and gently shoo it.

"But she was a pro, and everything was much more organized than it felt. For me, that was the charm. Even the tour players, you didn't come just to hit balls. If that was your intent, she'd put you out so fast. This was a place to learn.

"One of the lessons I'll never forget. I was working on something. Working, working, and I was making one of the biggest mistakes in golf, trying to make things happen instead of just letting things happen. I'd wound myself up so tight I couldn't perform. Ellen said to me, 'Why don't you just work on being average?' I can still hear her. 'Just work on being average.' Then she laughed, and I was laughing because she was right. The twist was, she was not average. She was extraordinary, but she did a lot of average things. She loved hot dogs. She liked drinking beer."

Dot, though pale, is more than gracious. Burns gets a first few words in edgewise, but in conversation Dot and I are off to the fair. We go from Harvey Penick to Michael Murphy to her aunt the great amateur—once herself Dot Germain, now Dot Porter—to homeopathy, qigong, gardening, this player, that, then to Plato, Max Perkins, Eric Clapton's music. It's a circular path and we're always back. "To know Ellen was to be taught by her," Dot says. "She believed no moment is wasted if in this game we're open to being taught by every little thing." Dot tells me how Griffin was at the center of the think tank of the National Golf Foundation, where all the great golf minds in this country—minds like Gary Wiren, Jim Flick, Bill Strausbaugh, Conrad Rehling—gathered for week-long seminars three or four times a year, how despite the respect for her and her great well of knowledge, even in the last years when she was so sick and tired and it took much effort to move, when she'd get a notice of or invitation to even the most rudimentary of seminars, Griffin would go. Friends would say,

"But, Ellen, you wrote the text, you know all that." She'd say, "But I might hear one thing, one word might lead me to something."

"She was always looking for something in the game, some piece to something," Dot says, "even if she wasn't quite sure of the something. She welcomed the unexpected. To the end, she didn't want to miss an opportunity."

In a few hours, when we're all tired, Burns and I leave.

Two days later, I thread my way back up that first narrow path to the simple, deep world of Dot Germain. She's invited me to stay, to take more time though she's on her way out the door, just for a bit, when I arrive. Three bounding dogs offer their lapping, loyal, canine company. After Dot drives away, the four of us—Molly the waterdog, Joseph the hound, Casey a mystery mix—bask in the warm sun of the glassed-in porch. It's such a peaceable place we all drift to napping until Joseph gets up and paces and snorts. He wants in for biscuits and tea. He wants biscuits, I decide on tea. I put the kettle on and find the Milk-Bone, making myself at home as Dot said I could.

She's left some things that might be helpful to me on the table beside the large, comfortable chair. Magazine articles, books, clippings, tributes. Tea in hand, I flip quickly through, scanning, until, folded and tucked underneath them all, I find this written by Dot Germain.

A Bit of Ellen

Ellen's story begins with some of the stories she told of her childhood. She must have been one tough kid. In spite of her mother's efforts to dress her properly, she was a tomboy and would have none of the fancy things her mother was trying to make her wear. She was boxing champion of block twenty-three and even later in life bragged that she had beat up kids to make a way for her and her little brother. One day her mother took her to buy new shoes. When she took off the ones she wore, there were these socks cut out at the toe and heel, cut to look like baseball socks, and feet all covered with dust from the baseball field. Her mother, a very proper social lady, screamed. Ellen frequently embarrassed her mother.

She loved calling herself an army brat and loved the many moves her family made. Each move was an adventure and a chance to meet new friends.

I came to know Ellen in the early seventies. I was a graduate student looking for a thesis topic and was told I really should go meet Ellen Griffin. "She'll help you get a topic," my graduate advisers told me. So I went to what was called "The Farm" and was captivated by it. I was a golfer and a physical educator, and here was a person who not only had my interest, but in her casual, easy way could break away from the ordinary world and teach in this beautiful, rustic place. As a knowledgeable amateur golfer who had taken many golf lessons in her life, I was also captivated by her extraordinary expertise.

I soon became aware that I didn't want any of her many ideas. I wanted her for my thesis topic. It would be a biographical thesis written in a nontraditional form, a way suitable for her. I became one of her students. During this time she made teaching look so exciting, I asked her if she would teach me to teach. Becoming her apprentice was a young teacher's dream. As time went on, I could predict her analysis of a swing. But, I could never predict what she might say to a student. It was like a master chef cooking by feel, unable to tell how it was done. Once the ingredient of the person was added to the mechanics of the swing, there was no telling what Ellen would say.

One time she was teaching a student who thought she needed to know very detailed mechanical knowledge in order to swing. Ellen told her to drop her club and follow her. Together they walked not in a small circle but a big, winding one around the pasture. Ellen stopped and then asked the student simply, "How did you do it?" The student's mouth dropped, and then they both really laughed. That student, I think, remembers that lesson above all others.

It's impossible to think about Ellen without remembering her dress. Students throughout her fifty years of teaching have wondered about it. She believed a single string of pearls could dress up any outfit. One person told her they'd never seen so many shades of green worn at the same time. Those of us at The Farm saw unusual layers of clothing topped off by any old hat. It's no wonder that when she told me she liked the way I dressed, I became quite concerned.

Ellen was great fun to be around and the type who could philosophize over beers, but on a personal level, she was a very private person. She did not need friends for sharing wounds or personal problems. She sorted through her life alone. Her most reflective time was 5:00 A.M. when she woke to write. At that hour, I think she used nature as her sounding board and confidante, a source for answers and inspiration.

Nature at the farm was unlike anyplace I'd ever been. It was magic, pulsing with the life of all who shared it with her there. Wild birds lived in the sanctuary of two stands of bamboo. All animals, guests, family, visiting pros, and farmhands were of equal stature.

I'd join her in the early morning as the birds flew in to be fed. It felt more like a ritual than a feeding. There was Cushing the cardinal, and Mock, and many others. Many knew Ellen personally, flocking all around her feet. The peacocks fed, too. Carol and Mann were the first of them in line. And then came the ducks, guinea hens, and chickens.

I have thought how the transition from the University of North Carolina, Greensboro, to the farm says so much about her. She'd taught physical education there for so many years, but she left the university without another job or retirement benefits. She told friends she didn't believe in retirement. She would create her own way. If worse came to worst, she would find a room in the county home, preferably a corner room with a lot of windows.

I'm sure many people thought she was nuts leaving in the way she did. But she trusted that whatever happened in the future would be right for her. Within a year she knew she missed teaching, and the idea of teaching golfers on a farm was born.

Friends like to say how she thrived on the challenge of insecurity. Her focus was outside the internal realm of personal problems and issues such as personal safety, and on the excitement of dreams and ideas. The way she lived her life is what brought vitality to her: Live in the insecurity of the unknown. Let go of the past.

She wrote a verse about faith: "To wonder why is useless. To know it happened and to believe that it will ever be so is important—never knowing when, but knowing, believing that it will—faith, faith, faith . . ."

Through this faith, she did not fail life. Never was this more evident than in her last few years. After her first stroke, when her brother, a doctor, told her, as she was just coming back into consciousness, that she had had a stroke, her first words were, "Did you count it?" After a second stroke, which left her speechless for months, she decided it was time to take Spanish lessons. Later, during months

in which she was fed through a tube, she read gourmet food magazines. I asked her how she handled it and her answer was very simple:
"Keep your focus on what you want." A picture of the farm and
teaching stayed in her mind. Another time while taking care of her, I
asked her one too many times how she felt. She snapped back, asking
me how in the world I thought she could get well if I kept asking her
how she felt.

The final inspiration came days before her last surgery. She called
Debbie Massey and me to her hospital bedside, but not for final good-
byes. There was no time for that. We were to take notes on the future
of education in golf. For several days we obediently took our yellow
pads to the hospital, taking pages of notes. But as clear and simple as
her instruction seemed, Debbie and I were not always certain of
the meaning. To Ellen there was a mysterious side. She would not give
the answer to larger questions nor would her striking, mischievous
blue eyes give up the thoughts that shone in them. It was for us to discover what her words meant and to learn to ask better questions.
Maybe that's the object of a great teacher. But the message of her life
is clear. When I think of Ellen, I think of things like faith, living life
with joy, and above all, touching base with the voice that tells you
what to do.

When I'm through reading, Joseph rests his head on my knee.
When Dot returns, he begs another bone and we have more tea,
Dot lying on the sofa, me not far away in the large, comfortable
chair. She tells me Griffin always said that the most important
thing in golf is connecting what is here inside (at this she spreads
one hand over her torso) to what is out there, the target. "When I
read golf instruction," she tells me, "I can't breathe. Because
there's nothing in it that's alive."

Through the next days we talk often of Griffin. I go through
books and letters and notebooks. Dot points me in many directions. A qigong master comes by; he holds gatherings now at the
Tee House for a few hours every Saturday. I don't touch a tape
recorder—the healthy food, a distant rooster, the brave squirrels
and birds, Dot's own brilliance—this seems to be a sanctuary. I
just try to absorb everything and keep it alive—my "one for the
road" on what we both agree will be, though interesting, a long
and varied journey.

The night before I leave I ask if I might drive the next morning to The Farm for a few minutes. "I'd like to see it once more, alone, in the quiet," I say. She says, "Of course."

It's a foggy 5:00 A.M., a light mist. Where the driving range once was I stand on a slight rise trying to rouse the farm to life. I try to see Griffin clearing the heavy fieldstones away by hand, digging in the deep Carolina clay, riding the old tractor and slowly sowing the right grass. Over here, the busy putting green dotted with balls. Over there, a bunker with traitorous lips. There a mound with grass so hardy and fat it glistens.

"Before the farm was The Farm," celebrated teaching pro DeDe Owens remembers, "I'd stop out and Ellen would be so excited. She'd point high in the air, she'd say, 'See the range—over there. See the green—over there. See the bunkers. Over there. Over there.' I'd look, and follow her hand. It was all real to her though nothing yet had begun to take shape."

As I stand, the farm recedes—the bunkers sink back to scattered patches of sand, the green to scruffs of coarse grass, the noise to quiet—and I am the only one here. But there are the words, Diane Glancy's: "There's the sky and the ground with nothing between them but a landscape of stories you can hear if you hold your ear to the wind to the land."

I gather up a bit of the sand, a small snatch of grass, and carry it with me, and let it fall slowly into the cup in my car. Driving out, careful of the lone peacock, I remember my knowing, without really knowing why, how important it was for me to get here. In the often exclusionary, phony upper-crust world of golf, Griffin— at home in floppy hat, green plaids, and when called for, her single strand of pearls—to her students, was teacher, adventurer, friend. "Some people deliver lectures, sermons, or speeches," she wrote, "but the ones you remember are those who deliver themselves." Taking her with me, I speed on to find the others.

Annette Thompson

AT A GAS STATION somewhere between Ellen Griffin's farm in central North Carolina and Savannah, Georgia, the Saab pops a radiator hose. A large cloud of smoke billows out from under the hood and I watch wide-eyed as beautiful sea-green coolant gushes out onto the parking lot. When I see that the problem is smaller than it looks, I catch a ride to a nearby auto parts store, jimmy on not quite the right hose (it's tough finding Saab parts in small Southern towns), and in less than an hour I'm back on the road. But the incident nicks my usual faith in the Saab, so when the two of us enter the long, palm-lined drive into Ballen Isles Country Club, I implore her to behave, not to even think of making a spectacle on these rich, flowered grounds.

Ballen Isles is a grand place. There are four towering entrances to the sprawling stone clubhouse. Built in the late sixties as home of the PGA, it was that until the early seventies when the association and investors parted ways. Since then it has become an equity member-owned enterprise. Residential. Posh.

Inside the main clubhouse there are at least ten lush carpeted ways to go. I'm early, so I head to the ladies' room, something I've started to make a practice of. Truth be told, I like to rest for a few minutes in the women's lounge, sprawl on one of the usually finely upholstered Victorian divans, and listen and watch the members scurry about. The inevitable floral decors I can do without, but the wall-length mirrors and amenities in the dressing rooms I've grown accustomed to.

From the lounge I follow another corridor to the well-stocked pro shop, where I poke through their selection of clothes and clubs and shoes. When I've had my fill, I announce my presence to the starter and tell him I'll wait on the veranda.

"You don't wear lipstick," a woman who I guess to be in her early eighties says to me. Whatever her age, it is clear she is trying to defy it with her thick makeup and younger-set clothes. She fumbles trying to pull a cigarette from its diamond-clasped case.

"Lipstick? No, I don't wear lipstick," I say softly back to her.

"Well, I wish I didn't have to, but my husband died. Now I have to find another one if I'm going to stay on in this club."

I immediately think of Marcia Chambers's fine book, *The Unplayable Lie,* which chronicles the woes of women in these private clubs, but I don't ask the particulars of this woman's predicament; instead, I go a different route.

"Do you know Annette Thompson?"

"Annette! Oh, Annette, she's a firestorm, like a burning arrow. Sweet, though. She's the swing savior around here, that's what my friends are always talking about. You could just eat her up."

"Does she wear lipstick?"

"What?" the woman says.

"Annette, does she wear lipstick?"

"Oh no, like you, she doesn't have to. Our generation, we never quite got to ourselves, we have to doll up." She flicks her lighter. "I'm lonesome."

"Does your golf help?" I say.

"Well, I think it would, but I don't play. I play bridge. But golf, I think I'm going to take golf up."

"Yeah, forget the lipstick, though it's nice on you. Get Annette and take up golf."

"Men like a woman who can hit a ball, right?"

"And you might like it yourself."

"That's a thought," she says, and taking one long breath, snubs out the newly lit cigarette. Immediately she's off, but she turns before the door inside and says, "What's your name?"

"Oh," I say, and I don't know why I don't give my name. "Just passing through."

"I like that," she says, " 'Just passing through.' "

Before I can take that up, a lean, very tan woman in fine clothes hurries up and puts out her hand. "Annette Thompson," she says. She's three hundred miles a minute but with focus, and we're off. She knows where we're going and just where we'll sit, down the corridor, around the bend, to another remote Victorian divan where out of every window are long, green views of perfect grass.

I'm guessing she's in her late forties, young for all her accomplishments: LPGA Master Professional; LPGA Teacher of the Year in 1985; national president of the LPGA Teaching and Club Division for four years; first "Master Teacher of Golf" for the Ellen Griffin Endowment; director of education for the National Golf Foundation; "teacher's teacher" and clinician in Japan; teaching professional at Ballen Isles since 1984; instructor at Vassar and Smith colleges and assistant professor and women's golf coach at Penn State University; member of the advisory panel for Titleist and FootJoy worldwide; contributing writer for *Golf for Women, Golf Digest, Senior Golfer, Tee Time, Women's Golf League,* and *Golf and Travel Northwest.* In addition to having written, edited, and coauthored more than a dozen books, including *Jack Grout's Golf Clinic,* the last book written by Jack Nicklaus's teacher, she's also created four major golf instructional videos and the audiotape *Women's Golf: The Mental Game.*

She was born in Pinehurst, North Carolina, a resort mecca for golfers who came down from the north in the winter. A few local full-time residents played the game, but Thompson was not born into one of the few families who did.

"It seemed," she says, "there were only two things that really worked in sand hills—golf and tobacco farming. I grew up on a tobacco farm and it really didn't take a smart person to realize that the golfers were having more fun. But I learned from the work. On a family farm, if it had to be done, you did it. Farming is the first great bastion of feminine equality. There are no men's jobs. There are no women's jobs. Just jobs. And if you're big enough, you can do it. Which was probably not a bad way to grow up."

It was Thompson, her brother, her mother, and her father on

275 acres. "In the middle of summer it was not unusual to get up at three in the morning to remove the cured tobacco from the barn, then harvest the entire barnful, then go and reset your irrigation and pick melons, then go to bed about eight o'clock and do the same thing the next day. I'm not trying to sound like Abraham Lincoln," she says. "Every kid in the neighborhood did that. You didn't know anything else."

She takes an unusual pause, then starts again. "On a farm you learn a whole lot about life, fast. I can remember some of my friends from college would go out to work with me in the field and before long they'd say, 'Okay, how long are we going to do this job?' I'd look at them in disbelief. It might be a twenty-acre field and we're on the first row and they're going, 'How long are we going to do this?' I'd say, 'Well, until it's finished.' 'Well, when will that be?' I'd say, 'It might be four or five days, but until we're finished.' It wasn't a question of how long, it was how long does it take because once that field was picked there was another one."

She is smiling, happy. "It's kind of like the Quaker thing," she says.

"You mean 'Labor is prayer'?" I ask.

"Exactly. It was very meditative. And sometimes I daydreamed. That's why, when I came to golf, I never thought the game was hard. When people get so frustrated, I can say, 'Come on, golf is not hard. Tobacco farming is hard,' and we laugh because certainly none of them would like to be there.

"And farming taught me something more about golf because farming is not fair. You can raise a crop and in a matter of minutes it can be destroyed. One of my most vivid recollections is the day before we were to begin harvesting when we had a fifteen-minute hailstorm and the entire crop, everything we'd sweated over, was wiped away. After that, golf, an odd bounce, a lipped putt, while in the moment it can be devastating, it wasn't anything like that day we lost a season's worth of work.

"Most of us have a real warped idea of the amount of control we have over anything. It's not that we can't control certain aspects of this game, it's that we think we can control everything. That's where our error is. Then God says, 'Wait a minute, just so you don't forget . . .' A fleck of grass throws a putt off-line, the ball is stuck in a tree or shoots this way or that. The elements, variables, the unexpected. That's golf. That's farming."

Thompson didn't learn to play until age twenty, when she was in college at the University of North Carolina, Greensboro. "In my hometown, dates were pretty much limited to the movies or the bowling alley, or the driving range. That was about it for entertainment," she says, "so I would hit balls with my friends sometimes and I found it intriguing. I asked my parents for a set of clubs and they got me a set of Patty Bergs from Sears. I went back up there to UNC-G and I stuck that ball on the first tee and I played golf. I didn't have a clue as to what I was doing. I started late and without instruction so I developed and repeated a flawed swing. Eventually Ellen Griffin—I didn't have her for a golf class but I knew her from another class—would come out in the late afternoon and watch me swing. 'Go ahead and loop it at the top,' she'd tell me. 'Don't tell anybody I said that, though. But you can't hit it unless you loop it, so go ahead.'

"I wasn't a physical education major to start with. I was an English major, but I wound up getting counseling from Ellen about switching majors, and she taught me more about teaching in general. I remember her saying, 'If you can get beyond the fact that we're not teaching you to do, we're teaching you to teach, you'll be okay.' She was big on teaching people, not golf. Later, she left the university to go to work for the National Golf Foundation as director of golf education. When I followed in that job I said to her, 'First I was behaving myself as an English major and you got me into phys. ed., then you got me into golf. The first job I had at Vassar College, you recommended me. Now you have me in the NGF. Why am I following you around?' And she said, 'I'm not responsible for all the things that go wrong in your life.' She had a wonderful sense about her, and I find that voice coming back in much of what I do."

Like the teacher I once imagined, Thompson laughs often. Her self-assurance is evident in the ease with which she moves, and this becomes her because there is no trace of arrogance, nothing haughty or verbose. "My biggest regret is that I didn't come to golf and get formal instruction early on." Though she plays well enough to have met the LPGA's handicap requirement of 10 or less, and she easily passed their playing ability test, which requires shooting 85 or less on a championship course, her game and her swing are not what she'd wish: "My biggest personal demons are that I'm not a very good player. I don't have a picturesque swing. Therefore, deep down resides the thought, Why do I have the right to teach? It's maybe like someone who's unusually short growing up in a family of very tall people—although you may suddenly grow and out-tall everyone, those first feelings stay with you."

But Thompson has no regrets, and learning golf as an adult has had its advantages in teaching. "In everything, every step of the way, I can empathize. It's the old 'Been there, done that.' Learning anything new, I know firsthand what my students are going through."

"The tobacco kid with a loop," I say.

"Right. Exactly."

Through the next few hours my head swirls with her expertise and I see clearly why tour players, scholarship athletes, hopefuls for LPGA qualifying school, beginners, and locals of all levels flock to her. She is what the woman on the veranda suggested, a full quiver of sharp arrows. She is a searing, competent master, the very best of what she never had herself.

Life's Load

Let me tell you what golf is and what golf isn't. Golf is a game about seeking perfection; it is not a game of perfection. It's a game of doing the very best you can in this moment. It's here and now.

Why do you sometimes see even a pro blow up during her last nine holes? It's because she senses the end is near, she's running out of holes. You may see her have a double bogey on the third hole and get right back, make four birdies, and make the turn at two under par. But if that same player has a double bogey on hole fourteen, she'll have a double bogey on fifteen, bogey on sixteen. Why? Because everything in her feels it—the end is near, she has less time to make it up. She gets out of living in the present and jumps ahead and tries to juggle all the parts together, and it can't be done.

There's a wonderful Japanese phrase I like to use that says, "A bridge was not built to take its life's load all in one day." What we often try to do is pack the needs of a whole round into a very small set of circumstances. "On this hole maybe I can . . . I really need a . . . Next hole I gotta . . . Then maybe . . ." I needa, I gotta, I needa—well, the Needas and the Gottas can't play golf. They self-destruct.

Remember this: A single bridge. A moment's load. Here and now.

Chocolate

Golf is unpredictable. No matter who you are, no matter how good you are, how consistent you are, how well you have been playing, how well you have the potential to play, the golf game is inconsistent. Long stick, small surface, round ball, fast swing, inconsistency written all over it. That's the inherent allure. The paradox is that everyone is working to take the allure away because they want to get more consistent. And when they do get more consistent, they want to be even more consistent. Everyone says, "What is it about golf? What is it?"

It's very simple. The most persuasive motivation you can use on an animal or a human is *intermittent reward*. If I want you to do something, I say to you, "Okay, do it, I'll give you a piece of chocolate." You do it and do it, and I give you the chocolate and give you the chocolate, and pretty soon you get sick and tired of chocolate and you don't want to do it anymore. But what happens if I say to you, "I know you love chocolate, so do this, and I'll give you chocolate," and you do it the first time, and I give you just a bit of chocolate, yummm, but the second time you don't get any chocolate, or the third time, or the fourth, so you say, "Well, if you don't give me chocolate this time, I won't do it anymore," and sure enough, the fifth time, chocolate appears. And the sixth time, and the seventh, you get chocolate again—"Oh, boy, I get chocolate again now"—then you don't get it again until the twelfth time. You will keep performing this task longer for that kind of reward—intermittent reward—than either getting it every time or never getting it. That's what golf is. That's the reason slot machines work. Same principle—you never know when you're going to win. And each time you think you're going to win. It's the old truth: There's always hope on the first tee.

"O Holy Night"

If you're good, you make your craft look effortless. In the holiday season, on television on PBS, every year, here's the symphony, and here's some soprano. The names change, but it's always the same, and she's singing "O Holy Night." And she's singing with a range of three or four or eight octaves, and there's no strain. There are no tendons or ligaments straining. There's no perspiration. She's just standing there doing it, and I say, "How long do you think she trained in voice lessons and what is inside her to make a range of three or four octaves seem effortless?" This is exactly why members come up to me and say of the LPGA players I work with, "It doesn't even look like she's swinging hard." I say, "Well, it's only an ounce-and-a-half ball, doesn't seem as if you have to swing that hard to move it." That player is swinging efficiently, and that's why it doesn't look as if she's working hard; she doesn't have any loose motion. Most recreational golfers have a lot of loose motion and that's why it's hard work, and that's why it's difficult, and that's why they get injured, and that's why they miss the golf ball.

Polish

What is a good swing? Some will say, "One that looks really good." Others will say, "One that hits the ball far and straight." "One with crispness." "One with fluidity and beautiful rhythm." Still others will say, "One that doesn't hurt the body." A good swing is different for different people. But some people will never believe they have a good swing because they're seeking the answer to hitting the ball better purely by an improved swing. The answer to hitting the ball better is by accepting an adequate swing, because once I accept an adequate swing, then I can polish it. Once I accept that I have a diamond and no longer a lump of coal, I am on my way. But most of us stand there with a pick and a hammer trying to polish a diamond.

Many good players have been ruined not by instruction but over-instruction. Once we have a diamond, we need to get a hold on self-acceptance. Most often there's a certain amount that has to be done, but we tend to overdo. We assume that if this is not perfect, what we need is a hammer and a chisel when maybe all we need to do is accept that this swing isn't perfect but it's a seven or an eight, and let's see what we can do to polish it to get it up to being a ten more often, understanding that we can use an eight all day. Now we need to be a nine or a ten putter, but we can use an eight swing. We too often forget that diamonds are polished, not hammered to brilliance.

RBU

This game is not hard if you think you can control a two-inch angled surface hitting a one-and-a-half-inch round ball on the end of a thirty-six- to forty-five-inch stick traveling at somewhere up to one hundred miles an hour. If you think that's easy, then the game is easy. What we have done as humans is make the game complex in order to explain why it's difficult because we don't accept simple things as being difficult. Walking a tightrope is an extremely simple concept: Put your left foot in front of the other. Stay in balance. Don't fall off. Simple. So is golf. Simple concept. And because of that concept people expect too much of themselves. They don't understand sweat equity when it comes to golf. The average golfer who practices ten hours a month does not deserve to be upset with herself. The tour player practices eight hours a day. When you do that, you can begin to start to think about being upset with yourself.

Golf is one of the few activities where we confuse perfect with good. The only golf shot you the golfer are happy with is the perfect one because that's the one that sounds good, feels good, is hit clean. I say, "Good, that was perfect. You can expect three of those today—three to seven perfect shots in a round of golf, relatively speaking, anyone from an intermediate to a tour player. That's what you can expect. About one or two an hour. That's perfect. The rest of the time you have to recognize what is good."

As a teacher I have to spend a lot of time helping people determine what is good. On a scale of one to ten, I ask, "What is that?" It may seem a two to you, but no, it isn't. In golf, that is a four or a six. You're playing golf, you're not playing you! You're playing a game.

Tim Gallwey's statement, "I want you to tell me how to play my game," is key in teaching. I spend time on the range helping people determine what's good for them. If you hit a shot imperfectly, but you hit it and it gets there and you don't lose a stroke, accept it. Always work for perfect but accept good. It's like this: From my home to the course, there are six roads I can take. I need to be here at 8:00 A.M. But as long as I arrive on time, it doesn't matter which road I take. As long as I'm here on time, you don't have to like it. It's like this: You are the golf hole, I am the golf ball. Now, I may not want to go all the way over to the beach. I want to go down Military Trail, but sometimes when I hit that ball, Military Trail is not what I end up driving along. I end up hitting the tree, going through the bunkers, and running up onto the green. I call it "RBU": Rotten but useful. Beginners have them. Pros have them. We all have them. We have to learn what good is.

Expect perfect. Accept good. Enjoy the rotten but usefuls.

Say It, See It

My tour players, I have them verbalize because if you verbalize, you visualize. If they're not hitting the ball well off the tee, I'll have them stand up there and tell the caddie out loud exactly where they're aiming. This does two things: It relieves some of the pressure, and you begin to visualize more deeply. The picture is etched more clearly and takes on a life of its own. If you're standing up there, all inside your head and trying to manipulate the ball to go somewhere, I want you out of that manipulative swing thought. I want you out *here*. I want you to see it—up, up over that tree over there. Say it. See it. Out loud. Verbalize to visualize. When you're having trouble, make your plans for the shot known to the world.

Sunday

I tell my tour players this: The only way to learn to play on Sunday is to play on Sunday. Playing on Thursday is not playing on Sunday. It has everything to do with conditions. The last nine holes on Sunday is a different condition pattern than the first nine holes on Thursday. I don't care how many tournaments you've played in.

Think about this: I'm holding a million-dollar check. I say, "This check is going into escrow. I will let you have it if, in six weeks when I come back, the two-by-four that I've just laid down here the length of that hole—if you can walk on it, I'll give you one million dollars."

Now that seems like a good deal. Put your left foot in front of your right, stay in balance, don't fall off. That's it. So you cancel all your work, and you walk for six weeks, you practice, and I come back, and I say, "Are you ready?" And you say, "I'm ready." And I say, "Good, let's go," and I pick up the two-by-four and you say, "What do you mean, 'let's go'?" And I say, "Oh, I forgot to tell you, the two-by-four's going to be between two twelve-story buildings."

Your eyes get the size of half dollars.

And why? I didn't change the task at all. What I changed were the conditions under which I expect you to perform. Now, tell me, who's at her best with her eyes the size of half dollars? The only way to learn to play on Sunday is to play on Sunday.

Them

There are so many personalities, and in golf we don't leave our personalities in the clubhouse. We play the way we are. We compete the way we are. Who we truly are, not what we've cultivated. To be really fine, we must know and accept and work with who we truly are. It's the Chuck Hogan line: "We can never play for them." We don't have to say who "them" is—them could be our partners, our husbands, parents, coaches, press, friends, whomever. In competitive golf—and I think to be really successful in anything—we must play for ourselves. Because the them is never happy, because if we win once they want us to win twice, if we win twice they want us to win three times, if we win three times they want us to be rookie of the year, if we're rookie of the year they want to know why we don't have the same season next year, if we have the same season next year they want to know why we're not in the Hall of Fame, if we're in the Hall of Fame they want to know why we're not still playing. This is the way life is.

That's why people are sometimes more comfortable as "losers" than they are as winners. I call it the litany of our discontent; we can sort of spew out reasons for why we didn't win or we didn't do whatever it was—play as well as we should—so we get very, very skilled at explaining why we didn't win. . . . "I could have done better but this happened and this and dahdedahdedahhhhh." We get so skilled at it that we don't even mind anymore. It's momentarily painful but we know how to do it, we know how to handle it because we practice handling it. We know how to explain it away.

But when we win, now we have to explain how we won and we risk rejection because everyone who didn't win might not like it. And what about next week—we're expected to win again. This is the way life is. That's why I have those who think they want to be champions do so much work on the inside. I tell them, "You have to know how to win physically, with skill, you have to know how to win mentally, with focus and intellect, and you have to know how to win emotionally, and that means being strong enough to think of yourself and to accept yourself as a winner with no attention to 'them.' " Because until I get it somewhere in here, in the heart, that I'm a winner, I may win in spite of myself but I won't become a winner. I'll join the flash in the pans—won once and never heard from again.

The Zen of It

Yes, there's the Zen of it. But I don't call it that, I call it the old "Hit it, go find it," which implies that kind of nonattachment. Simple. You just try to keep yourself in the here and now and centered, which is finally: "IT'S A GOLF SHOT. HIT IT, GO FIND IT." Arnold Palmer used to say that. Hit it, go find it, hit it, go find it, be able to putt. That's not a bad way to play. That's one of the reasons Palmer and JoAnne Carner were such immediately popular players when they came on the scene, because they had that ability to play with abandon, not to go through a lot of controlling. They hit it and went and found it. Carner said the reason she was such a gallery favorite was because she spent so much time on the other side of the ropes looking for her ball. They both had the ability to stand up there and swing and then go find it without seeming to labor over keeping it in control. They seemed to let it fly and not have so much attachment to it. That's one of the reasons they so endeared themselves to galleries, because we all long for that. And mastery of the short game.

When you can putt, it's much easier to trust the old "Hit it—it'll come down somewhere." If only we could move ourselves to the great freedom and fun in that.

Two Things

People don't understand two things: You have to learn to putt the ball and then you have to learn to make putts.

People think they're the same thing, when one is technique and one is the use of the technique. Learning to putt the ball is simply the mechanics, in the same way that you learn to drive a car so you can go places, not for the sake of learning to drive a car. Going to the market you don't think, Okay, now I'm going to use the skill of driving the car. You simply go to the market.

What happens when people try to learn to do the mechanics of putting while trying to make putts? One part of the brain is being told that this must go in no matter what, which is the objective of putting, and another part of the brain is saying, "The putter's lined up wrong, watch your hands, take it back straight, not so fast." There's a cacophony going on. If the club is coming through wrong and it happens, as it sometimes does, that the ball rolls in in spite of yourself, at the expense of proper mechanics, you'll develop a habit that can work only under certain circumstances. When conditions change, when there's more pressure or you're on a green that's faster or has more breaks, then the inefficient mechanics you've been able to use under certain conditions will no longer hold up. You'll be off.

Learning to putt is learning to use the mechanics under all conditions and learning to read and to sense the feel of how much a putt is going to break, the speed of the green, the grain, all these things. There are often tour or scratch players who are very good putters naturally and nobody ever interrupts them and they just continue. But the one thing that happens if your mechanics aren't good, no matter at what level, is that they will break down under certain conditions. So learning to putt is the learning of solid mechanics. Learning to make the putt is learning to use those mechanics under varied conditions. The player who is skilled in technique is going to spend most of his or her time evaluating a shot on the green, reading the nuances, not thinking about the mechanics of how she's going to roll the ball because she's already learned that, much in the same way she's already learned how to hit a 7-iron. The decision is, Is it a 7-iron or an 8-iron? not How do I hit a 7-iron? It's the same with making putts.

What happens is that a lot of people stay in "putting stroke" the same way they stay in How do I hit a 7-iron? and forget to play a 7-iron shot. That's very common. Too many people play golf swing, not golf.

Get on with It

You're never going to get down to be a single-digit handicap unless you get one stroke below where you are now. That's the first step. The lower you go, the harder the strokes come off. The other thing to understand is that the game is not predictable, it is intermittent. You have to learn to accept that, learn how to play bad golf shots because when you've hit it poorly, you need to know how to move on and be committed to the next shot at hand. Someone said to Davis Love III: "You came on tour with potential and you didn't materialize right away. What did you do to start to play to your potential?" He said, "I'll tell you. It's down to one thing. I used to hit a bad shot and I'd walk to that bad shot talking about how bad it was. 'If you're such a good golfer, if you're that good, you wouldn't have hit that shot,' I'd tell myself. Then I'd arrive at the bad shot. It was in trouble, and I had no idea how to get it out of trouble. I hadn't thought about it until I got there so I'd have to rush myself and more than likely I might hit a poor second shot, too. Once I learned to say, 'Okay, it's all right, you're a good enough player to get it out of there, let's go see what we can do about it,' things changed. I'd spend the time walking to that ball planning how to get out of that situation. Snap! I turned my game around."

I can't tell you the number of people who don't understand that simplicity. Of course you can't just be a Pollyanna and be positive all the time. You can be upset about hitting the shot, but I'll give you about twenty seconds to do that. Now, get on with life . . .

Success

Golf. All it is, is golf. A 64, 69, 72, 76, 84, 108, or a 118. It's not good or bad; it's just golf. It's just there, and that is what I relish. I rel-

ish the opportunity the game gives me to try to beat me. I'm not trying to beat you, I'm trying to beat me, trying to beat *it*. I'm trying to
solve the problem, the opportunity of what this golf shot gives me,
what this hole, what this day gives me. That's success.

Gloria Armstrong

IT'S DECEMBER IN OAKLAND, cool and rainy. Gloria Armstrong has well over ninety students but they're preparing for Christmas now, and with that and the weather, the lessons are few. In a small apartment at the top of a hill, she spends weekdays at her computer, traveling the Internet, designing the single Christmas card she'll send to students and friends. Weekends, she'll watch the women pros through the waning days of the present season play the JCPenney Classic, the Diners Club Matches, Wendy's Three-Tour Challenge. She tapes each day of every stop, searching and analyzing each swing.

"Gloria Armstrong is one of the most generous souls in golf." I'd heard that many times, and her melodic voice on the phone led me to expect to be welcomed, but I hadn't imagined the genuine warmth. At sixty-eight, she's a little heavier now than in her playing days, but that only adds to the feeling that, even as a stranger, I'm loosely wrapped in her intelligent care.

As a player she never dreamed of the Hall of Fame. On a tour that at the time paid its weekly winner $1,000, she fought to come away with last-place prize money. There was no trust fund, no family money to help her along. Her father was a linotype operator for *The Oakland Tribune,* her mother learned to fly and joined the WASPS and ferried planes all through World War II. The two divorced before her mother left for the European theater. Armstrong was eleven. She saw her father sporadically, on weekends, and spent a lot of time helping out on a relative's farm until the war ended and her mother came home.

"She went to work for Lynn's Ballroom in downtown Oakland as a secretary and a pilot," says Armstrong. "The owner bought a Stagger Wing Beechcraft, and I used to fly with her. But one weekend when I was supposed to go with her, she called and said, 'You can't go with me because Mr. Lynn's invited a whole bunch of people. They're going up to a wedding and I'm flying them. It's a full load. There won't be room for you.' It was just as well because over Buchanan Field the plane caught fire and they were all killed."

Gloria was sixteen. "From then on I was a great believer in things being 'meant to be,' " she says. "I was alive and I might not have been."

While her mother was flying transports over Europe, Gloria's father led her to golf. "When my parents divorced, Dad and I started to play. I think he thought it would help me, and it was a way for us to be together. Even though we had to be separated during the week when he worked, I was fortunate to have a father like him because he wanted me to do everything at a time when most women were restrained. He didn't have a lot, and what he could have had for himself he sacrificed for me. He also loved flying. We both did. Even though my mother was killed that way, I got my license when I was seventeen."

Armstrong developed her game on public courses and without a teacher, but soon became one of California's premier players. Even so, in 1954 when she wanted to play in the state amateur championship, she couldn't because she didn't belong to a country club. "It was one of the ways they kept blacks and those like me without much money out. Dad said, 'You can join Richmond Country Club. I can help with that, but that's it. You won't be able to do anything else. Or I can take you for two weeks and you can play the tour down in New Orleans and Beaumont, Texas.' "

Armstrong chose the tour. "I was a nervous young lady. I didn't know anyone or what it was all about; I only knew that I wanted it. My game must not have been real good or real bad that first stop, because the only thing I remember about the whole trip is that it got hot and I had my caddie put his coat in the trunk of our car and people around were laughing because you didn't do that with a black person in the South at that time. Coming from California, I didn't know about that and I wouldn't have abided by it even if I had. Same with the cups at the water buckets: COL-ORED, WHITE. I saw no reason not to just use the one I happened to grab and I did."

She turned pro the next year. "Back then, Bonnie Randolf and I used to play every week for that last hundred dollars. There were twelve of us out there and eleven places. A hundred dollars meant I could go to the next two tournaments."

Winters, she had a job putting bikes together at Montgomery Ward; another year, selling airplane parts at Air Parts, Inc. Without the funds to practice in warm-weather resorts, she took whatever was necessary to go on, and in the spring when the tour began again she hauled a small trailer stop to stop, 7,000 miles through the season. Sometimes she took in sewing, working late into the night, with often only three or four hours between the stitching and the tee times the next morning. And she also gambled—small stakes at cards, low-wager Nassaus. "People always told me I had a good swing; I never thought I did. But I must have to have stayed out there that long doing it as I did. All those miles, especially doing all the driving [others sometimes hired her to drive the whole distance so they didn't have to], I'd get to the course and my hands would be vibrating. I couldn't feel much for days but that steering wheel, and I was a feel player. I'm not one for 'what-ifs,' but sometimes I just wonder if I'd been able to feel I might not have done better. I know I wouldn't want any player I was working with doing that and then playing a tournament."

There is nothing of excuse or regret, only clear curiosity. Her eyes move with a luminous intelligence. I could listen way into Christmas if she'd let me. The scrapbooks are out, and the old, now rare magazines—early copies of *The Lady Golfer* and *Golf World*—so well cared for, truly in mint condition. We talk and talk because she is still as fresh and gone on the game as I am, even now, at sixty-eight.

Because a good friend of mine lives in this town, I've heard some of the local legends about Armstrong. If a student of hers hasn't practiced, she won't give them their next lesson, regardless of the money. She has taken average local players, men and women, and moved handicaps from a 27 to an 11, from a 19 to an 8. One man passing through heard of her and offered three times her usual rate if she'd see him between his flights; she refused, because she was volunteering, instructing kids at the course's academy and she wouldn't leave them to assistants. And the favorite: the very flashy guy who showed up with all the best equipment, arrogant, show-offy, who cursed every shot and the game. Near the end of the session, she reached in her pocket and handed him back his money, saying simply, "Stick with sailing or your water polo, something you enjoy." When I ask her if this is true, she thinks, then, half-remembering, she smiles and says quietly, "I don't know, probably."

Along the way she has had lessons from the best teachers. "I've been lucky and I've taken something from each one of them. Gardner Dickenson, Sam Snead, Harvey Penick, Jim Flick. Later Chuck Hogan. You always get help. And I worked for Davis Love; I baby-sat Davis Love III and Mark. I worked for Davis for ten years at Atlanta Country Club. He was so generous both as a teacher and a friend. One year for Christmas he bought me a television and a ticket home for the holidays. And of course there was also Tommy Armour.

"I worked and studied with Tommy for many years. He was my main teacher. I'd pick him up every morning at nine and we'd go to the golf course. Then I'd take him home at five. The only day he didn't go to the golf course, Thursday, he'd play bridge with the ladies. I played the last few holes with Tommy that he ever played. When we got to hole three at Delray Beach, he said, 'Take me in.' And that was it."

Gradually she made her way back home. Fittingly, for many years Armstrong's lesson tee has been the public course, Lake Chabot, in the hills of Oakland where her father first took her to learn to play before the war. She has a long memory and is grateful: "The one thing I can give back to golf—I can't pay back money to players who helped me out—but I can teach and pass on to somebody else." She is an LPGA Master Professional; 1970 LPGA Teacher of the Year. She, in fact, is a treasure trove: "Everybody wants to learn faster than they practice. Patience is most often the last thing we learn. I teach patience by having patience. I out-patience them.

"The biggest thing is finding a way the player is going to understand. I have enough knowledge; I will find the key. It's not whether I can see. I can see. It's how I get them to feel and understand. It's having a lot of different ways of saying things. Sometimes I have to go home and sleep on it, mull it over in my mind. I lie awake at night thinking, What did I forget to say? What can I say to help them? What am I missing?"

She is not a modern swing doctor. She takes no more than four lessons back to back, and she never has. After that, she says, she cannot give her best. She believes no teacher can.

Though she has helped pros win, she is no less concerned for beginners. Here, she says, is a huge misconception. "Many think anyone with knowledge can help those just starting," she says, "when, in fact, you have to be a really good teacher to teach beginners and not start them on the wrong track."

Evelyn White, a journalist and author, is one of her students at Chabot. "I'm a black woman, forty-one or -two at the time, just coming to a game that has not had a history of welcoming me. I'd heard about Gloria Armstrong. I drive into the course and the first thing I see, and this is before Tiger Woods, is this towering white woman surrounded by a group of little black boys. The kindness was evident, and the keen attention. The boys were swinging away like Willie Mays and Gloria's saying to them calmly, 'Let the club do the work, let the club do the work.' And they're looking up at her like 'Hey man, the lady's making sense,' and I knew right then: This is the teacher for me."

When Gloria was still competing, she was also helping Kathy Whitworth win. "Gloria is a great observer," says Whitworth, "and I look to her because, like Harvey Penick, she keeps things simple. She never tried to change me much. When I got offtrack, I'd ask her to take a look and she would say, 'Well, you used to do this when you were playing well,' and in that, she would trigger something. Once when I was on a streak, I was winning but not playing well and she stayed out at the range with me to get me going again. I was feeling so good at the end of our session, hitting the ball so squarely, I said, 'What do you want when I win?' And I did win. At the end of the year at a tournament in Mississippi, I gave her a little party, champagne and the whole thing. It was so good to see in her face, she knew I'd remembered. But how would I forget? She was still out there competing herself, but was always willing to help anyone who asked."

In 1962 *Life* magazine said of her: "To Gloria Armstrong, the Tour is something more (or perhaps less) than either money or adventure. Gloria is 35, and has spent 10 years just making it as a pro. 'The tour is my family now,' says Gloria. 'I've drifted away from the outside. This is all I can do now, play a little golf ($4,000 won last year), teach golf in the winter . . . it's one way to live.' "

In her mind she has received much more than she has given. But for all she has given, she has received what for a teacher may be the greatest gift—a student with supreme talent, one with a heart as big as her own. As seventeenth on the money list in 1956, Armstrong made $2,357. Eighth on the money list in 1998, Pat Hurst made $612,329. In 1962, her best year, Armstrong earned a total of $7,200 in prize money. Hurst, in her very first professional tournament took home $7,189. Hurst plays in a world far from Armstrong's tour—the small traveling trailer, meatballs cooked in coffeepots, clothes hung from air vents. It is a world of five-star hotels, eager sponsors, six-figure endorsements. A world where women can at last aspire to "having it all"—the game, a husband or partner, a family, and celebrity, too.

Because of Hurst, the stand below the television in Armstrong's small Oakland living room is stacked with videotapes. Armstrong knows every sequence and is ready when Hurst E-mails or calls.

"I was around eleven and a half or twelve when I went to Gloria," says Hurst. "She has been my only teacher. Some teachers have a model swing they like to teach, but Gloria taught me *my* swing. She taught me to deal with *my* swing because under pressure we always go back to what we do unintentionally. She taught me to really feel and to look at and understand my divot. We've been working together so long she knows what I'm talking about no matter what I say.

"We communicate sometimes without her even having seen

my swing. I can describe it on the phone or in E-mail and she can say, 'Try this or this,' and she knows. Last year, before Michigan, I was hitting the ball really bad and I phoned her. She said, 'It sounds like you're doing this and this and you should think about working on this.' I did, and I won.

"Even when I was growing up, when she was giving me lessons, if I didn't understand she'd throw another avenue at it, the same concept said in a different way. Every time I left my lesson with her I felt confident because she knew my swing better than I knew it myself, and each time she'd try to pass a little more of it to me.

"Growing up as a junior golfer, as an amateur and then turning professional, there's not much I can give back to her besides playing and playing well. When I was a junior golfer, I made this present for her for Christmas, a board full of all my different newspaper articles. I put stuff like 'I won this because of you,' and she cried. It meant so much to her, and it still does. Every time I call up, I rarely call her just to say, 'Hey, let's go to lunch.' I call and say, 'Gloria, I need help.' 'Okay, when do you want to come see me? What time?' I'll say, 'Well, what do you have today?' I always say, 'today,' and she's always there for me whenever I need her, despite her schedule. She'll say, 'How's four o'clock?' To me that means everything because I play golf every day and sometimes I might need her right now, and she understands how important that is."

Hurst is well aware of Armstrong's own days on tour. "She has so many stories, but they're rarely about herself. I had her come up to Seattle last year to see the tour up close. She said it was such a shock because it was so different, the way we handle ourselves compared to the way they handled themselves back then. They were in the hotel rooms, they were thinking about their swings, the course, the weather, the game, discussing it. When we get back to our rooms, we don't do any of that. It took her by surprise to see how it is now.

"She and all her buddies, all the old-timers, they're the ones who've allowed us to be out here playing for the kind of money we're getting today. We're getting paid to do something we love, and it's these early women who put in their time, gave up whole parts of their lives to make it possible.

"To have this kind of teacher who's been through it all—I know that's really rare, and lucky.

"We've been working together for seventeen years, more than half my life. I trust her and I think she also trusts me. Everything she teaches is about trust. I can go a year without seeing her because in teaching me that's what she's worked toward—she's taught me to help myself. She's made me understand what to look for, where to look when I get off, and that's allowed me to go out on my own. What it comes down to is that she's led me to, and given me, myself."

The Broom

The hardest thing in golf is to learn how to score without hitting the ball well. Some days you're on, some days you're off and you've still got to score with what you've got. On the course, you cannot be thinking about your swing; you've got to be focused in on the ball and where you want it to go. If you're "Do I take it here?" "Am I bringing it here?"—if you can't trust your swing, you're finished, you're going to be lost. That's the problem with amateurs, they're analyzing all the time; they're always after the perfect swing. Well, some days you go out and hit the ball fantastic, some days you go out and it'll go all over the course. Some days you're on the range, and it hooks or slices, and you go out on the course, it hooks or slices. So let it hook or slice, don't try to fix it once you're in the game. Score with what you've got that day.

Great players know what the ball's going to do, and they know they're not going to strike it perfectly every time. You can make a great swing and hit a lousy shot just because your timing is off. There are also a whole lot of players out there who can't swing a lick at it in any way that looks pretty, but they manage to get it in the hole quickly. That's because they work with what they've got.

I remember Peggy Wilson, a good, good player in our day, usually a fine golf swing—a great student of Harvey Penick. A reporter asked her about her round one day. "I played real good," she said, "considering I had the perfect swing for digging out stumps."

Golf is just like that. It's a fantastic, frustrating game. One day you're on, and the world is your oyster. The next day you may not be able to hit the ball with a broom. I tell my students, it's those days with the broom that really show what you've got.

Gambling

Some out there have personalities that don't let them gamble. I can see that a lot because when they're under the gun on Sunday, they can't even get the ball to the hole, they always get it on the front edge of the green. No one's going to win a tournament that way. At that level, on Sunday, you don't win it just getting it on the green; you got to get it close so you can have a chance at making the putt.

When you watch golf, you watch human nature, because golf involves all the emotions—your physical ability, your mental ability, and what's inside. To win you need to know when to risk and when not to. That's why, I think, in practice players get better by gambling. You get to really test and know your nerve under the gun. If you have any competitive spirit, playing for your own money, whether ten cents or ten dollars, makes you better.

As a kid, I played for a quarter. I didn't have many quarters. A quarter meant a lot to me. Later, after I turned pro, Marlene Bauer, the tour's leading money winner at the time, would take me out and we'd gamble with Tommy Armour and his partners. Tommy was a big believer in the wager as teacher. I'll always remember the first time I went out with Marlene. The two of us were playing Tommy and this other fellow, Gino, who was about a 16 handicap. At the time I didn't know anything about "presses," but Marlene was following all that.

We got on the eighteenth hole, and she came over and whispered, "If we don't win this hole, we're going to lose seventy dollars." And I had about thirteen dollars. I have never forgotten that because, words just out of her mouth, she knocks it out of bounds. So I hit my usual heeled shot down the middle of the fairway. It's a par 5 and, of course, Armour hits it down around the bend. He's set up perfectly to the green in two. Gino by now is walking along because he's out of it, way off to the right in Palm Meadows. So I hit my second shot up so I have a 7-iron in, and Armour hits his up to the right and leaves it short, left of the green. Thinking only of my thirteen dollars, I knock that 7-iron on so stiff I make four, and we ended up tying the match. It was after that that Armour started to work with me. He showed me how to play a lot of short shots that I didn't know, and he showed me how to play with total concentration—how, as he said, to be on the inside.

Wagering, he believed, tests you inside. I didn't have the money to get into high stakes, but I learned from it because there were times playing with him, us against two other guys, I'd bet my usual dollar but Tommy would put a wager out, and I hated to lose his money. There were days we'd be playing for stakes I couldn't pay in months. That put the pressure on, the so-called fire in the belly. It taught me his favorite lesson: Inside you may be doing this @#*#@**@*#, you may even be shaking, but I learned real quick that you must think only about the shot you're going to make, not the swing you're going to take. You've got to get the ball to the hole—that one thing. Everything else is dreams.

Never having had much extra, I'm not one for high wagers. I think the simplest bet accomplishes the same thing. Play for lunch, for a quarter, for who cooks dinner or does the dishes, play for a soda, a nickel, but play for something. Something on the line will call up that little extra drive and, with time, make any golfer better.

Casting

Most women, 90 percent of the women who cast, cast because the first thing they're told when they learn to play golf is "Keep your head down and still." The only thing they can do in doing that is cast it from the top in order to hit the ball. By casting, I mean hitting at the ball immediately from the top, flipping your hands at the ball. The wrists should have cocked by the time you're at the top. Casting is uncocking those wrists like you do when you swat a flyswatter. The shot's over, you've spent all the whip you have by the time you're back to waist level.

The worst piece of advice anyone can give anybody is "Keep your head down and still." Number one, it doesn't allow freedom; you're frozen. Number two, it creates terrible posture. Right off, before you start, you're finished. Number three, it destroys weight shift. It's impossible to get your weight through.

I want my students to have freedom. That's how you create speed. For clubhead speed you have to have motion, not loose-all-over motion, but contained, efficient motion. If you're standing hands frozen, head frozen, elbows frozen, do you have motion? Standing head down, chin down, all scrunched up, the mind's quickly going to try to figure and plot. Everything inside you is going to be telling you to swat at the ball.

Washrag

There's something from Harry Pressler I like to use with my better players. In golf it's so important that the hands meld together. Harry made this easy. He used to say, "Take your grip, and when it's there, wring your hands lightly on the club in the same motion you would use to wring a wet washrag, but ever so lightly. This will meld the hands together as one unit." And it does. But you must not let tension in. When you see good players up close, you see them all try to lighten their grips. You can see them visibly lighten up. The better the player, the more important light grip pressure. Remember, light grip pressure and a melding.

Where You Are

For the better player, control of distance is the prime thing in learning to win. Most club players, after they've hit a good shot, let's say with a 7-iron, they don't think to walk it off and see exactly how many paces they've hit that 7-iron. Even to halfway good players I say, "How far do you hit that club?" They'll say, "Oh, I don't know—a hundred and thirty." Well, that's not good enough if you want to be right on the pin. I make them go out and learn and get to know. I say, "The next time you play, when you hit a decent, solid shot, you walk that shot off and see how many paces you hit it. Pace it to the nearest distance marker." I don't want to know how many yards but how many paces, for the simple reason that each person has a different distance in the step they take. One might take a step that's four feet long, another that is two and a half feet long. We each need to do it by our own pace. If you're a young player or a club player without a caddie, your own pace is what you have to go by.

Pat Hurst will pace even short shots around the green, because for a good player in contention, that feel and confidence in distance is an edge. Winners don't guess, they know exactly where they are.

The Rifle Sight

Many players don't realize that the leading edge of the club is like a rifle sight. If you don't get that leading edge lined up correctly, you can't hit the target. You must be precise. The leading edge has to be perfectly perpendicular to the line of flight. To have any chance at all of returning the clubface to square at impact, which is the only way you will get solid contact, you must be perfectly square at address.

For some reason, even though we can all get sloppy in this, beginners get into a panic. They swat at the ball as if they have a baseball bat in hand. There are two major problems with that. First, in baseball the ball is moving at a great deal of speed toward you and in order to reverse the direction of that ball you really have to swing hard at it. Second, the clubhead is not a baseball bat; it is not smooth and nicely rounded and consistent in its shape. It has one, and only one, spot at its center that must be perfectly square at impact.

In order to help my beginners understand that none of us can go at the ball as if we have a bat in hand, and also to get them to see how speed is not the first consideration in a solid hit, I have them raise the club straight up over their heads as if it were a lightning rod on top of a tower. They take their grip and then raise the club straight up above their heads. Then I have them bring it back down and place the bottom of the club on top of the ball. The object is to raise the club and bring it back down to touch the top of the ball. Simple, yes, but to do that they cannot rush. They begin to understand that they must have control of the clubhead to do this, as simple as it is.

Another way of talking about it is to say that it's like eating with a fork. You don't just rush the fork back up to your face as fast as you can, you'll jab yourself in the face, or an ear, and hurt yourself badly. From the plate to your mouth, even though you no longer have to think about it, you're careful with those tines so they're on target. Most players swing too hard because they believe that force alone equals speed. But that isn't true in golf. Clubhead speed creates distance, of course, but that's secondary to solidly connecting to the right spot. "Spot" is by far more important. Long shots come off the center of the clubface. Adjusting your rifle sight squarely to the ball with the ball dead center of the clubface is key.

The Zone

There's a huge difference between those who are out on tour and those who are winning on tour. Those who are winning are attuned to everything—the wind, the grass, the sounds, the smells, the air, everything. It isn't blocking out, it's taking in. It's being so fully aware of the moment that you're protected by it. No one can get at you. All you have to think about is what you're going to make that golf ball do. You don't have to worry about your swing or any outside thing because it's all inside yourself. People talk talk talk about the zone. When outside is no longer outside, when outside blends with inside, you're there. That's the zone.

Sound

No one pays enough attention to just how much we play by sound. That's why it's so hard to play in the wind, because the wind destroys your hearing so that throws off your timing. Sound is so much more important than people realize. That's why the game is so hard for deaf people or people who are hard of hearing; they can make good contact, but it's hard to repeat it because they can't hear and identify the sound. When you start hearing that good contact, your mind gets a sense, a feeling, between the hearing and the hitting. Your brain, your insides, make a connection with that sound, so sound becomes a big part of timing.

I really try to make my students realize that not only is the wind doing something to the ball, it's doing something to the sound. I try to make even beginners aware of it, how important it is to listen and feel. Try to hit the ball squarely, listen, then try to reproduce that sound. The more you hear it, the better you're going to swing it. Start out short, hear that "click." Hear the click of hitting it squarely. Sound happens on the outside, but you have to hear it and get to know it and feel it on the inside.

Armour always taught how to be on the inside, and that's what I think I've taught Pat Hurst, and what I try to teach each student I take on. How to play when you're nervous, when even your thumbs are shaking and your stomach's flipped. How do I make good contact under those conditions? Sound is so much a part of the answer. That click—listen for it, the familiar sound of hitting the ball squarely. It's so important.

All our physical organs change every day. Our hearing, our eyesight, our fingers, our hands. That's why some days we don't hit it quite as well. Our hearing's not quite as clear or the wind's blowing, it doesn't sound the same, it throws off our tempo just a little bit. That's why you need to get that sound inside you during practice, so you can hear it even when there's noise, even when the wind's howling. Sound, it's a big part of trust. A big part of winning.

Shirley Spork

WHEN SHE LEAVES a first message on my answering machine, she signs off, "Shirley Spork, founding member, LPGA." It is not so much prideful as no-nonsense, matter-of-fact. Though she likes all kinds of fishing, stream to deep sea, and woodcarving, her interests have not scattered far. Golf has been her life.

She grew up in Detroit, Michigan, where her father was an electrical engineer and her mother a clerk in a local pharmacy. Her family's house was across the street from an eighteen-hole course, though neither of her parents played. Summer after summer, Spork curiously watched the comings and goings there until dusk one evening when she was eleven. She scaled the high stone wall that separated the fairways from the street and, under cover of bushes and trees, she studied what went on. She found her first golf ball before she left that night, and from then on it became a ritual. She waited for the pile to grow, then one day carefully washed each ball and began selling them to passersby on the street. After a couple of years, when she was thirteen (in 1940), she decided it was time to start to play. She took money from her golf ball earnings and went down to the Kresge Five and Dime and bought a putter from the dollar bin, then a 7-iron. Each night it was up over the wall and there she worked alone to improve, staying well after dark.

Spork wanted to turn pro right out of high school but her parents said no, and in the fall of 1945 they drove her to Michigan

State Normal Teachers' College in Ypsilanti, where she promptly began classes. In 1947, she won the National Intercollegiate Championship, and not long after she started playing pro events as an amateur. "In 1950, at the Weathervane Women's Western Open in Chicago, Illinois," Spork says, "I was eating breakfast with Marilynn Smith and Babe and George Zaharias before the first round of play. Babe said, 'Hey, Kid, why don't you turn pro? You're tops in Michigan. We need more players on our ladies tour.' I said, 'Well, Babe, how do you turn pro?' Babe got up from the table, took her right hand and plunked it down firmly on top of my head. 'Kid,' she said, 'you're a pro. Go tell 'em on the first tee you're playing as a pro.' I did," Spork recalls, "and I was one of eleven lady pros playing in that tournament."

As Spork was finding her way, the LPGA, too, was only beginning to take shape. In 1949, at the Eastern Women's Open in Essex Falls, New Jersey, businessman Fred Corcoran had been on-site signing up any lady pros who might be interested in playing on a tour the following winter. Patty Berg, Betty Jameson, Babe Zaharias, Helen Dettweiler, Betty Mims White, and Helen Hicks all signed on, and collectively they became known as the Ladies Professional Golf Players Association; they picked Patty Berg as their president. The next year Corcoran filed papers in New York State to incorporate the organization, which would be named the LPGA.

In September 1950, four months after Babe had anointed Spork a bona fide "pro," Fred Corcoran presented the LPGA charter at a tournament in Wichita, Kansas, and all women professionals present were made official founding members: Patty Berg, Betty Mims White, Marlene Bauer, Shirley Spork, Helen Dettweiler, Betty Jameson, Babe Zaharias, Alice Bauer, Sally Sessions, Marilynn Smith, Louise Suggs, Opal Hill. That was the LPGA's official beginning.

Before I meet Spork, I call her a hundred times from the road. I'm seeing others as I wend my way from Wisconsin toward her in the high California desert, adjusting my schedule as I go. She does not grow impatient with the necessary changes, or that I've now mixed up locations and forgotten that at this time of year she's in Palm Desert, not El Cahon, California. Though she is serious, altogether direct in manner, each time I phone she finds her lesson book and reserves a new chunk of time.

At seventy-two, she is a teaching professional at Monterey Country Club in Palm Desert, California. It is a gated place where members drive the predictable Mercedeses, Lexuses, and Lincolns. I sit with her beside the pool. She is a sturdy figure with strong, solid shoulders. Her clothes are fine, though practical. She wears a light brown-flecked wool mountaineering hat with six small, colorful souvenir pins all in a line above the brim. It's this choice of hat as much as her kind eyes that endears her to me. She is ardent about the LPGA and the game.

"In the first few years of the tour, the players gave a golf clinic before each event. I usually followed Patty Berg's narration. I was the young trick-shot artist." She used two-way clubs, hit shots right- and left-handed with a fishing-rod-shafted, extra-long club, big tees, and anything else she happened to invent.

At each stop every player was expected to give personal interviews and make an appearance at local sports events—baseball games, boxing matches—to promote the tour in that town. Radio spots drew the local folks out to walk with players along unroped fairways. "Prize money? The total purse was usually a thousand to twelve hundred dollars and paid out in eleven places," Spork says. "The players? We were like a band of minstrels. We usually stayed at the same motel or tried to get private housing arranged by tournament sponsors. We'd leave the eighteenth green on the final day and drive until dark, then start again the next day and the next to cover the long distances between events. We tried to bunch together to share expenses."

Players often found a church to attend Saturday nights or Sunday mornings before their noon tee times, in that way creating the "familiar." Spork generally placed a small check in the church's collection basket. "At one stop in Waterloo, Iowa," she says, "the good monsignor, an ardent golfer, noticed I had not finished well that week in the prize money. I received my check back with a note saying: 'You need this more than God does. Also, if you are ever in our area again, we have a good cook at the rectory. Stop by any time.' "

The courses they played were usually 6,500-plus yards and

events were often scheduled at new sites so owners could promote memberships. Often, the courses were not in the best of condition. Once, in Burneyville, Oklahoma, for the Opie and Waco Turner Open, the husbands of some of the players were asked to set the cups on the greens. The usual tool used would not go though the hard, pebbly soil, so the hole was dug with a trowel and that same pin placement was used throughout the tournament. "At that stop, as well as a few others," says Spork, "the greens were so full of weeds the local rule allowed us to pick them before we putted. But the players loved this stop because we were able to make daily money. There were payouts for chip-ins, birdies, eagles, low rounds, as well as the final. Refreshments were free. One year they even brought in Miss USA to entertain."

As if to add some grace and light to the picture she's creating, Spork again mentions Babe Zaharias. "Louise Suggs's father, who was a former baseball player and scout, was a pro at a course in Carrollton, Georgia. He'd taught all the caddies to retrieve our practice balls using a fielding glove. It was a beautiful sight to watch the Babe send out 150-yard eight-iron shots to her caddie—shot after shot, he simply reached out for her ball, not moving a bit."

At sponsor dinners, players would often entertain. Betty Dodd and Babe played guitar and harmonica and sang. Others would join in. Marilynn Smith regularly played piano and Spork would sing "Night and Day."

The first television coverage the LPGA received was in the early fifties at George S. Mays's Tam O'Shanter All-American Open in Niles, Illinois. It was the highlight of the women's tour schedule. "We talked for days about what we'd wear and how we'd play the eighteenth hole, which was the only hole the TV camera was going to cover.

"As I recall, the hole was a long par four where you had to have a good drive and a fairway wood or long iron into the elevated green, which sat across a river with an overhanging tree. I hit a good drive and a five-wood onto the green. I made certain as I walked across the bridge and all the way around the green that I smiled and casually marked my ball with the plastic bingo marker they'd given us on the first tee. I tapped the marker down with my putter and strode to the edge of the green, making sure to face the TV camera. As my opponent went to putt, I looked down at my putter and saw my marker stuck to the sole of it. I strode back onto the green when it was my turn to putt and faked replacement of my ball and picked up the marker. My opponent said she hoped she hadn't stepped on my marker. I said, 'No, it was right here on the end of my putter all the time.' "

One of the first promoters of the LPGA was Helen Lengfeld, a leading nationally ranked amateur through the twenties and thirties, as well as the editor and publisher of *The Golfer* magazine. As a personal friend of Alvin Handmacher, the retail clothes giant, she secured his interest in helping to establish the Weathervane Golf Tour, where events were played in the Midwest, Texas, the West and the East, and the scores from all four events were totaled to arrive at the grand champion. The final event was played in New York, the home of Handmacher clothes, and all the players received an extra-generous supply of golf skirts, blouses, jackets, scarves, and hats to supplement what for most was a small wardrobe. "I waited for that one through the year," says Spork. "Most of us on the bottom end of the purse really appreciated it."

In her competitive days, Spork represented Golfcraft, the company that grew into Titleist, and in an envelope of materials she has for me, there is a 1951 ad for "Shirley Spork Woods and Irons." SUPERB! it says at the top of the page, and there stands the much younger version of Spork, in her early twenties, leaning on a large staff bag filled with clubs bearing her name—her face and eyes mischievous and bright.

Golfcraft sent Spork—a first for a woman professional—to Europe to give exhibitions and clinics that same year. She went to Scotland, England, Wales, and France. "When I got off the ship," says Spork, "I wanted to go straight to St. Andrews and just play an anonymous round. The Old Course was a dream and I couldn't wait. It was October and already cold with the winds off the sea, so I sent my manager to track down some insulated underwear while three guys and I, each with a caddie, went off the first tee. Well, at the third hole, there were about ten people; on the fifth hole, fifty people; the ninth hole, one hundred people, and each hole after that more and more. My manager comes back and tells me, 'All these people are here because in town all the store windows say, CLOSED—AMERICAN LADY PRO AT LINKS. They just shut their shops and came out to watch. So we get to Road Hole 17, and the manager says, 'Well, they're all out here. You better do something to entertain 'em.'

"So I got out my big tee and did some trick shots, and that was so well received that at the end of the round I was invited by the secretary of the Royal and Ancient Golf Club into the clubhouse. To this day I think I might be the only woman golf professional ever invited into the closed confines of the men's locker room, meeting room, and offices. They showed me around the whole place. At their request I gave a swing demonstration standing on top of their boardroom table for all the officials and members present—all males, of course!"

That night Spork stayed at a nearby inn and its pub was packed with curious townspeople. "Someone came in and gave me this A. Patrick club. A. Patrick was one of the original club makers from Musselburgh. The man who gave it to me said that when he took down this house there, the club was inside the wall. An A. Patrick, 1853. It was called a long-nose play club. That night I became a golf collector. I've never forgotten that gesture.

"For me, there was nothing like being at St. Andrews. Long before, I had heard the stories and the history, how the golf hole we play every day is its size because when they were building that clubhouse, there were four-and-one-quarter-inch drainage tiles left over. One day builders sank one of them into the ground to maintain the hole. Prior to that, the earth was just scooped out; the tile made the hole secure. From then on, the hole became four and a quarter inches, what it has been and hopefully will remain forever."

Spork returned from Europe wanting to be a club professional. She worked first at Pasatiempo Country Club in Santa Cruz, California. In 1952, twenty-six, a woman, and single, she applied for her first head pro job at Ukiah Municipal Golf Course in northern California. "Because I was a woman, townspeople, golfers who'd attended one of my many clinics, went to the city council to put in a necessary good word. I became greenskeeper; golf pro; keeper of the clubhouse; custodian of the meeting rooms used for civic meetings, folk dances, Boy Scouts; and in the rainy season I continued to play the tour."

In 1954, she was offered a position at Tamarisk Country Club in Palm Springs. There she taught the celebrity members—Jack Benny, Kirk Douglas, Danny Kaye, Harpo Marx, Dean Martin, et al. Over the years, she has held teaching professional jobs at Tanforan Golf Club and Indian Wells Country Club in California; Sugarbush Golf Club in Warren, Vermont; a second stint at Tamarisk; and presently, Monterey Country Club in Palm Desert, California.

But the growth of the LPGA remained a primary focus. In the late 1950s, she was appointed by the LPGA to a committee with Betty Hicks and Barbara Rotvig to design a school to train those interested in becoming teachers. With the help of Ellen Griffin, Jackie Pung, Marilynn Smith, Mary Lena Faulk, and Mary Ann Reynolds, the committee opened its first National LPGA Golf School for Teachers at the University of Michigan, in midsummer of 1960. Its purpose was to "promote interest in the game of golf, provide vocational opportunities in teaching, merchandising and golf promotion for lady golf professionals."

In the mid-seventies, Ellen Griffin asked Spork to take a full-time position traveling the country for the National Golf Foundation to promote quality education in the game and to teach teachers to teach. She did this until 1978, when she returned as teaching pro to Tamarisk. Spork and DeDe Owens are the only people to be honored by the LPGA as Teacher of the Year twice, Spork receiving the award in 1959 and 1984. In 1998 Spork was presented with the LPGA's highest honor in teaching, the Ellen Griffin Award. Her LPGA workshops for teaching professionals number way over three thousand, and since 1979 she's had her own school for women golfers of all levels at Singing Hills Resort in El Cahon, California. But "I've never taught anyone to play golf," she says. "I've taught them how to learn to play golf."

One of her protégés was a young kid from Idaho, Shirley Englehorn, who, before a life-threatening fall from a horse, was everyone's candidate for greatness. After the accident, Spork and a friend flew to Englehorn and stayed for a month.

"I've often thought what that fall must have meant to her,"

says Englehorn. "What it might have been like for her seeing me unable to move, her having devoted so much time to my training. She never let on, not once, to what must have been a crushing disappointment. When everyone else thought I was finished, not once did she let me see that in her face. After, forgetting herself, she focused on me—and that's how she was all those years in her patient caring for the LPGA."

Spork buys me lunch and we continue talking. When it's time for a lesson, I ride with her in a cart to her lesson tee. The sun is warm and there's a desert breeze. On that oasis of velvet ground, flowers bloom everywhere. "This is the life," I say, and with a wide smile she remembers Walter Hagen: " 'Wine, golf, and song. Drink the wine; hit the shots; smell the roses.' What could be better?" But I know it's more than that for her; she's carried a dream for the LPGA for a long while, and she's worked and worked and not yet given up on a greater vision. I think of the first message she left me in such earnest, "Shirley Spork, LPGA, founding member," and what that really means for her. She is single and has no children; the LPGA has been all of that. I try to recall the lines I once read in a book of May Sarton's, but not until I'm back home do I find it—Sarton quoting from Florida Scott-Maxwell's *The Measure of My Days:*

> A mother's love for her children, even her inability to let them be, is because she is under a painful law that the life that passed through her must be brought to fruition. Even when she swallows it whole she is only acting like any frightened mother cat eating its young to keep it safe. It is not easy to give closeness and freedom, safety plus danger.
>
> No matter how old a mother is she watches her middle-aged children for signs of improvement. It could not be otherwise for she is impelled to know that the seeds of value sown in her have been winnowed. She never outgrows the burden of love, and to the end she carries the weight of hope for those she bore.

Shirley Spork, LPGA, founding member.

Five Eighths

I'm a founding member of the LPGA. I've been around a long time. I've taught champions, I've taught amateurs, I've taught beginners. I traveled the country for many years for the National Golf Foundation teaching teachers to teach. I can tell you what I've seen: We're all too impatient. We live in an instantaneous society; no one's ever satisfied. What I know is this: Golf is like eating an elephant. You can only eat it one bite at a time. I'm seventy-two years old. Given everything, at this point in my life I figure I've eaten five eighths of the elephant. If I'm lucky, by the time I leave this earth, hopefully I'll have eaten a little more.

The Simplest Advice

Some of the simplest advice I give is: Once you get into a problem situation always get out the easiest way possible. Don't expect a miracle. Don't follow a poor shot with a stupid one.

If you're in the trees and rough and there's an opening two feet wide, don't expect to get through that little opening. Just get it back in play. Even if it means going backward. Most of us when we get into a problem situation—a bunker, a hazard—we get deeper and deeper into trouble. We add more and more strokes because we think we can make up for the poor shot. Well the poor shot's done; don't complicate it by a foolhardy, desperate one. You can't make strokes up. You have to go on and play a sensible solid shot. That's the only reliable way to get from A to B to C to D in the fewest strokes possible. A to B to C to D—that's the miracle.

Grip Size

Proper grip size is important. If the grip is too small, you'll hold it too tightly. There are problems when a grip is too large as well, but it's better to be too big than too small. Unfortunately, because of old ideas in manufacturers' minds, most women play with undersized grips. You can usually judge this by the size glove you wear. Generally, if you wear a women's small or medium, you need a standard women's grip; if you wear a women's large or a men's small, you should be playing with a men's standard grip. With women's clubs off the shelf it's often a mystery what "standard" is for the manufacturer. Having clubs regripped is not expensive and very well worth it.

Aim

Even pros have problems with alignment. What I use to help players improve is the image of tying a string to your target: On approach shots, mentally tie the string to the flagstick or, on long shots where you can't reach the green, if you have an aerial target, tie it to the top of a tree well beyond the hole. Then pull the string tight all the way back to you until you can trace the line to your master target; bring your eyes back to the ball, find a little spot out along the line six or eight inches in front of the ball, square the club up over the line, then set up squarely so you can keep extending your back hand out toward the target over that line and make sure your index finger, on that small extension, is pointing down the target line with the toe of the club pointing up at the sky. Take a half swing back, then extend through. If you work this little motion into your set up and make sure your feet, hips, and shoulders are square to that line, you'll be directly on target.

A First Step

One of the best ways to understand timing and tempo is to take one club, say an 8-iron, and practice hitting it different distances. Hit one a short distance, a medium distance, a far distance, and then vary that. This is not practice to see how far you can hit it. It is practice in shot making. This practice will give you an understanding that you are not smaller than the club, or smaller than the ball. You can experiment with controlling the ball by controlling your timing and tempo in relation to the ball. Hit an 8-iron 100 yards, then 80 yards, then

60. Feel what you need to do in order to do this. That's a first step in becoming a player.

Ease and Balance

All good shots are made up of five actions: analyze, visualize, center, swing, hold the finish. You have to analyze what you are going to do; visualize the shot; center your attention on the ball; swing the club; and hold the finish. If you can hold the finish, you're in balance. If you have energy left and have hit the ball squarely, it will show in your finish. Do not use all your energy. All good players know this.

What I see every day is people coming out and going at the ball with everything they have, which leads me to wonder what would happen if those same people went to the racetrack, got in a car, and floored it all the way around. Well, I'll tell you: They wouldn't get all the way around. They'd spin out and crash. Yet that's what people do every day on the golf course. What they don't understand is that all good shots have a reserve of energy. This is critical. The key to distance is not whaling away and falling all over your feet. The key to distance is ease and balance.

A Happening

You have to be very selfish to be a tour player. Like a great violinist, you give things up. You must practice. Then you practice some more. You have the desire, the drive, then hopefully you're sitting on the corner at the right time. Life has something to do with it. You get picked. Not everyone does.

Through the years the "champion" becomes the golfer who hits it closest to the hole and makes the putt. They all got there, they're all qualified. When you get to a certain level, the person who is winning is getting good breaks. The person who is not winning is getting bad breaks—the ball when it hits, rolls one way or another, this or that. When it's your turn to win, you win. You can't count on winning, winning is a happening.

Rain

People come to me when it's raining. They say, "I guess we don't have a lesson today." I say, "No, no, no, you have to hit balls in the rain." So I stand out there and I teach them to hit balls in the rain. Because golf is not perfect conditions if you want to be a player. If you get to know a bad climate, you play better because you learn how to adjust.

I remember playing a tournament as a young amateur at Plum Hollow in Michigan. To reach the eighteenth green, we took a rowboat from the place where our drives landed to the green. It was the only way we could get there. The green was elevated. We hit the approach shot, got in the boat, and away we went. We had our umbrellas and each a big towel. The towel, the glove, whatever you wanted dry, you hung under the umbrella, enjoyed the rain.

I remember as a young player playing at the National Intercollegiate. It rained and rained and rained, but no lightning, so we played. I had only one pair of shoes. They got soaked all the way through. Sopped. I had no others. This worker in the clubhouse put them in the oven for me. The next day, the rain had stopped, and I won't forget, through that kindness, I played in dry shoes.

Peggy Kirk Bell

*T*HERE'S A SHIRT a friend bought me, which despite being lovely spends most of its time in my closet. It's far and above my finest—French, I'm told—the purest, soft white cotton. But still, I can never help but look at it suspiciously, not able to forget that it cost more than five cords of wood at Wisconsin prices. So in it, I'm seldom comfortable, which to me is everything in clothes. I twist and turn and fidget, ever mindful that I mustn't stick my sleeve in jam or spill soup down its middle. Nonetheless, when packing for the road, I folded it in plastic with a few good others for special occasions and tossed it in my trunk. Today at Pine Needles, I've taken it out. I know that this place, an old legendary Donald Ross course, is a cut above—site of the 1996 U.S. Women's Open (and its projected site in 2001)—a resort that entertains many well-dressed people.

In the parking lot, hidden among the cars, I pull off my T-shirt and rush into this fine one. I loosen the collar from its buttons and flip it up old-Hollywood style. Dodging the steering wheel, I run a brush through my hair and check the rearview mirror, twice making sure my cowlick's pressed down. Out of habit I peruse my pants legs for lint, then head up the walk to greet Pine Needles, the sly old dandy of a course first carved out seventy-some years ago.

The lush fairways are tight. Beautiful large-leaf pines stand as a snare for errant shots along almost every hole, the tall beauties shimmering in the red cast of neighborly dogwoods.

"When you drive into Pine Needles and you get to looking around," Marge Burns and others have told me, "big and beautiful as it is, I want you to know Peggy and her late husband, Bullet, nursed that place, like a child, back to health.

"They worked eighteen-hour days, both Bullet and Peggy. The great lodge you see now, they pounded a lot of the nails themselves. Upstairs rooms stayed empty, half finished, until the completed ones earned them enough to continue."

Burns tells me how in the 1940s the place lay dying. Designed in 1927, it failed during the crash of 1929. In World War II, a military training center rolled over its grounds. Later, it became a hospital. The remnants of the once great course were fading surely back into the sand hills of North Carolina until the fifties, when the Bells arrived and beckoned it back into the world. Now rows of bright bushes and flowers wave and welcome me under the midday sun. The old, sprawling, rustic lodge, all aglow in its lacy burnt-orange gown of pyracantha, sings out.

I've been waiting to meet Bell after all that I've read and heard about her: "golf's finest lady"; "an elegant exercise in excellence"; "the classiest lady of the fairways." But those tags aren't what's brought me here. It's her old competitor's words: "a true character"; "an original"; "one of the Babe's closet friends." I know her credentials: She is an early member of the LPGA, a Master Life Professional. She played professionally from 1951 to 1966. She won the Titleholders as an amateur in 1940, was LPGA Teacher of the Year in 1961, LPGA Professional of the Year in 1981; she received the first Ellen Griffin Award in 1989, was presented with the Bobby Jones Award in 1990, and runs Golfaris, one of the finest golf schools for women in the country. But words such as Betty Jameson's mean more:

"Peggy's been a sketch in everybody's life who's known her, a figure no one could imagine. We all have a fragrance. Sometimes some of us, we're like something that's wilting. But Peggy's always fresh. She has a spontaneity and a sense of humor that're both devilish and angelic. On the course she would give you a wave or a pat or a look and you'd always go off better for it."

As a young player just preparing for the tour, Dot Germain took a job working for Peggy: "I was hired as a nanny but what I did—I squeezed orange juice for breakfast and was responsible for the kids' dinner. What that meant was taking a basket to the lodge and bringing back whatever the kitchen had prepared for the guests that night. It soon became clear that Peggy had given me the job so I could practice at that wonderful place, which is what I did the rest of the day. Peggy knew what that time would mean to my career. That kindness, that's Peggy."

Germain also speaks of what others wonder at in Bell—her mind and imagination. "At the pro level, on tour," says Germain, "the real challenge and necessary ingredient beyond technique is imagination. A golf shot requires reacting to each shot with all the player's senses engaged. Knowing a shot by a sniff of the wind, the feel of the ground through your feet—more than the TV announcer's take: 'Well, she's pulled out a six-iron . . .' Because every shot is different, there's an immediacy. A highly skilled player takes in information through the senses—that's the input—but the test is: What shot does she create from that information? That's a measure of a player, that's the magic.

"I was too late to see Peggy out on tour, but what I saw in her at Pine Needles day to day—she always reacts in her own way to her life and her teaching. It's like she's hitting a shot with her life, she's hitting the shot with her teaching—there's that same immediacy, that same spontaneous imagination."

And Bell is fun. "I played my first state tournament in 1939," says fellow teaching pro Carol Clark Johnson (recipient of the Ellen Griffin Award in 1994). "I was fourteen. Peggy Kirk was in college. We all stayed at the top of the Columbus Country Club and before going out on my round I stopped at a fountain to get a drink. You know, you just fall in line with a whole bunch of people. Well, we're all standing nicely, and all of a sudden the one at the spout turns around and squirts water out from between her teeth, smack into my face. I turned to my aunt and said, 'That girl just spit water in my face.' That's how I met Peggy Kirk Bell the first time.

"You look at her now, this lovely, tremendously successful woman—flourishing business, beautiful family, tops in teaching—well, she could pull that stunt in a heartbeat, she's still the same!"

As I've wound my way from one former pro to the next, I've

heard what's called "the lobster story" repeatedly. It was Johnson who, all those years ago, masterminded the prank and tells it best: "At one of the tournaments, we were all staying at this hotel, sixteen floors up, huge for the day, and since Peggy was always scheming, playing tricks on everybody, we wanted to get her back good. She was rooming with another player, Naomi was her name, and when they went out, we went in and put a live lobster in Peg's bathtub. It was a big guy, a four-pounder, and it's sliding around, up and down. We hid in the closet and waited to see what Peggy would do. Not long after, sure enough, she comes in and we hear Peg say, 'Naomi, you want a Coke?' So we know she has to go into the bathroom to get the ice and soon we hear her fussing with the glasses and then all of a sudden—are you ready for this?—she yells, 'Hey, Naomi, look what came up through the pipes!'

"That's Peggy's mind! Everything—whatever can be imagined—is possible.

"Sixteen floors up, and that's what she said. She's always game for anticipating the amazing. We'll always love her for that."

When I walk in and finally set eyes on Bell there at Pine Needles, I flash quickly back to something my mother told me early on. There are some people in life everyone should meet, people whose presence has enough light and power to make those who glimpse them just a wee bit different, ever after. I see quickly that Bell is one of those. Not because she is stunning with her high, classic, Hepburnesque cheekbones and strong, graceful form. Not because her clothes have a subtle, unmistakably Parisian flair. But for how those clothes fit. They don't. They merely ride along, as if on the wind. Not because of mistakes in size or tailoring (those are exactly right). But because it shows—her heart—unmistakably open and free and large.

We shake hands, and as if tipped off by the gods, she remarks on my shirt, then herds me into a magnificent dining room all huge beams and glass. At a first table we meet her family (two daughters, a son, and a son-in-law, all of whom now help run the place), then stop to greet the receptionist, a busboy, two waiters, and many guests.

In her late seventies, so vital and fresh, Bell still strides like a player. Her face is bright with the places she's been, her deep eyes wizened by that varied map. "Let's go through the buffet right off," she says, "then we won't need to interrupt ourselves for that."

The buffet is two long tables of colorful, divinely smelling, alternately steaming and cool, crisp food. I take a plate and follow her down the line. I'm so busy I pay no attention to what I choose though I'm hungry and see clearly it's finer than anything I've had in weeks.

At the table, briefly remembering the shirt, I think to use the large cloth napkin as a bib, but looking around instead spread it haphazardly on my lap. She tells me right off of a speeding ticket she's gotten that morning. A habit she, even now, can't seem to break. "It was a fifty-five-miles-per-hour zone and the cop told me, 'You were going seventy-two.' I said, 'No I wasn't, I was going seventy. I always drive seventy.' I said, 'You're a mean cop.' I could see he wasn't going to let me out of it anyway."

We both laugh, and with me still studying her face and neither of us paying much attention to our plates, we begin. She was born in Findlay, Ohio. She had a twin brother and a sister two years older, an active, loving mother, and a successful father who owned a large wholesale grocery business with centers in Findlay, Columbus, and Marion. "I was always going to summer camp in New Hampshire," says Bell. "I loved camp because I loved sports. But then one spring my mother said, 'Peggy, you're off to college this fall, you're too old for summer camp.' I thought: What in the world am I going to do in Findlay, Ohio? It ended up that God, as usual, knew what He was doing; a man from Marathon Oil was being transferred to Texas and he had to sell his bond to get some money back from his membership at the country club. It was still sort of Depression times, so he went to my father's office and said, 'Now, Bob, you need to join the country club.' And my father said, 'Well, I don't know why I'd want to do that, my wife and I don't play that silly game.' And the guy said, 'Well, maybe your children will.' At dinner that night my father announced that if any of us wanted to play golf, we now belonged to the country club."

"Though I didn't know a thing about the game, I was happy, and my father was happy, because I was a tomboy. I wanted to go to Cleveland and play softball, and he said I couldn't do that, but here now was golf, a sport he thought had a little more class. (He didn't believe in girls working. In those days women were to stay home and keep the home fires burning and raise the children. Men were supposed to provide.)

"So the next day I stopped down at my dad's warehouse, and, with everything else, he sold every kind of sports equipment—baseball, football, basketball, every kind of uniform—all in one small area of the warehouse, and I went in and asked this man who ran it to give me some of those golf sticks back there in the corner. He put together a little bag—a three-wood, three-iron, five, seven, nine, and a putter—and gave me three balls, and I was off. When I got to the country club, I went in and I said, 'Where do you start?' They told me, 'Right over there.' Well, I went over and hit it off that tee and knocked it in the woods. I hunted and hunted, and I couldn't find the ball so I dropped another one, and I hit that in the woods, and then did the same thing again; I never made it to the first green. I came back in—I'd spent two hours hunting for balls—and I said to the pro, 'Who's the teacher?' And he said, 'I am.' I said, 'Well, how do you hold this thing?' I was holding it like a baseball bat, and he said, 'Would you like a lesson?' and I said, 'Yeah,' and he said, 'Tomorrow morning at nine o'clock.' I said, 'Well, gosh, I'd like to learn it all today.' But I went back the next day, and every day that summer. Lessons were fifty cents, caddies were ten cents. I was seventeen."

A good athlete, Bell was off to a quick start. "That first year I played in the club championship. Nobody was any good. I didn't win it that year, but I won it the next five or six years until I stopped entering." That fall she went off to Boston to Sargent Physical Education College, part of Boston University. "The next summer I read where they were having the first National Intercollegiate Championship in Columbus, Ohio, ninety miles from my hometown, so I drove down there and entered, and I'm pretty sure I was the worst player in it. I'd only been playing about four months.

"Patty Berg, who'd turned pro maybe a couple of years before, she was there and gave a clinic and I thought it was just amazing. She'd say, 'Now I will hit the ball from right to left;

that's called a hook,' and she did it. And she could slice it, and I thought: Isn't that marvelous, she knows where it's going! I was just hoping to hit it.

"So I met Patty there, and she gave me a golf ball, and I still have it. We were all staying at the dorm for fifty cents a night, even Patty, and it turns out that just as I'm pulling out of the course parking lot, who comes walking along and asks me for a ride but Patty. My dad had just bought me this Packard convertible, a really sharp car, and after Patty Berg sat on the front seat, I wouldn't let anyone sit there for a week. 'Don't sit there!' I'd say. I was just in awe of Patty."

The next spring, the end of her sophomore year, Bell's father sent her an airline ticket to fly to Florida during spring break. "There was about four feet of snow. I had to shovel to get out of the dorm and get on the plane. I got down there and I said, 'I gotta get out of that snow business.' I wrote to Rollins College, went down there, and started playing golf every day."

Back home during summers, Bell entered tournaments in the Toledo, Ohio, district, which provided the opportunity for her to play Inverness and other fine courses. She soon won district and then state, and was on her way. "I'd taken lessons since I'd first started playing, so I had a pretty good swing. I valued the swing from the start and never stopped trying to improve it. When I got out into the world and got to meet better players, I got to play some golf with Glenna Collett Vare. Talk about a champion! I couldn't take my eyes off her swing because right off I noticed how her left foot came up quickly and was slapped down even faster. She'd twirl it up and set it down as fast as you could wink. I said to myself, That must be it! She's won six national championships, I've got to get that foot action!

"I had a pretty slow swing, and all of a sudden I started pumping my left foot up and down like Glenna. Helen Sigel Wilson, who was playing with us, noticed me and all these new motions and said, 'What on earth are you doing?' 'I'm getting Glenna's foot action,' I said; 'I'm working that into my swing.' She said, 'Are you crazy? That's probably the worst thing she does!' "

Bell and I laugh. Her voice is a low, gravelly pleasure that floats with only the finest ruffle of age. I ask her to tell me the story about herself and Glenna at the Curtis Cup in 1950. "I was terrible at finding four-leaf clovers," she says. "Are you good at it?" she asks. "I never had any luck with that. Glenna found them all the time, that was another one of her gifts. When I played that year in Buffalo, Glenna was the captain of the U.S. team. The night before the first day's play she posted my name for singles competition. I was petrified. I was scared to death I'd lose.

"So I went to her room that night and pleaded with her to take my name off the list. 'Please don't play me,' I said, 'I'm afraid to lose.' The Curtis Cup is such an important event, it's not you, it's your country you're playing for; it's a great strain, and I was all tied up in nerves. I remember almost begging Glenna. All she said was, 'I'm captain, and you're playing.'

"The next day I was one down in my match with three holes to play. Glenna was watching from the side of the fairway, and she called me over and asked me how I stood. I told her I was one down. She walked off and came right back holding a four-leaf clover she'd just found. She handed it to me and said, 'Go get her.' I won on the eighteenth. I still have that clover."

Sweeping across the years she talks more of Glenna, Berg, the tour—one generous tale after another. When the waiter asks if I'd like coffee, I hold out my cup even though I've not drunk it much in the past. I want to ask her about the stories I've heard.

Jameson has said, "Those days, by car the tour was a long haul, mile after mile. Peg flew like the wind in her little open Packard, but, like everyone, she got tired of pushing that. She had the means, so she got herself a plane instead." Jackie Pung has said, "It was a one-fan plane. Off she'd tear, up and down in that noisy thing." "We all worried," Marilynn Smith has said.

"Tell me about your plane," I say. "It seems no one can forget you and that plane."

"I learned to fly from Gloria Armstrong," Bell tells me as I test the coffee. "We were paired at the first pro tournament that Gloria ever played, New Orleans. I made the remark, 'Ah, I just hate to think of driving to California again,' and she said, 'If I was playing golf like you do, I'd have an airplane.' I said, 'Yeah, but I don't know how to fly.' Gloria said, 'You can ride a bicycle, can't you?' I said, 'Yeah.' She said, 'Well, that's all flying is.' So the rest of the round I kept after her, talking all the while we were playing, because by then I was playing lousy.

"Finally she said, 'You buy an airplane, I'll teach you to fly. There's nothing to it.' "

As Gloria tells it: "Peggy talked all the way through that round. The next week in Beaumont she wants me to take her to the factory in Wichita and help her buy a plane. Well, my dad drives us, and we go, and we start looking. She looks at a brand-new one and says, 'That's too much,' so we find one with sixty hours on it. It was $6,900 without the radio and $7,300 with it. Peggy says, 'Do we really need the radio?' At the time, we didn't, so I say, 'I can fly without the radio. I'd prefer to have it, but I don't need it.' I was trying to save her money, and she's thinking that the radio's for music and that she can do without music.

"The tour was going back to Phoenix, then on to San Diego, and on up to Reno. The plan was that I'd fly it for her along that route, and we'd stop in Oakland, and she'd stay with us before Reno and learn to fly. Well, that's finally what did happen, but between the factory and home, that's when all the experiences started.

"We set off without a radio. We had such head winds all along the way, rough, rough air and one misadventure after another. But we got to our stops and played our tournaments. Then into California, trying to land in San Diego; as things turn out, it's dark, and I don't have a radio. I go into my procedure to go into the airfield without it, just circling around and around, waiting for the green light, and the third time I say to Peggy, 'Looks like they're not going to give us the green light again.' I'm coming in toward the airport, square with the runway where I could land if they'd let me, and just then, they give me the green light. Well, that fast I pull the throttle back and dump the flaps and we just dive from about eight hundred feet. We land and we're on the ground and I look over and Peggy is ghostly pale, white as a sheet, and I say, 'Peggy, what's the matter?' She mouths to me— she can't even say it—'I thought I was going to die.' I said, 'Well, didn't you see the green light?' She says, 'Didn't you know I was color-blind?'

"She got that radio put back in as soon as she could, and she did get her lessons from my instructor when we got to Oakland. The scary part was, she had to get back east for the Weathervane tournament and took off cross-country with only around eight hours solo."

"I thought I had a few more than that," says Bell now, fork waving in her hand. "But, anyway, you don't need many; once you're up there, it's as easy as Gloria said." She continues, eyes squinting as if seeing the past, "I took off for the Weathervane from Sacramento. I'm going along and heading east and I start thinking I should soon be over Donner Pass. I think: That mountain looks awful familiar. Well, turns out it's Mount Diablo. I'm heading due west out over the Pacific!"

"Did flying do anything for your game?" I ask her as the waiter takes our plates.

"Well," she says, "nothing else is important to you when you're up there flying. Everybody down below seems very small. It's a very free feeling. Golf at its finest is played that same way.

"But flying, there really isn't much to it. You go up, you come down, you get a feel. When I think about it, though—years later, I did get in a snowstorm. I was following the railroad tracks and all I could see was white. I said, 'God, you get me down, I'll sell this plane.' Pretty soon I saw a wide-open field and came down. I walked and found a house. I called Bullet straight from there and said, 'I'm selling the plane.' He said, 'You can't just leave it there. Wait it out and get it home.' I said, 'Do you want to kill me? Now, the good Lord got me down, I better sell it.' But I listened to Bullet. I waited out the storm and flew it home. But not long after, I did sell it, for eight thousand dollars. That plane paid for the swimming pool out there. Did you see it when you came in?"

"I did," I say as the waiter pours me another cup of coffee and I watch myself add cream. We talk of the long hours, the work, the years woven into this place. How the spirit of its history—of its people, events, and happenings—are felt here in it.

She goes to the rest room and is quickly back, and before she's even seated I ask, "How did you meet Babe?"

"Babe," she says, leaning forward, straightening wisps of stray hair from her face, "I met her first during the 1945 Western Women's Open. Her mother had just died, and I asked her what she was going to do. I just assumed she was going to withdraw. She said, 'I'm gonna win it for my mother.' And she did.

"It was a couple of months later she called me up from California and said, 'This is Babe. You going down to Florida this winter?' I said, 'Oh, yeah.' She said, 'Well, I am, too, and I need a partner for that International Four-Ball and you might as well win a tournament.' The thing was, she wasn't boasting, she'd won something like seven tournaments in a row, including the national championship. Well, we got to the tournament and there were big galleries. Babe always packed them in because she was known for all sports. And I'm walking around sort of nervous and she says, 'What's wrong with you?' because I played every practice round with her and she'd never seen me like that. I said, 'Oh, gosh, Babe, I'm kind of scared. If you lose this one, it'll be my fault.' 'Aw, I can beat any two of 'em without you,' she said. 'I'll let you know if I need you.' So I relaxed and she won the tournament."

Through the next hours we talk of the Babe—some stories new, some I'd heard or read many times, but what I'd missed was this tone and rhythm, here now, bringing all the caring, the love, the admiration alive. "Babe could hit it," she says, moving her arms a bit to emphasize. "And she wasn't big. Only five-six. But she was so strong in her hands and forearms. Her hands were so strong she could hold it very softly; that's what made her touch so fine and her short game deadly. And boy could she putt."

Bell reaches with one arm over her opposite shoulder, touching her back, "Babe always talked about a muscle back here. She believed this muscle here behind her shoulder had something to do with her distance. She didn't have a pretty swing—it wasn't flowing—but it was powerful. She'd come through, she'd be over on her left side and she'd spring way back on her right on her drive. On the take away her left heel came off the ground about two inches, then her first move from the top was slapping that heel down so she was right there at impact. That power, I guess, was its own thing of beauty. In the rough, where I'd have to take a sand wedge and just blast the ball out, she'd take whatever club she needed and just swing right through the grass.

"On the green, five- and six-footers were 'gimmies,' and her wedges, she could lay 'em flush right to the pin.

"The Babe, I was pretty shy when I met her," Bell continues; "she helped me with my confidence. What an example. According to her, no one had ever been better at anything. And I do mean anything. She'd even show us how good she was at ironing. We'd be in my room and she'd be ironing our shirts and she'd say: 'Look at this—I'm the best ironer there is.' And she probably was, too. She was a marvelous cook, and she could knit, and she'd like to talk about how she'd sewn curtains and won first prize at a Texas fair.

"And men loved her. She'd tease them in the galleries, 'Don't you fellows wish you could hit it like that?'

" 'Babe,' they'd say, 'how do you hit it so far?' 'I just loosen my girdle and let 'er fly,' she'd shout out. They never tired of that. And she never wore a girdle in her life.

"The press was always waiting for her after practice rounds. One time I heard her tell them she had a seventy. 'Babe,' I said later, 'you didn't have a seventy.' 'Well, I should have,' she said. 'Anyway, I tell 'em what they wanna hear.'

"Like when I had my first baby," Bell goes on, scratching the arm she reached back with before. "Babe came charging in, saying, 'What are you going to name her? You're going to name her after me, aren't you?' I said, 'No, I can't stand the name Mildred and neither can you, Babe.' 'Well, then call her Babe,' she said. 'No, she's got to have a real name,' I said. 'Well, then we gotta find something that looks good in print.' We thought for a while and I said, 'What about Heather?' 'No,' she said, 'I think it better be Bonnie. Bonnie Bell will look great in print.' So it was Bonnie. Everything Babe did, she thought of the press. And lucky for our early tour she did."

"What do you think made you so close?" I ask.

Bell moves her hand to her chin and rubs her fingers over her cheek, thinking. She brushes back another loose strand of hair. "I had a home in Florida and she probably knew she'd get a free room. She was always looking for something for free. And she got it . . ."

"But you were friends," I say, wide-eyed, "that wouldn't be." Then I see she's kidding.

"Babe was the best friend you could have, but she did like

getting things free. And she always did. You know how Rolex is now a large sponsor on the tour? Well, when I was presented with the Ellen Griffin Award in New York, with it I was presented with this Rolex. . . ." She pushes up her cuff to show me, then takes it off to read the inscription. Lightly there I touch Griffin's name; it's warm. "When they gave me this, I got up, and I said: "The story's always been that Arnold Palmer was the first one on tour to receive a Rolex, but I'm going to tell you another story [because that day, like every year, they were presenting every winner at that luncheon with a Rolex—Player of the Year, Rookie of the Year, the Vare Trophy winner].' So I said, 'Rolex has been on tour longer than most people know. In 1950 or 1951 Babe was in New York for the *Ed Sullivan Show*; she was going on to play her harmonica. And on that trip she was walking down the street, and she looks in a jewelry store and sees this Rolex watch for women. In those days they made only men's. So she sees this and says, 'Look! I gotta have one of those. It's a woman's!' So she went in and got the telephone book and called up and found out where Rolex was. She got in a cab and went over to the office, up into this skyscraper, walked into the office and said she wanted to see the president. The receptionist there wanted to know if she had an appointment, and Babe said, 'No, you just tell them Babe Didrikson Zaharias is out here.' The woman was a little perturbed that anyone would think she could just walk in and see the president but in a matter of about a minute, the president's out there in the waiting room grabbing Babe's hand, saying, 'Hey, Babe, how are you?' And she said, 'Good, but I gotta have one of those watches.' And he said, 'Sure, Babe, we'll meet at Toots Shor's tomorrow for lunch.' He was going to get the press there. 'And then,' he said, 'we'll go out to Winged Foot and play golf.' That's when Babe said, 'Well, George needs one, too.' And the next day, her husband, George, got one, too."

There were always clothes, clubs, shoes, Bell says. And the gifts from Amana when Babe and George were building their house—a stove, a refrigerator, whatever Babe would want. And the horse from tournament sponsor Waco Turner. "A real nice horse," Bell says. "And at the end we almost got her a plane. I said to her one day, 'Babe, you gotta learn to fly because Bonanza will give you a Beech and I'll fly it, too.' (The Bonanza Beech was about thirty miles per hour faster than mine.) So that fall she took up flying and she soloed and was really doing it, and then her cancer got so bad . . ." Bell's voice trails off and her eyes move to look out the window. "It was real hard seeing her at the end. She never made it back to play. Never got the airplane. . . ."

We both look out the window. I twirl my fork, quietly check my shirtsleeves for crumbs and stains. Through the afternoon I absently drink more coffee, and as we get further lost together in other days, I study her closely—the beauty, the abandon, the directness, the generosity—wondering if enough memory and mimicry could steer me that way. "You sure are something," I say right to her. And rarely have I meant it more.

In 1990 she got the distinguished Bobby Jones Award for sportsmanship and service to the game. "That was a very high honor for me. I was shocked. Sometimes people get awards and I hear and I think, Now how in the world did he or she get that? Well, in this case that's what I was saying about myself. I didn't know how they were giving it to me. I almost had a nervous breakdown trying to get up and give the speech because I'm up there thanking the United States Golf Association and here are all these hardworking people on committees and things, great gals who've worked for golf all their lives, and I said, 'Gosh, all I've done is enjoy the game. I don't feel I've done anything.' "

Though golf seems everything to Bell, it runs only a close third to faith and family. That morning she's been out helping her church and Habitat for Humanity raise a house. "Raise a house— you ever do that?" she asks.

"All that lumber and hammers and boards. I love it. You see something rise there just from nothing, and soon there's a house for some family."

"You pretty good with a hammer?" I ask.

"Sure. And lifting, too. I still lift," she says, raising her arms.

We both get up now and are off to the rest room in tandem. On our way back, down the steps to a lower dining tier, Bell spots a group of women just in for a session at Bell's school, Golfaris, once the only one, now one of the best in the country. "You-all get settled all right?" she asks them after she introduces me. Then she tells them she'll be seeing them bright and early in the morning. But before we go on she makes a point to say that women are the fastest-growing segment of the golf population but also, sadly, have a disproportionately high dropout rate. At that she stands like a great general, arms raised, and says, "Don't you ever quit. Don't you ever quit this great game!"

Back at the table we talk about Griffin. "Back then, there was nothing for women. Shirley Spork was just trying to get going in California. There weren't any women golf pros. I remember sitting in the LPGA meetings, and Shirley and Ellen kept saying, 'We've got to do something about the teaching division,' and they'd all laugh. All anyone was interested in was the tour. There was very little as far as schools then, even for men. At first I worried we were too far out of the way here; who would come? But Ellen said, 'If you got the product, it doesn't matter where it is, they'll find you.' That's what happened. Ellen convinced Bullet to let us use the lodge during a cancellation he had in February. We had two weeks to plan it. We decided I'd hit balls and she'd talk. The first year we had fifty-four women, the next year one hundred and fifty, the next year over two hundred. This was in the late fifties. You know the rest of the story."

We talk more of Griffin's effect, then I ask Bell to treat me to the story of the first lesson she gave. Her eyes get big and she laughs, remembering: "When Bullet and I first bought this place, of course I was the pro, I had to teach. But I hadn't quite realized the difference yet between playing well and teaching. The first lesson I gave, I told this poor woman, 'You gotta grip it right!' Then I kept her there, must've been two, two and a half hours, until finally she asked if she could leave. I went over just about everything I knew, and I didn't know much. Every few minutes I'd give her a new thought. I figured I had to teach it all in one day, get her set for the tour right then and there, and she was just starting. I don't know if I ever saw her again. I think she probably quit."

We turn finally to her great love for Bullet. Warren (Bullet) Bell was the greatest male athlete in Findlay, Ohio. He got his name for his speed on the basketball court and went on to play in the NBA. "Peggy was crazy for Bullet," Betty Jameson has said. "He was like some Greek god, Peggy's idol.

"When Bullet asked her to marry him, she was as excited as when Babe asked her to play the International Four-Ball!"

On the tour, Bell played with great passion and love, and in 1966, she left for the same: "I always loved the game, I was crazy about it," says Bell. "What happened with the tour, I got married and then I had a baby, and Bullet and I worked all that out fine with the travel and the kids until Bullet got heart trouble in the early sixties. I went back and forth and tried to juggle until I came home once and Bullet told me clearly he needed help, he didn't want to be left alone. I never did leave him again."

"It's lucky Peggy had Bullet to keep her on track," Shirley Spork has told me, "because Peggy's so generous she'd have given it all away . . ."

I remember this later that evening when, despite my protest, she takes me to the front registration desk and asks the receptionist to get me a bed and a dining room courtesy pass. "You got to sleep. You got to eat," she says. She herself is off to Raleigh to give a speech.

There at the desk before she leaves, as she searches for her keys, she asks when I'll be back and gives me a pep talk to speed me on my journey, telling me to remember her hero Patty Berg's words, saying them to me now loudly. " 'There's a difference between the wish to win and the will to win.' " I should remember that, she says, when I get tired.

We embrace, I shake her hand, she squeezes my shoulder, and looking straight at me says, "Thanks."

"I think it's the other way around," I say, holding up my room key. Winking, she turns and is down the hallway.

Later that night as I settle into the room she's given me, I take off my fine shirt and toss it aside. Miraculously, it has escaped without incident, no splotches of jam or butter or juice. My head, though, unaccustomed to the coffee, is whirring. In bed, I drown myself in a sea of books and papers, trying to find peace. In my mind I go over the grounds of that great course as I walked it a few hours before at dusk.

Lying quietly and still, I visit again the practice range, which, I believe, must be one of the best of all time—the huge practice bunkers, the teaching shed, target greens, lights, a hill to help players master uneven lies. Then suddenly I'm talking again with a waiter, seeing pride in his eyes as I swallow my dinner and he gives me his take on Peggy: "We'll have groups here, Ms. Bell'll be called to the phone—Betsy King wants her, or this one, or that, all winners' names—well, soon she'll be back to the table, just the same, always the same, just making it clear in her voice and small ways that the game belongs as much to us little guys. The thing about her," he says as he leans closer, "you don't know what to expect. It's so hard to tell when she's pulling your leg."

As the night wends on, I pick up a magazine, a book, read this, highlight this, flip back to that, and, finally, nod off, having settled into the words I've found of three-time U.S. Women's Open Champion Hollis Stacy: "Peggy's never cared what the world thought of her. She went out and helped start this tour. She's a nonconformist. We had to have people like that to help lay the groundwork for the LPGA. I admire her for having the fortitude. I admire all the pioneers. Playing golf wasn't in fashion for women back then. Today, it's easy to forget that."

What Babe Gave Me

The thing I should have learned and didn't: I can remember we'd played in a tournament and I'd go to the practice tee. And Babe would not go practice. She might go putt or chip a little bit, and I'm out there beating those balls and beating those balls, and she'd say, "What are you doing?" I had the feeling that if I hit more balls—more than anybody else—I could win. And she said, "You know what? I can go back to the hotel and lie down in bed and fix my golf swing. I don't have to hit balls." She had the mind for the shots and for the swing and for just visualizing her swing and then repeating exactly that. She had tremendous vision both with her eyes closed and open.

I quote her a lot. She used to say to me, "Once you win, it gets easy. All you got to do, Peggy, is win one and the next one is easy." And what is that? That's nothing but the confidence that you can win. That's what Babe gave me.

Slipping Around

One of the best things to happen for courses and greens is the use of soft spikes. I was at this big golf shop the other day trying to find something for my son-in-law for his birthday. I went in there and picked up the FootJoys or one of the shoes there with soft spikes, and I said, "Now, how long do these spikes last?" You know what he said? "Fourteen rounds."

You got to keep changing them. So you can't possibly walk on cement with them or you wear them down. Most people don't even know that, they just go on and keep playing in the same old spikes. I about flipped when he told me that, and these were the latest. So check your spikes and change them when you need to or you'll be slipping around.

Glenna's Lessons

The first time on the tee that I met Glenna Collett Vare, I was just getting going and she'd won six national championships. I must've asked her, "What do I need to do to get better?" She said to me, "Well, write down the weakest part of your game." So I wrote that down and looked to her with great expectation. Then she said, "Now go out and practice it."

Another thing anyone unmistakably learned from Glenna was "play fast." Glenna couldn't stand to see anybody waste time. She'd go around eighteen holes in two hours. She'd go through everybody on the course, and everybody let her through. She couldn't stand to stand around. "It's a game," she said. "You play. You don't have to think." To her, golf was simple. She had one very clear strategy: Swing the golf club, go to the next shot, get the ball in the hole!

Cheaters

I've seen some cheaters, and they don't last.

The Model

Posture determines your swing. You have to have good posture. I was playing with Sam Snead one time and he said, "You'll never hit a long iron until you get your rear end out! You got to start bowing to the ball. You can't get the club back to the ball inside if your fanny's under, there isn't room." And he was right, of course.

A lot of players, women especially, tend to tuck their fannies in. They've been told to round it under.

One day I was teaching this woman who was a model, and she's got her fanny rounded under, and I said, "Look, you got to get this posture down because your posture determines your golf swing. You got to get your fanny out!" She said, "All my life I've been told to round it under, because I'm a model." I said, "Well, then you go back to modeling, you can't play golf."

So not long after, I'm still on the lesson tee, about three-thirty in the afternoon, and she's coming down the eighteenth fairway and she hollers over and she has her arm and her club up in the air and her fanny way out, and she's waving, "HEEEEY!" When she finished she came rushing over and said, "I never hit it so well!"

As Snead was trying to tell me, when you have your fanny under, you're going to pick the club up, you're going to throw it on the outside, you're never going to be shifting. You're going to sway. You can't turn if your fanny isn't out. Correct posture eliminates the sway.

I make a big point at the school, I demonstrate for students how they look with their fannies tucked under and their knees flexed big, and I say, "Now does that look better than this?" And I show them where I have my knees straighter and I just bow to the ball. That way they see it and do it.

To feel this, just lay your club down at your hip joint, just lay it right across your lap, and just push back, that will push your fanny up. (It's not like sitting down on a bar stool, that's the worst thing for set up that a teacher can say.)

I tell students, "Lock your knees and bow, then barely soften your knees." That gets them out over the ball. Or I have them stand straight, put the handle of the club on their tailbone and run it vertically up the middle of their backs so the clubhead's up flush with their head. Then I have them just bow at the hips. If they're in the correct position, neither the handle of the club or the clubhead will come away from them. This teaches them to bow at the hips, not at the waist, which is what you need to play good golf.

What Strength Can Do

If you want to improve your game, not just for distance, but for feel, you got to get stronger. You don't have to join a gym or get a lot of expensive equipment, but you do need routine and repetition. One of the main things is: Do a lot of stretching. Keep stretching the different muscles and hold that stretch. Stretching is key in making you strong.

You've got to do a lot of walking. It's very important your legs stay strong. I have a stationary bike and spend twenty minutes on it every day.

The other thing is weights. Weight work on the right muscles, along with stretching, will really help you build the strength you need for golf.

The tools we have today for improving your swing, it's unbelievable. But you have to watch out for gimmicks. Even so, some teachers have some very interesting techniques. Gary Wiren's "fan" is one of the best conditioning and golf-strengthening tools I've come across.

I've had students pick up twenty yards from swinging that fan maybe ten times a morning.

In Florida I have a trainer for conditioning because I know how important it is to keeping my game. At any age you've got to keep your hands and forearms strong. The stronger your hands are, the lighter you can hold the club—the weaker they are, the tighter you get and that destroys the shot.

One of the Babe's big advantages was that she had strong hands so she could hold them softly on the club. That was key to her incredible feel. She was strong all around. What people overlook is that strength will not only help you gain distance, it's vital to your short game, too.

Golf's Many

In my years I've seen quite a lot. I've seen some take up golf because they like to ride in a cart. They love to ride around in all that fresh green, to get out and feel the air rather than sit at home. I know some who are crazy about the game because of all the good-looking clothes. I've got a cousin, all the money in the world, she could never spend it. I go over to play with her at her club and she says, "How do you get dressed and ready so quick," and I say, "I'm going to tell you how. I have white shoes, and a white glove, and a white visor, and you've got six visors in every color, a glove in every color, and shoes in every color; your locker is just stacked. You've got to figure out all those colors before you can play. You're a stylist. I just want to get the ball in the hole." But that's the great thing. We're all there for something. This stylish woman, she plays four times a week. Just to hit it makes her happy. A solid hit is what she's after. She has a boy-friend now who likes it, and that's really motivating. She's eighty-one years old.

Kathy Whitworth

*F*OR AMERICAN PLAYERS, the U.S. Open is something special—this country's national title. No matter where it's played, the spirit of the Open seems to come to life that week, asking, Whose life will change come Sunday? Who will stand with the names Patty Berg, Betty Jameson, Babe Zaharias, Louise Suggs, Betsy Rawls, Mickey Wright held high on the trophy raised above her head, having through these four grueling days proved herself the best in the land?

The players have readied themselves, steeled their minds, perfected their swings, come armed with the finest equipment, donned their most charmed attire—a special visor, gold-ringed socks, a lucky ball marker, a magic hat. They will shoulder the pressure, play each shot, perform and hope, but much of what makes the Open special is the shared sense that the course alone knows the winner and it will reveal its secret in its own sweet time.

"For any tournament of such importance, most players carry a deep sense of the 'meant to be,' " says 1981 U.S. Open winner Pat Bradley. "We'll give it all we have, then dig for what we don't have, but someone's number has been pulled. The answer will come late Sunday."

This year, it is Blackwolf Run, a harrowing course along the Sheboygan River, just off Lake Michigan in eastern Wisconsin, that will provide the answer for 1998. This was lucky for me, three and a half hours away at Thistledown; I could drive, not fly, to it and stay at a friend's, not another hotel. I am there early Monday morning to watch the week unfold.

Though I know to expect a much larger press tent than at regular stops, I'm not prepared for 250 chairs spaced along long tables draped in cobalt blue cloths as if set for an elaborate social affair. The huge TV screens, ringing phones, computers, fax machines, copiers are many more than usual. The interview room is rimmed with still cameras, video cameras, and top-notch sound recorders. The thoughts and ramblings of players are printed out for us within minutes of hitting the air. The course is set long, the second longest in Open history, but most praise its personality and welcome its test. For me, it is smooth work; whomever I need to see shows up on time. I'm done by Friday and without spare time to be a fan, I think anxiously about cutting out, getting back early to my own desk and bed.

But a small, stubborn voice bothers me. A few days before I came here, one of my young junior girls, seeing advertisements for the event, overhearing me say I was going to attend, mustered the courage to ask quietly, "Would you take me there?" Had I not been working, or if only thinking more clearly and farther ahead, I would have arranged to load all of Thistledown's kids in a bus and make a day of it as other youth programs have. I would have had a hard time saying no to any of them who might have asked, but with this one it's worse. Postponing no, I've said, "Maybe. I'll call you later in the week," when I should have known the stage was already set for yes.

Torie is ten. When she says she wants to be on the LPGA tour, she's not dreaming. It's a goal she works toward every day. It's not outside her but something real and alive she carries deep inside. She moves with it; you can see it. She has become a fixture now at Thistledown; men crowd around to watch her hit straight 220-yard drives with her old junior driver, to watch her finesse half wedges, and roll putts with her very soft, deft touch. Despite such unsolicited attention, she is steady—always the same, never cocky or anywhere near showy, boisterous, or bold. She doesn't only love the game, she needs it and she knows it. It has helped her without being fazed to accept the diagnosis of childhood diabetes that was discovered last spring just three weeks after she took up the game. When doctors told her and her mother about the three-a-day shots necessary to control the disease, all Torie wanted to know, her mother said, was if it would affect her game.

The first day I met her she moved winsomely, as if from far off, out of the past. I flashed immediately on *Field of Dreams*. In backward-turned cap, baggy shorts to her knees, and wild, shoulder-length hair, I thought, Oh my, who is this? Not unusually tall, she is perfectly solid through her shoulders and chest, as if it's there that all her world rests. Her brown, perfectly round eyes drilled me as she walked up that day, though she was grinning from ear to ear.

"My grandpa says you're the best woman here. He said I should see if you'd help me. I wanna work on getting on the PGA."

"The LPGA?" I ask, not guessing she's truly meant what she's said.

"Well, the LPGA, I guess then, that'd be a start."

Not wanting to dampen new dreams, I amend quickly, "That's right. You could start there and see what you think."

We play round after round, day after day, for three weeks before I leave on many trips. Whenever I returned, there she'd be, my lively shadow. On nine holes she broke 50 quickly, improved to consistent low 40s, and on a recent scholarship application to help replace clubs she's far outgrown, in answer to "Please provide a brief bio and list of tournaments played and place finished," she printed simply in a scratchy hand, "I played in nine tournaments and won them all."

That Friday I would like to leave the Open, but I hear that voice, and phone. I stay that night one hour west so the ride she's begged will have only a two-and-a-half-hour drive early the next morning to meet me. Though up at 4:30 A.M., she's her usual self—button-eyed and shining, determination so evident my mother has come to affectionately call her "The Little Bear." She's not a kid who giggles and chatters. She is quiet and watches, and despite the rich country out the Saab's window, she spends most of the way studying me.

I tell myself as we go along that though I'm not at my desk, this is all good. I'm leading her today—for her dreams—to better, bigger heroes. Though for my work the day is shot, I'll relax for eight hours and see the Open through her eyes.

As we come onto the Kohler exit, the traffic lined a half mile back, we sail along the shoulder with our pass. Nearing the American Club, the grand hotel where those players with the amplest funds stay, I spot Liselotte Neumann out with her dog. Before I say a word, Torie says, "There's Lottie." Lottie? How could she know that? I think. She's turned in her seat and I see her give a small wave, then turn back. "I guess she didn't see me," she says.

We forego a courtesy car and I walk her in through the main gate so she can get the full effect. Busload after busload of fans arrive from distant lots, and I can feel every molecule of hers racing as she gathers it all in. "I don't know if I'm ready for all these people yet," she says. At first I think she's hesitant to go in. "You're not claustrophobic, are you?" I say.

"No," she says, "I mean, I don't know if I'm quite ready to play in front of them yet."

I try not to let her see my face because she would not understand a smile in response to her belief and her seriousness. "Well, by the time you've practiced your short game all those many hours, you'll probably feel at ease," I say.

"Probably," she says.

Her beige Titleist cap is turned backward, and she says she's going to use it to collect autographs. In the souvenir fan tent she admires things but never pauses extra long or looks longingly. She buys a hard plastic divot fixer for $1.50.

As we make our way down the knoll, below, in the distance, I see Kathy Whitworth, tall, strikingly handsome, all in yellow, coming toward us on the path. I talked with her three days before. This yellow is so good on her I wonder if she had in mind the movie *The Last Emperor* ("Only the emperor wears yellow") or if she knows the I Ching: "A yellow lower garment brings supreme good fortune . . . It is the symbol of that which is reliable and genuine." Most likely not, but anyway, I think that it suits her.

Four days ago I happened on her in a back dining room of the clubhouse eating lunch with Patty Berg. She's moved about through the winter—even the letters I sent through the LPGA came back "Address Unknown"—but I was told by many, most recently Betty Jameson when she phoned in excitement about the Open, that even without an introduction Kathy will speak with me. "Kathy is lovely. The best. Oh yes, very approachable, yes."

On Tuesday morning, I watched on the practice range, at the ninth and eighteenth greens, and between tees, as school kids took advantage of the more relaxed practice round routine, tearing after any player, poking programs, visors, shirts, caps—anything to be signed—at players, very often unaware of the name, concerned more with quantity than person and feat. Three times as I stood talking with players I was hurriedly handed a pen and asked to add my scribbling to the array. "I'm not a player," I said, and had to point to my running shoes before they'd believe me.

It must get old, I think, for players week after week, though it's their job and most do it willingly. Somewhere, by the end of the season, it must leave a mark. But it's great for the game, and I'm gladdened when twice I see women well past sixty admiringly hand a program to Se Ri Pak, a cap to Pat Hurst.

That practice day, just shy of one o'clock, I rounded the eighteenth green and headed up through the clubhouse, cutting through a back dining room en route to the press tent. It was there I found Whitworth and Berg alone. I went five paces past before it registered, then turned about-face and stood for a minute, weighing whether I should interrupt. Kathy's back to me, Patty facing me, I walked up, saying, "Excuse me," and with my lightest air explained myself. Five seconds into it, I realized Jameson was right— it was easy. Neither could have been nicer. Having secured phone numbers and plans for further conversation, only later do I dwell on the contrast—the obscure players chased after and hounded, while up there, the two of them alone. "There's nothing unusual in it," Whitworth says later, "nothing any of the players of either Patty's or my generation don't well know. We've had our day. The torch has been passed. Even the best of us can walk around unrecognized by most."

As Whitworth and I greet each other on the path that early Saturday morning, Torie, too, is unaware. She's tying her shoe as we speak, and I don't tell her who Whitworth is until we've walked away. Then, "I gotta get her to sign my cap," she says, and she runs to catch up with her from behind. From a full thirty paces

I see Whitworth smile, bend, then pat the kid's head. As Torie comes away, delighted with her prize, Whitworth smiles knowingly and waves a final time.

"I didn't know any pro would be that friendly," Torie says. "I don't know if I can get that tall. I'd like to stand that high."

Though Whitworth is only five-nine, one inch taller than I am, she evidently seemed six-seven there to Torie, and as we continued on to the practice range, I hoped it might be an omen. Who better for her to meet first than Whitworth?

In 1985, Whitworth passed Sam Snead's record of eighty-four tournament wins and proceeded on to her eighty-eighth victory, four more than any player in history, man or woman. She won with a swing that was not picturesque but was perfectly rhythmic and decidedly hers. She was an intense competitor, a fighter, but gracious and fair. "What I did in being a better player does not make me a better person," she's said often. "I'm not smarter or more intelligent than someone who digs a good ditch. I am proud for myself and what I did and that I gave it my best shot. When they ask me how I'd like to be remembered, I feel that if people remember me at all it will be good enough."

In speaking with her, I found her to be open, succinct, tracing her years straightaway, simple and clear:

"The times I've been asked, 'How do you achieve success?' I've most often said, 'First you have to get yourself born in a small town.' I was born in Jal, New Mexico, a small company town subsidized by the El Paso Natural Gas Company. A little course there provided employees without a lot of money a place to play. When I started, I paid my daily greens fees, but when it looked like I was serious about what I was doing, Mom and Dad got a sort of associate membership that allowed me to play. If I'd come from a larger city, I'm not sure my family could have afforded that. Also, there wasn't a lot of play on the course, so some days I'd have it almost to myself. This was back in the late forties when women in sports were rare, so I was a big duck in a little pond. I was a classic tomboy, too, and fortunately a nearby pro, Hardy Loudermilk, saw me and took an interest. Harvey Penick eventually became my teacher, but Hardy Loudermilk first worked with me and wanted me to do well so he unselfishly sent me to Harvey. Then, when I came home, he helped me continue in whatever Harvey wanted me to do and was there to make sure I got it right, so I can hardly say Harvey without saying Hardy.

"I had two men who were extremely kind and not the least bit egotistical or set on imprinting their stamp or personality on me. That was so lucky. In a big city, I'm not sure I wouldn't have gotten lost in the shuffle. And this is what I tell a lot of young players: You don't have to have state-of-the-art equipment; what you need is opportunity. That's what that small town gave me. I certainly didn't have the most expensive clubs or balls and certainly not a finely manicured course. I played with my dead granddaddy's clubs, and I found a lot of my balls out in the sticks, and, boy, when I hit one out there, I went and got it. I say to parents, 'You don't have to buy them a Big Bertha, just give them a chance. If they really want it, they'll find a way; they don't have to have the ultimate in anything.'

"When I started, I didn't know what golf was. Maybe it was something I was meant to do. At the time, it seemed it was something I fell into. A friend of mine invited me to play, so I borrowed those old clubs my grandmother had saved. I liked the game right off because it was something I could do alone and work at. At first, there was no driving range at the club where I went to play, so I practiced a lot in a cow pasture. Me, the cows, and the mesquite bushes. That's how it was.

"Another thing helped: I played bass drum in the school band. I was always blessed with rhythm. I just loved band. I didn't realize it, but I was the leader, especially in marching. How fast we went on and off the field depended on the rhythm of that bass, and I know, though I was unaware of it at the time, that helped me in the golf swing.

"My parents did all they could for me, and when Hardy wanted to send me to Harvey, my mother drove me that great distance—everything is a great distance when you grow up in West Texas or southern New Mexico. While I had my lesson, she would stand right behind and listen to what Harvey said. I was glad to have her there because she took notes. I still have some of them written on an old paper bag.

"As I went along in that area, I was fairly well recognized as an up-and-coming young player, so I was invited to play in a lot of little events and exhibitions where I got to meet Mickey Wright and Betsy Rawls, who were doing exhibitions for Wilson. I just popped up everywhere they went in that country. I'm sure they must have thought, Who is this little kid coming out everywhere we go? Eventually, they invited me to play in a nine-hole exhibition with them and oh, what a big deal. That was another advantage of being in that remote area: There weren't a lot of local players to choose from.

"There's also, though, another thing about growing up in a small town. You're just really green behind the ears. When I won the New Mexico State Amateur it qualified me to play in the Titleholders in Augusta, Georgia, which is the women's equivalent of the Masters. So my mother and I knew that was the command performance. I had an invitation to play and we thought that meant I had to do this. It was quite a financial burden on my parents because we couldn't travel by car. My mother and I got on the Greyhound bus. It was a day and a night and then we got to Augusta the next day. We stayed at the Bon Air Hotel, which is this huge, huge, white hotel on top of this hill where all the players stayed. They even had my name posted on the back of this chair, which to me was really impressive.

"We got signed in and settled and then went out to the golf course. The eighteenth green sits just down below the hill, directly below the doors of the clubhouse, and my mother and I are there looking down. Betsy and Mickey were visiting and talking and they looked up and saw us and just did this sort of classic double take, like, 'Who? Her? Her again?' I knew in my heart they thought, 'My god, that young woman is everywhere.' But they were really nice, and Betsy Rawls had her mother there and they took us out to dinner one night and were very kind.

"I had this small plaid bag I had ordered from the hardware store my mom and dad ran. I did have some real nice woods and irons that Hardy was able to get for me, but the caddies there didn't want to caddie for me. They thought it would be so embarrassing to carry that funny-looking bag. I don't remember how I did it, but I finally got some guy to carry it. It didn't bother me because it was the best I had so it was good enough for me. I wasn't embarrassed about it, but I was embarrassed that I was a poor player. I didn't know diddly-squat about anything. Mom was a great trooper, though, and we had a wonderful time. Come to find out later, she was talking about how we were both scared to death. I knew I was scared and didn't have a clue about anything, but I thought for sure she did. If I'd known she was as scared as I was, I would have gotten right back on that bus and gone home. That's why, when I actually won the Titleholders six years later as a pro, it was so exciting for both of us. It held special meaning.

"I turned pro in 1958, but it took me a long while to win. When you're a kid, nothing seems to come fast, it seems it goes on forever. I felt I had come close to winning several times in 1960 and 1961, but I didn't win. I lost a couple play-offs and I thought, Well, maybe I can't win. Maybe I just can't get it over the hump. But those years were important because I was learning how to lose. I was putting myself on the line and learning about coming up short. Some people can't accept that, which is why there's the old saying, 'Either they're afraid to win or afraid to lose, one or the other.' We say, 'Well, I would've won but dah dah dah. I would have played better but I didn't feel well, or . . .' There's always a reason. We're afraid that if we really try and give it everything, and then don't make it, how do we accept ourselves—and that's too bad because there's nothing wrong with trying and falling short. It's just another way of finding out about ourselves.

"Starting out, I wanted to be the best in the world. I got that knocked right out of me at the very beginning. Then I thought, Well, maybe I'll just be . . . maybe I'll make some money. I had to put my goals and priorities back into the right sequence. To become the best player in the world I had to do certain things, and one of them was to play better. How you become the best player in the world is not by giving up on it, but by understanding that maybe you won't be. Self-acceptance is the key. I had to accept myself as a nonwinner before I won.

"As it turned out, and I look back on it, I'm so glad that I didn't win, because I wasn't ready. I would never have been able to handle it. I look at the girls who win when they first come out and they just have a hard time because then their expectations are so high it gets unrealistic. I had a lot of experience under my belt, so when I did finally win in 1963, five years later, I was ready.

"I didn't win by myself. I had some wonderful people out on the tour who helped me. Patty Berg was by far wonderful, and Gloria Armstrong really helped me, and Jackie Pung. Jackie was very good to me. We would travel together some and she helped me with my footwork a lot, with rhythm and using my legs. She made me so aware of that. Talk about rhythm, this woman had it, her swing was wonderful to watch. And there were Betsy Rawls and Mickey Wright. These women are each so smart, so intelligent, and they were very giving to me. When I asked for help, and you have to be very careful about asking for help, they never turned me down. They were my great heroes, really, wonderful models to follow. And I've tried to live my life as best I can with that in mind, because models meant so much to me, and being in the fore, you don't know who's looking at you. Someone is almost always looking. You don't walk around thinking, I'm going to influence these people today. You just live and do the best you can. I just feel very lucky to have had those people to emulate."

Torie's day at the Open stretches well on toward dark. We've tromped the grounds, seen the course, the clubhouse, the press tent, the locker room, the TV production truck, the rules van. She's watched from inside the ropes, gotten, I believe, her fill. Her cap is now full of autographs she's run down herself: Annika Sorenstam, Mjhari McKay, Barb Mucha, Rosie Jones, Pat Hurst, Helen Alfredsson, Se Ri Pak, Laura Davies, Jenny Chausiriporn, Liselotte Neumann, but as we drive toward home it's Whitworth she asks about. "Does she have a secret? How far does she hit it? What did she name her putter? How'd she get so tall like that?" The questions come one after another, a wide departure from her quiet watchfulness, and I no longer turn to find her looking at me. Her head is in Rhonda Glenn's *The Illustrated History of Women's Golf*, which she's dug out from the backseat. She's found Whitworth under the title "The Modern Monarch," and reads aloud to me, though she stops often and flips to the back pages to announce various victories and records: "Leading money winner eight times; Player of the Year seven times; seven-time winner of the Vare Trophy—what's the Vare Trophy?; six major championships; Hall of Fame, 1975; seventeen career holes in one—are they kidding?; captain of the first Solheim Cup, 1990, 1992; four-time president of the LPGA; first woman to cross the mark of one million dollars in career earnings. Boy, she must be rich. Does she play video games?"

"I don't know. I know she likes to fish."

"I like to fish," she says, but absently. As I bring the interior light up to bright because it's gotten dark, I see she's flipping the pages back and forth more rapidly. She's realized something: "Hey, all those wins, she never won the Open."

"No," I say.

"I wonder," she says. "Being so nice, maybe she got tired. If she rests up, do you think she could come back someday and win it then?"

She's looking at me hard now. "You never know, she might," I say.

In a different light I might have asked a question that would have led her further, but I am tired and choose the easy reply, careful as always with her to choose nothing that thwarts, even though I know true passion endures. "I'd like to play her," she says.

"That would be the deal, wouldn't it?" I say.

We hit a detour that winds into the unfamiliar, and the next time I look over she is asleep, one hand between the pages. I close the interior light and drive us on, listening through the quiet to her dreams marking our way through the dark.

Never Give Up

I kid Betsy Rawls a lot of times, saying, "You just don't know how many things you've helped me with over the years just by my observing you." It's the truth. Unbeknownst to her, I've learned so much.

One of the big things I once heard her say, and this may seem so obvious but when she said it it took on new meaning, "You must never give up." She said, "I work harder for a seventy-five or an eighty because when I'm out there playing, no matter how bad it gets, I fight over every shot, I never give up." That's a mind-set you learn, something you discipline so it becomes a part of you because it's so easy to give up. It's so easy to say, "Gosh, I can't play today." The hard part is to keep trying. And I've found that if you keep that attitude, then when things are really going your way, you just shoot the lights out because you're still grinding as hard as you can on every shot and it becomes a discipline. It becomes part of you, so when things do go your way, that's when you shoot your really great scores.

Se Ri Pak made that comment at the Open when she won and I thought, Good for you. She said, "I never give up. I never give up." And it was true. Near the end Jenny Chausiriporn was on the fringe in two for what looked like an easy par and Se Ri was in the hazard on a steep bank in deep grass a few feet from the water. She had to take her shoes and socks off to make the shot. She went in there, set up, and stuck it close. She hung in there. That's what you do. You play yourself through everything, you stick, you keep trying no matter what.

Bring It on In

Patty Berg is into her eighties now, and I don't know anyone who's done as much for women's golf. The thing about Patty, with all her great victories, is that she lives in the present. Never have I caught her dwelling in the past. She keeps up with all the young players, many who are, I'm sure, barely aware of her, and she remains so sharp. She called the Open early in the week when we were there. She said, "Well, it looks like it's really going to boil down to the people who are in the best condition physically." And that's what happened. In the play-off we had two young players who were in great shape, and as it turned out, to win there you had to be—it was a marathon. Patty could see that with Blackwolf Run playing that long, and the wind, it would beat the players up. And there's always the stress and strain of any Open; that, coupled with the rough and that type of golf course, meant these girls were just absolutely going to get beaten to death.

Tournament golf especially takes a lot out of you physically, and people just don't realize it because golfers aren't thought of as athletes. But to compete, you have to be an athlete. The stress and the pressures, the strain of holding your emotions in check through four days, the walking, the wind, you're exhausted when you're finished. It takes deep stamina to get you through to the end. Club players especially need to check their scorecards, compare their last holes, especially in tournament play; if there's a drop-off, conditioning is one of the places to start. To be your best, like Chausiriporn and Pak on that grueling test, you've got to be able to bring it on in.

The Big Head

A big key in my career was Hardy Loudermilk, my first teacher. He came back into my life in a big way after I had won eight tournaments in 1963. I played pretty well, and then the next year I was playing okay but I hadn't won anything. I was really not too happy about it. Toward the end of the year, we were playing our last tournament in San Antonio. I came into town and my mother was with me because we were going to go to Japan from there. Anyway, the three of us went out to dinner and I was just crying the blues about how I had been playing in all these tournaments and not winning. Well, Hardy finally spoke up, and for me it's not what a person says, it's who says it; someone else could have said what he said that night to me, and I wouldn't have heard it the same way. Anyway, I kept crying the blues, and he said, "Well, I think you've got the big head. Yes. And I want you to know it." Just like that.

It hurt my feelings so bad and I thought, Wow, I can't believe he told me that. Of course, you never think of yourself as having that happen, but I knew Hardy wouldn't say that unless it was true. He wouldn't say it just to be mean, so it went straight into me. I went out to play a practice round the next day, and even there in the Pro-Am I noticed it, I was moaning and groaning over the slightest thing. I thought, Man, oh boy, this is bad. This is not going to work. I was taking winning for granted and grumbling over everything.

That dinner was a big moment. It's not nice to tell about myself, but fortunately I had someone who cared enough about me and who had the wisdom and strength to say, "Hey, you have gone over the top—you're not as great as you think you are. Winning is a gift." I worked really hard that week. I won the tournament. I appreciated what I did well and I never, ever took winning for granted again.

Imagination

When we were on the tour, one of the things the LPGA did every week was to give a clinic, usually every Wednesday afternoon before the tournament started. Patty Berg would emcee, and those of us helping, usually Mickey Wright and Betsy Rawls and me, would hit balls. We'd have to hit the shot she called out, and I can tell you that for me it was the best experience in the world. If you didn't know the shot, you had to learn it. That's where Patty was so great. We spent six weeks down in Florida with her learning to do this clinic, and Mickey has cited this, too—it was great experience and I think a huge reason why I played so well. We practiced different shots all the time, and I became far more imaginative as a shot maker.

Patty would stand up there and say, "Well, now we're going to hook the ball, this is what we do, dah, dah, dah, de dah," and we would have to do it or look like a fool. Today, there's so much emphasis on the perfect swing and swing technique, a lot of players forget a big part of golf is imagination. We had the advantage of traveling together and experimenting and learning these shots, so it was easier than doing them yourself, but if you truly want to be a player, you have to get out and learn the shots one by one, which often calls for improvisation. Students would benefit so much by just taking a club, forgetting everyone else, and going off alone to try different shots. Learn what produces what and the feel of the shot you just took. Get out there and learn what you and the club can do together. You need to feel, then you need to repeat the shot in practice over and over so you remember the feel.

It was from all the practice at the clinics that I knew where I was most of the time in my swing. If I got in trouble, I always felt that if I had a swing, I could manufacture a shot. My teacher Harvey Penick always said, "Don't try to play a shot you haven't practiced." Well, I practiced those shots all the time. Given all the places you can end up on a golf course, imagination in practice is the thing.

Thinking of Harvey

I've had some success as a teacher, but I'm not as good as I hope to be. I had the most wonderful model in Harvey Penick. He had a remarkable love for helping someone hit the ball better than they'd ever hit it before in their life. He'd say, "Their eyes light up, and I just get goose bumps." Teachers with the feeling and genius and generosity he had are few.

I can't teach without thinking of Harvey. I travel and often do a lot of three-day schools. I tell those who come we're only going to work on two things, grip and set up, because we have only three days. A lot of times they'll come to me and say, "Well, I went to so-and-so's school." And I'll say, "What did you learn?" They were on the tee from dawn until dusk and they didn't know what they'd learned, they couldn't tell me. I say, "Well, that's not the way it's going to be here."

I do as Harvey did with me. He wouldn't let me do anything until I got the grip. He said, "Until you get the grip, there's no sense in going on." For three days, all I did was grip. He said that until you put your hands on there without thinking about it, you can't go any farther because you won't be able to think about the other. We worked grip grip grip; that's all there was to it. Harvey knew, genius that he was, that he could have taught me a lot of things, but if I couldn't grip the club, if I couldn't stand on my feet in solid setup and balance, what good was the other? It would all be off.

People need to remember that being a great player doesn't make you a great teacher. When Harvey heard I was going to be teaching, he told his wife, Helen, "Call her up and tell her she needs to get down here. There are things she needs to know." So Helen called, and I thought, Okay, sure, and I went down there. I said, "Okay, Harvey, I'm here. Help me." This was before all his wonderful books came out. All of us were always saying, "Please write this down somewhere." We went over and over a lot of things, and I said, "Well, gee, Harvey, you never told me about this." And he said, "Well, you didn't need to know that as a player. You need it now as a teacher."

One of the last things he told me was, "Please don't let them grip it in the elbows." I didn't realize why at the time he was teaching me. He was just so much grip, grip, grip. But now as a teacher I know why. He always said, "You're going to swing it like you grip it." Most people grip it in their shoulders and their elbows. They have so much tension up there it kills all the feeling and distance. Harvey wanted to make sure the grip did not extend above the hands. "Ease," he'd say. "Ease in the elbows and shoulders."

What Counts

It might have been my dream as a child, but as it turned out, I'm not the best player who ever lived. In my mind, Mickey Wright is. I knew right away that I could never swing like Mickey, nobody could ever again swing like Mickey. Her swing is just so great. It has its own fine mechanics, that's one thing, but mechanics can be learned. Mickey's swing is great because of who she is. I won eighty-eight tournaments, but if she'd been able to overcome the pressures that her greatness brought her, she would have won a hundred. Sometimes, when you win a tournament, it's more of a relief than anything. You're just glad it's over. I think that's how it got to be for Mickey. She would have been quite happy to just play at six o'clock in the morning all by herself, do the best she could, and then let everybody go out and shoot at it. The notoriety, the public acclaim—much like Hogan, all of that was just not in her makeup.

I didn't have the greatest swing; I just did the best with what I had. That's all I think anyone can ask. In 1973, I'd been winning on tour for ten years and I hit my own burnout. At one tournament I could hardly sign my name I was shaking so bad. It was exactly as Ben Hogan said: "It's like water dripping on rock. Eventually it will take its toll over a period of time."

You're always trying to get better. You're always pushing, pushing, pushing. Because you're number one and that's why you're there, you need to win. Winning is ingrained. It's been your intent for as long as you can remember. There's the old cliché, "The fun is getting there. The hard part is staying there." And that is the hard part about being number one. Now you've set a level and you must maintain that level. What happened to me in '73 was that I just couldn't handle it anymore. I had to find another way to play, to play without the pressure of staying number one.

For any player, when you first start to win, it's a lark. It's so exciting you can hardly believe it. You accept that the fun is being there under the gun in the excitement of competition. The key is remembering that, because as you go along, the pressure can change that.

By the time I'd won sixty-some tournaments I was really feeling the strain of that push. I needed to back away but I wouldn't. What was happening instead, I'd have a really good round, and then the next day I'd go out and shoot an 80. This didn't just happen one time, it was happening more and more. It was frustrating. It took a friend of mine to make me see what I was doing. She said, "You find yourself in the lead and you find some way to get out of it. You subconsciously blow a hole or blow a round just to take the pressure off." And of course that was what I was doing. I was blowing myself out of the tournament so I wouldn't have to be there.

I had to face that and begin to understand that I could still try to win but it was okay to take the next week off. I let up on my schedule and worked myself back to where I could feel the pleasure of being there. It didn't have to be a fight.

In a few years, though, the strain was back full force. Early in the season in 1977 I won the Dinah Shore, and I'd played real well the first part of the year, so I found myself being the leading money winner again. I remember thinking, "I can't do this. I've got to get out of this situation." I was thrilled to win the Dinah Shore, it was my seventy-eighth victory, but I didn't want to be the leading money winner anymore. I didn't. The pressures, the feeling of being caught up, all flooded in and I started backing away again. Soon I missed a cut and I remember being so tired after it was over that I couldn't get up to go have lunch. I always tried to win when I teed it up, but at that point I had won and won, and I no longer wanted to carry what you carry as number one. I had to see myself just as I had when I was first on tour and wasn't winning; I needed to cut down on my schedule so that when I did play I could feel the fun of being there that I'd felt in the beginning. I went on to win ten more, but only because I got back to knowing the fun of it, the thrill again of being under the gun. You have to guard that, because that's what counts.

In the beginning, you worry about, "Oh, I made a mistake. I'm not going to make any money, or I'm not going to make the cut, or I'm not going to do this, or I blew that." But you eventually learn that winning money, making the cut, and winning tournaments sort of take care of themselves; if you play well, they'll happen, and to play well, you can't be thinking about all that stuff. That's where the discipline comes in. You have to be tough on yourself.

You cannot give in, you cannot give up; you have to get out there and be the best you can. Work on your game, not someone else's. Stop trying to be the best in the world; be the best you can be. Betty Jameson always says, "You can't win until you know how to lose," and it's true. Winning comes after self-acceptance. When you're in the right mind about it, the fun is being there, and winning takes care of itself.

Winged Foot

THOUGH I'M SPRAWLED under a large maple, restful and quiet, Matia, my teacher, reminds me, "She who walks in haste, cannot walk with dignity."

"You sound like a fortune cookie," I say.

"That is from a fortune cookie."

She hands me a photograph she's come upon, creased and grainy, stuck amid a stack of other photos. Women golfers in knee-length skirts. Two loom large in the foreground and fill the image. The taller of the two, face turned away, touches the shorter one's shoulder. I can see that something has happened.

"What do you see?" Matia asks.

I don't want to be wrong. I could try to guess. I can see something is out of the ordinary.

"Should I know these people?"

"Jackie Pung and Betty Jameson."

It's the 1957 U.S. Women's Open. I'm told that in the photo Pung has just lost the title. She has scored well enough to win by one but she's out after signing an incorrect scorecard. The total is correct, but one hole was mismarked in error. Jameson's hand is posed in consolation, regret, apology. She's out, too. On a par 5 each wrote the wrong score for the other. And they've both signed the cards.

I learn the story and now wish I could remember the exact words, because in them I feel I am present. We are all present. It was a lovely day. The crowd was huge, all of Manhattan on the grounds of Winged Foot, the famed course in Mamaroneck, in Westchester County. The great Tommy Armour darting between the ropes following his two prized students, delighting in "his girls," paired, making their run: Jameson a confident, brilliant beauty with a charmed artistry that expressed itself in a forceful way; Pung fluid and rhythmic, face and carriage brimming with light and ease, on the greens often breaking freely into the hula in glee.

That day, Pung triumphs. Jameson finishes well behind. They are rushed shoulder to shoulder to a single card table amid a mob at the edge of the eighteenth green, the media firing questions, their handlers prodding. With nowhere to sit, they stand and exchange scorecards. They glance at them. With the totals apparently right, they sign. Quickly, Jameson is off to reflect. Pung is rushed to microphones, cameras, celebration. The hour turns. The hole-by-hole error is then discovered. Both are disqualified. Finished.

Betsy Rawls, one stroke back, is the winner—the U.S. Women's Open Champion.

"Oh, no," I moan. By now I'm sitting. "They must have felt terrible. Both of them." I look with new eyes at the picture.

Matia continues the story and I hear that after that day, that error made in the haste of all that frenzy, scoring tents became customary, pitched to the side at each tournament's finishing hole. From that day, chairs and cover and refuge were provided for the players to sit in peace with their cards (a ritual already in place for the men, already a practice at tournaments run by the Women's Western). From then on in all major events, the tents were always there, dubbed in remembrance, "Pung's Pavilion."

"Pung's Pavilion?" I say, smiling.

"They took a collection for her. Passed a hat, a cup. She went home with that."

We're quiet. A breeze picks up. In a few minutes Matia says, "Winged Foot, 1957. Who won that day?"

Thinking it's a quiz, to see if I've gotten every detail, I'm about to say, "Betsy Rawls," then I realize she's asking something else. Still, it has to be Rawls. She played well, did everything correctly. Of course Rawls. Anything else betrays the rules—for sure, the record books. It's the right answer, the dot-the-*i*s, cross-the-*t*s answer. I look at Matia. What would she say?

"Who won that day?" she asks again.

Because my life is not neat as a pin, because at heart maybe I'm yet wild and shabby, or because I believe that trees and birds do make a sound in the forest when I'm not there to listen, I say, "Jackie Pung. She won, she won where it counted." When Matia says nothing, I look in her face for disapproval, then at the photo again to reconsider. "Who did win that day?" I ask her.

Still she says nothing. When my eyes raise to look at her, "Ssssh," she says, chin to the sun, dozing.

Betty Jameson

"What happened at Winged Foot was the most horrible thing that happened in my golf career. It was just innocence and ignorance and carelessness on everybody's part. I think it might have been the residue of mortal minds run rampant because we were all in a frenzy. I was going to win that tournament and so was Jackie, and she did win it. When I left the green, I was just very upset because I hadn't played as well in the afternoon. But we were really digging in, giving our hearts to it. Jackie was playing up to a champion and had won it outright. And I stole it. Not because of anything that happened out on the golf course, but because we didn't know what had happened. We were totally unaware of it. On our cards, on the fourth hole, we had written the wrong scores down for each other. We were a hundred yards apart. I went to the right for my drive and she went to the left. And we never saw each other until practically the putt. Neither of us played that hole well and we were so glum about it we thought each of us had gotten one better on the hole than the other, and we didn't check it against each other. We just wrote it down. We had a history playing together, and we just thought we knew. And we not only had a woman parading around with a placard that showed how we stood, we had a USGA woman walking around with a scorecard marking it down. When it was over, we were rushed to check a score in that bedlam on the edge of the eighteenth green. All of Manhattan was loose around that table. Jackie was so thrilled to win, and I was so down to lose, that we did not do what was supposed to be done.

"When this one USGA official found out that I had signed a wrong card, he came racing out in his Presbyterian Sunday school manner and said, 'Betty, we're going to forgive you this time, but you did—you committed the cardinal sin. You signed a wrong card, but we're going to overlook it.' We got back and the press, not the USGA, had discovered it: The total was right, but the figures didn't add up. Then Richard Tufts, the USGA president who knew golf in and out, came out and told me what I had done. 'I'm sorry to tell you, Betty, but Jackie is disqualified.' And that man, he felt bad about it. He told me again and again over the years how sorry he was. I was down in the dumps. I couldn't have been sorrier. It was the blow of blows.

"And the thing is, it never goes away. As recently as a few days ago, at a McDonald's at breakfast, this fellow came up. He said, 'You know, I was there at Winged Foot.' He started telling me about this Hawaiian girl who had won. I said, 'Jackie Pung.' He said, 'When she won the tournament, we collected money for her, everybody in the locker room and the clubhouse.' It got to be more than the prize money, everybody threw in. But that wasn't what she wanted, she wanted the title."

Jackie Pung

"I couldn't believe I made that error, that's number one. I made an error—I had to accept it. It was mine; I can't say it wasn't. There are photos, and in one of them in particular, I look at that picture now and I've got my head down and my hands on my eyebrows. This is when they called me back to the table. And then there's another of Betty Jameson, with head bowed and her hands on my shoulder. It was such a big thing going on. I never sat down, I just signed the card. I saw the bottom was right and just signed it.

"It got to be so big. Tommy was there going up and down the stairs trying in his way to straighten it out. Babe was in the locker room, her voice raised to Betsy, saying, 'Give the trophy to Jackie. You know the title belongs to Jackie.' It was especially hard because I'd wanted to win so badly. Betsy had beaten me in a play-off for the 1953 U.S. Open. Had I been able to win that I would have had the U.S. Amateur title and the Open title in the same year. Now I'd finally won. But then it was gone.

"My teenage daughter Barnette was there with me at the time

and I took her to New York for a whole week to be with my people. They were having a gathering of hula dancers at the Lexington Hotel. I had won, but I had lost, and I had to be in what I had left, what remained, and I could feel that with my people. What I found there was, they were back to what I call my Hawaiian loveness—responsive love, people hugging and happy to see each other. They didn't know what I carried, they were just happy I was there and I was happy to be with them. I needed fun. After a week with them, I was ready to go back to work.

"It was big; it took so much out of me; I realize that now. But in golf we have errors, and also acceptance. So little is perfect. Golf is always forgiveness."

The gallery, members, press, Tommy Armour, even some competitors that day asked that the rule be overlooked, the error forgiven. But of course that could not be. Mary Dagraedt, LPGA Master Professional and the first person to be certified as a Rules Official in this country—man or woman—reminds players the rules are there to protect them from themselves, the field, the elements, and often, the unforeseen. As a former coach of national champion collegiate teams, Dagraedt knew the rules back and through and insisted her players did as well. In any match, she felt each one of them had a five stroke advantage over those who didn't. "The rules," she teaches, "are there to help, not hurt a player. Learn them and you'll come to know that." As Dagraedt suggests, though Winged Foot spectators were quick to blame and berate, it was not the rules that day that did not forgive, but rather, a rickety card table, assumption, and haste.

Betty Jameson's great career was winding down. Jackie Pung's next win came at the Jackson Open in 1958.

Jackie Pung

IN LATE NOVEMBER OF 1997, at the age of seventy-six, Jackie Pung received this letter: "We are writing to you regarding Winged Foot's 75th Anniversary plans.

"On Saturday, September 26, 1998, there will be a special golf event . . . for all the former winners of the major championships over the years at Winged Foot: i.e., Betsy Rawls, the winner of the 1957 U.S. Women's Open; Jackie Pung, the actual winner, briefly, of the 1957 U.S. Women's Open. . . ."

The letter went on to name other former major champions, men and women: Billy Casper, Suzie Burning, Hale Irwin, Roberto DeVicenzo, Fuzzy Zoeller, and Davis Love III. But Pung had stopped reading—she was honored, she had been remembered not for her error but with the words "actual winner."

Her journey to that Open in 1957 had been a long one. She was born Jackie Liwai in 1921 in Honolulu, 2,500 miles from the nearest continental landmass, a distance that made it the most isolated place in the world. Her mother was French, German, and Irish, her father a native Hawaiian, who had ventured off the island early. With his flute he had gone to New York, where he had joined a Hawaiian musical group led by a man called "Johnny Pineapple." At the time, Pung's mother was finishing high school in a Memphis convent. She met her husband-to-be when the band played Memphis. And she fell in love—first with the joy in the music, then with the flute player. "My mother was young but she was strong," Pung says. "She told her family she was going to go to New York and then with him back to Hawaii. Marrying a Hawaiian was not the thing to do. My mother was given money and completely disowned. When I was born, they were still young and just getting started. I stayed at first with my grandma so they both could work. My father was working in the boiler rooms of cruise ships. My mother was a salesclerk."

But her father loved golf. He played the public courses when he could, and when she was six, he started bringing Pung along. "I would caddie, and at that time there were no tees. There was water and a bucket of sand on each tee and part of my caddying meant mixing the two and carefully forming a little sand mound where my dad teed up the ball. I loved that job. I wanted to play but Dad said, 'Be quiet and observe,' so that's how I learned. I watched and watched. By the time I was ten he let me play, and when he saw that I could be good, he did all he could to further me along. I had wonderful parents—Dad with his golf and mother with her direction and love. . . .

"People think of Hawaii as a golf paradise, but that's not how the public courses were in the thirties," says Pung's daughter Barnette. "My mom scratched her way along rough fairways often on a few holes surrounded by a racetrack. That's how she learned. Those first courses were beautiful because she was grateful and made them so. She didn't get to play on better courses until she'd proved herself."

"By the time I started playing, my father had left the cruise ships and was a male nurse at the state hospital," says Pung. "He was chosen by a wealthy family for private duty with a mentally ill patient, Sam. Our family was moved into a large house on large grounds so Sam could have a family, but his high window was barred. I would play outside and climb trees, and behind those bars I would see him. But when I played golf, Sam could go out and he walked along with my father in the rough and took his exercise as I played. That affected me. It made me feel God had given me a gift and it was golf, because walking the fairways Sam and I were both free. Golf became beauty and freedom to me there under the heavens, the three of us beside the canals."

At age seventeen, she won the Hawaiian Women's Championship, a championship she took three more times. At nineteen, she fell in love with an island champion swimmer, Barney Pung. They were married, and in a few years, with two daughters, Sonia Leilani and Barnette, only a year apart, they settled into a close-knit Hawaiian family lifestyle. Despite her ability, a professional golf career did not seem likely for Pung, but she loved the game and did not give it up. She took jobs as a waitress, an army payroll clerk, and a taxi driver to keep her golf career going. In 1948, she borrowed $1,000 from a bank to continue playing. That money went quickly and she had to take a job as a salesclerk to repay it. But in 1952, in her final match in the U.S. Amateur Championship in Oregon, the road opened: She was five down after nine holes, three down after eighteen, but after a quick prayer at lunch, she says, she came back waging a relentless rally, caught her opponent, and sealed the match on the thirty-fifth hole with a birdie to win, 2 and 1.

She was the first Hawaiian ever to win such a big title. Five thousand of her countryfolks came out for a bright parade and day-long luau, and for her feat she was selected as Hawaii's number one athlete.

Though her way was clear to join the fledgling LPGA tour, she faced the challenge of becoming one of the first to weave the role of professional athlete with that of wife and mother. "I missed those I loved," Pung says. "Barney, my children, my island. I wanted to go home but I believed strongly that the spirits lead us and that golf was a gift the spirits had given me to help bring peoples together."

In 1953, she turned pro. "I'd be gone for months on the mainland and when I came home, my girls would act like they didn't know what I was doing there. That hurt me deeply. I was sad much of the time, but I kept going because I believed in my purpose."

In her bright Hawaiian clothes, she was a gallery favorite in an often snobbish world despite her difference. "I was five-four, two hundred twenty-five pounds, and I could hit it. I had tempo, I had rhythm—I had the hula! And I got a good sponsor, Mr. Hand-macher, and a great teacher, Tommy Armour, behind me. I came to the mainland an amateur and Tommy turned me into a professional. Not so much by anything he did with my swing. But he

helped me learn to handle the media and golf's people and introduced me to players who also helped me, like Toney Penna and
Gene Sarazen.

"The tour wasn't anything like it is now but we still had to
have a certain amount of polish. Tommy helped me with that, expertly.

"In private, though, we all had a lot of fun, though things in
those early times were never quite smooth. I remember I met Peggy
Kirk Bell; I flew from Hawaii and I landed and got to Peggy's and
it was snowing. And I'm wondering, How am I going to practice?
I had no car. Peggy was flying her airplane and I was catching a
ride with her, so off we go stop-to-stop in her one-fan plane, under
and up and above the clouds. Once we were flying down to the
Zaharias's course in Tampa and Babe had said we could land it
right there on the course, that she'd have someone out there give
us a signal. So all of a sudden we're ready to land, Peggy's flying
and I'm supposed to be looking for the signal. I said, 'What's the
signal?' Turns out Babe had a guy out there rolling toilet paper
down a long fairway. That was our runway, that was our signal!
After a few jaunts with her I thought, I better get a car!"

Her first year on the tour, Pung finished fourth on the money
list, earning $7,382. In 1954, she was eighth and made $6,291. In
1955, she climbed a spot and earned $9,259, winning that year at
Sea Island and Jacksonville. Though she finished well into the
money those first years and all delighted in her good nature and
light-hearted hulas whenever the opportunity arose for celebration, off the course Pung faced what fellow players did not—preju-
dice. "I couldn't eat at restaurants. I couldn't stay at hotels and
motels. I had to make arrangements to stay at private homes.

"Sometimes I would bring my white mother on the road with
me and that made it a little easier. But once I had my sponsor Mac-
Gregor arrange an exhibition in Tennessee so we could see where
Mother's people were buried in Memphis, because she hadn't been
back since she'd been disowned. So I got to take Mother back to
Memphis and we saw the grave sites, but we went to visit one of
the cousins and they wouldn't let me go upstairs. I had to sit in the
car. When Mother came down she said, "We're never coming back
here.""

"There were times we'd go into a restaurant and sit down," said Gloria Armstrong who, with other players, traveled with Pung. "They wouldn't serve Jackie and her daughters so of course we'd all get up and move on."

"Pungie," her fellow players called her on tour and still do to this day. "The Jackie Pung story is a famous one," the LPGA publicity brochure wrote in 1957. "It's the tale of the rise of a middle-class Hawaiian housewife to one of the most colorful careers in modern-day golf history." "Pungie was our joy," says two-time Titleholders champion and the early tour's great ambassador Marilynn Smith. "She lifted all of us up by the great dignity in who she was."

"On the tour I brought my hi-fi and my records with me," says Pung. "I played well enough that I didn't have to be on the tee until noon. After I had breakfast and my prayer work was done, I'd get in front of the mirror and dance the hula. You extend your arms, you do the hand motion, the fingers. Then from the waist down, you are pivoting with your leg work. The hula is all flexibility and feel. It's a connection, a transfer between the spiritual and the physical, and that's what golf's about. It's no different than ballet, an expression of the spirit within ourselves. I would celebrate with the hula sometimes on the greens after a win or a long putt. Sometimes at parties. 'Lovely Hula Hands,' that was my song."

The hula was danced on the eighteenth of Winged Foot that day in 1957. "Coming up on the eighteenth, the gallery was lined tee to green. Jameson was well behind but I knew Betsy Rawls was right on my tail. I knew I had to sink that long putt to win what for me was a long battle."

The putt never faltered, just rolled quietly, without fanfare, found its heart, and settled firmly into the bottom of the cup. Pung had won. She did a brief hula, then grabbed her fourteen-year-old daughter Barnette, who'd broken into tears, and they embraced there in triumph.

September 26 is sunny. The drive from Manhattan's Upper West Side this Saturday morning without traffic is no more than forty minutes. Often alone, I'm happy to be driving this time with a friend, a nongolfer without birdie aspirations or an agenda. We turn off the Hutchinson River Parkway and not far down the way, turn in. It is all subtle, no eye-catching entrance or even a wooden sign, just two old large stone pillars anchoring the open historic gate. Inset in the stone, raised on the dark bronze metal, the weathered words, WINGED FOOT, PRIVATE.

"Slow down," I say to my friend, "I've got to see this." For me, it is instantly captivating and I sit up in my seat. This very way so many of the greats entered. This place with huge stands of maple, oak, and elm—of vast lawns manicured and combed, the warp and woof of the grass proudly showing itself to the sun. The bubbling brook and old stone bridge, the footpaths that trail into the likes of a lovely English glade. Winged Foot. "Like the Crystal Palace," my friend says. And now he not only slows but stops the car there under the tall old trees. We roll down the windows. A light breeze is fluttering the flagsticks, mocking the bees. When I've counted the distance, allowed the worlds between here and Thistledown to settle, we drive slowly up the winding road toward the clubhouse. Two workers are raising a banner—WELCOME WINGED FOOT'S 75TH ANNIVERSARY.

There is an old carved lion in front of the clubhouse, a charming stone baronial building with turrets, small-paned leaded windows, slate shingles, and copper flashing. A royal domain. The parking lot is lined with Mercedes roadsters, Lexuses, an occasional Bentley, the predictable Cadillacs. Bag boys are there and ready. I lean against a stone post marking the entrance to the pro shop's front walkway and wait while my friend goes back for something he's left in the car. At least the trees are familiar, I think, resisting the impulse to heft myself up on top of the stone stoop and sit.

I'm dressed appropriately. Except for my mismatched earrings, I'm polished and expensively pressed and, fronting my best posture, could pass for one of Westchester County's corporate elite. The place, I'm told, is a haven for Wall Street, for the conspicuously successful, and for the generationally rich. With appropriate carriage, no one will suspect I'm there after scorecards and pencils. "Will you bring us a pencil?" my high school team had asked, one spurring on the other. "We might never get to a place like that." When my friend returns and we head inside, we see there's a large scorecard and pencil box propped as if just for us on an outside wall. I grab at least enough for my team and drop them into my bag. On the wide, lovely terrace, a large span of tables are set for members to enjoy a long, gleaming, breakfast buffet. But it is a quiet morning, only one couple seated. We help ourselves and slowly take in more of the place.

"It's so quiet here," my friend says. "Is golf always this way?"

"It's the ancient code," I say definitively. Another friend, just learning the game, had written me: "From the outside, I can see clearly that golf is its own world. The minute I open my mouth, it's 'Sshhhh, you're too close.' 'No, stand here.' 'No, don't stand there.' 'Ssshhhh, no, she's approaching the ball.' 'Sshhhh, no don't step there. . . . ' There's all this secret, esoteric information, an ancient, courtly code and you either know it or you don't. I don't. But I learned in just a few minutes that golf is its own kingdom, and you have to whisper. Like talking to the queen of England, you're expected not to speak above a certain decibel. I'm told there's mystery to this game, there are secrets; when my otherwise friends 'sshhhh' me sternly with such hushed reverence, I begin to believe it. Has a pact been made? What is it?"

After I eat and gather a few unruffled place mats—a colorful map of the east course—for my players, I poke around the recesses of the clubhouse. A long hall is lined with photos in an endless glass case. Bobby Jones, Tommy Armour, A. W. Tillinghast, Billy Casper, Hale Irwin, Fuzzy Zoeller, and behind a door beside the phones, a photo of Betsy Rawls. In the darkened bar, above the rows and rows of bottles of what I imagine to be the most aged and smoothest liquor, carefully lettered in gold on dark mahogany, is a list of the men's club champions dating back to 1925. Around the corner in a small inlet to the dining room the names of the women champions, all of them since 1930.

I find my way again into the sunshine and walk to stand near the east course's elevated green where Pung and Jameson signed the card that day. "The shot heard round the world," Jameson has named it. I stand there trying to call it all to life. But a passing member interrupts me. "The trees here are known as 'the friendly trees,' " he says, making conversation as he walks by.

"I noticed that," I say.

"Certain ones will throw your ball right out into the fair-way."

"Handy," I say, then notice my watch and hurry inside.

Pung should be arriving in a few minutes, the head pro tells me. I've spoken with Pung at length on the phone. She's told me about this anniversary event, sent me a copy of Winged Foot's letter, but she will not be expecting me.

I look through the clothes, the clubs, the putters, and then I see her entering the shop flanked by club pros—the wide, gliding presence of a much loved and revered ancient queen. She carries the deep rootedness of earth in her body, the steady light of her Hawaiian ancestors in her gentle face. She is smiling, dressed head to toe in Winged Foot logo apparel—cap, blouse, slacks, all of her in varying shades of green.

I go to her quickly and hold out my hand and am welcomed as though we've known each other for all time, just the way we've talked—her voice from day one as calming as a warm saltwater sea. Through the next hours I will shadow her on this her day of honor—of return. Barnette is with her—in 1957, fourteen, today, beyond fifty, though youth bursts from her.

We're introduced and Barnette tells me right off, "A man came up to me last night," she says. "He said, 'I was a member here that day back then. I want to let you know I put ten dollars in the pot. If only we could've given her the trophy.' "

Pung had received a little more than $3,000 that day the membership passed the hat. The official first-place prize was $1,800.

"I remember that putt on the eighteenth," Barnette says, continuing. "When it went in, I was already in tears. It had been such a long road for us as a family. First the separations; then, when my sister and I were older, trailing Mom from stop to stop. When she wrapped her arms around me on that green, it was like it was our victory—there was a lot of family in that embrace.

"But then it was over. Things happened so quickly. I remember them taking Mom into a closed room. I knew—there was a sense something was brewing. Then she came out crying. I'll never forget her words: 'I'm not the champion anymore.' "

Barnette blinks resolutely. There is sadness still, now in this moment. "A lot is fuzzy, but I remember clearly some of the members and a USGA official saying to me, 'You sit here and help count the money.' And I remember we got invited to be on *Ed Sullivan* to talk about the whole thing."

We laugh and together walk with her husband and my friend trailing behind, the first nine holes of the east course, where Jameson and Pung had walked along that day. Today Pung is playing with three different foursomes of club women all with their own games and questions. This is not a day without preparation. The club has pitched a huge tent, hired its caterers, sent invitations to tonight's black-tie affair. Pung flew from Hawaii to Barnette's home in Houston, the extra days allowing her to adjust to the time and to go see her old friend Jackie Burke.

Whitworth, Armstrong, Jameson, Wiffi Smith, all have told me if I ever saw Pung's swing I'd never forget it. "Playing golf, my thoughts were always on rhythm and timing," she's told me on the phone, and here I see it with my own eyes. But how does one describe pure perfection—a player so fluidly, smoothly, moving all of herself back, hovering for that one pure split second, then turning down and through the shot fully, totally connected, on up to a finish, not a trace of movement miscentered or out of place—this is Pung. "The hula reminds me—timing and soul must be connected if you're to get all of yourself into the swing."

The women are chatting and Pung chats back. Her caddie John has given them all an article describing Winged Foot and Pung's comments on what happened. This was Pung's idea. She's long tired of the topic. "Back in '57 and on through the years, the day overtook me. All the reporters, people ask me. I felt that I just wanted to make up a carbon copy and give it to everyone—I'm not Winged Foot. I'm Jackie."

When we come to the fourth hole, "Old Soak," where it happened, she plays it as any other. There is no pause or reminiscence to memorialize, just her long, steady shots to the green. Between that hole and the next she tells me, "The older I get the more I feel I'm on a spiritual journey. Golf has been a path." Standing under the high elms she says, "I'm happy to be remembered. I'm glad people know I'm alive."

She'll step up now and on "Bootleg" drill it 230 yards straight down the fairway. She's found her timing, her rhythm. She scatters no shot. But when she sets up on her approach, she's aimed too far left. Barnette sees it immediately and whispers to me. All along as we've walked, with uncanny precision she's critiqued her mother's play. From 120 yards out she's expertly zeroed in on the undulations in the greens. She knows the game, reads it like a seasoned caddie. "I didn't really start playing until well past thirty," she says. "But the game was there inside me because if I was going to be with Mom I had to walk the fairways. I got to know golf like other kids got to know riding a bike. In many ways I hated it, but I loved Mom, and people like Patty Berg, the Babe, Wiffi Smith, Betty Hicks took me under their wing. They were like family. It was just all the time after the last putt on Sunday, packing the car, packing the car, packing the car—that was the worst thing."

There on the fifth, she tips her mother off on a break on a treacherous putt the caddie and Pung have not seen and Pung sinks it cleanly. "My boss tells me . . . ," Pung says proudly to us all, showing her deep affection for Barnette. On the next tee, "Trouble," the 172-yard par-3 sixth, when Pung swings, the club sings out in perfect sweetness, the ball travels high, hits once on the green, and lays down six inches from the stick. "That was almost the hula," Pung says as her foursome and small gallery gather close to measure and raise the "if-onlys."

The day has grown warm. Pung wipes her brow occasionally. She is the most solidly formed, vital seventy-six-year-old I've seen, but it has not always been that way. In June 1998, *Diabetes Forecast* put her on their cover. "I like to say that I carried my own weight," she told them laughingly, "about two hundred fifty pounds of it. When I was on the LPGA circuit, I used to eat three thousand calories a day, but I was able to wear it off with my golf and walking.

"Still, it was hard to break that two-hundred-pound mark. I love to eat, and I can't even say I have big bones. It's just fat and a certain amount of heredity."

She was diagnosed with type two diabetes in 1994. "But I

think I was diabetic for maybe twenty years before that. I began to have the hardest time feeling my grip and my swing. You read about the tingling of the feet. All of a sudden I felt that, too. And that also hurt my game."

But Pung is a lesson in care and recovery. She began working out at a health club. She takes long walks swinging a golf club. She does squats, stretches, and she eats healthfully. "I love lentils and big vegetable salads. I also love pasta and rice and all kinds of beans, and now I feel my feet and my grip again. It's never too early or too late—*e malama pono o komino*, 'Take care of your body.' "

The day grows long at Winged Foot. There are more holes, more chatter with foursomes, TV crews, a video shoot for the party tonight, cameras, and a bench set up by the eighteenth. A setup man fusses with her hair, brightens her lipstick, birds sing out from the trees, the breeze is light. As we wait for them to roll, I sit with her on the bench and she tells me, "Even though I was the first Hawaiian in the LPGA and toured from 1952 to 1964 with comebacks in '71 and '76, every time TV or anyone mentions my name, it's still in connection with that card.

"I'm a *kupuna*. No one ever asks me about that."

"A *kupuna*?" I say.

"A grandmother," she says with a smile. "I got seven of them. A *kupuna* is a grandmother, an old one, a spiritual guide for the family; that's what I try to be now for mine."

Her husband died of lung cancer in 1978. Her older daughter, Sonia, died from diabetes last year.

"That must have been hard," I say.

"We all go on. Hole by hole. Stroke by stroke. That's how it is with families."

In a minute, they roll. The video's interviewer loves Pung with her eyes shining, her voice so lulling and gentle, there beside the eighteenth, it seems part of the wind.

Another ten minutes and she's herded inside and, when finished in the pro shop, we find the most private, remote divan and talk. She tells me of herself as teacher. "I try to impart timing and rhythm to my students by the way I speak to them. By the rhythm in which I speak to them. How we speak, how we move is very important, just as seeing is not always with the eyes. Through that rhythm and timing of my words I try to convey to them the good I have in me. That's what any true teaching is."

We talk of many more things—golf shoes, pitching, putting, Gene Sarazen, and as we go along I see she is very tired. But I also understand it is I who must say, "We'll stop now." It's clear that, as tired as she is, she will push on, keep going, as she always has.

At the front entrance beside the old lion we wait for her car with Barnette and her husband and my friend. We all agree that this return, it's been a day. "A gift," Pung says. And aloha doesn't mean good-bye. As she goes off with the rest for tonight's black-tie affair where she will finally be honored as the 1957 "actual" though brief winner, I go about checking on a fax I know Jameson sent to Winged Foot. Jameson had told me the night before on the phone, she'd gotten up early and had worked and worked to compose it. She'd been so engaged she'd forgotten her hairdresser, and it was late afternoon when she finally was happy with the words and got to the place to send it—all the streets were quiet, no one was about—the clerk had said to her, "To bring you out in this hurricane [Georges], this must be pretty important." "A little wind and rain, I was so intent I couldn't mind that," she said.

The fax was read at the party that evening:

CONGRATULATIONS TO WINGED FOOT

How wonderfully fitting that in celebrating your wonderfully historic 75th Anniversary you are paying tribute to the great and gracious Jackie Pung!

No mere words can convey the admiration *and* affection that I feel for Jackie. But this I know: No champion has ever proven herself more heroic and *gracious* than Jackie did, that day at Winged Foot, in 1957.

Arms all around the blessed Jackie!

BETTY JAMESON

Tommy's Lesson

When I was a student of Tommy Armour there were a lot of days I just sat back and watched him on the range because I knew one day that I also wanted to be a teacher. Of course I got many things from watching Tommy, but what I understood so clearly was that you find a player's biggest flaw and work to change that one thing—you don't take the wheels off a wagon. Tommy would work with the biggest flaw that caught his eye until he had it corrected and got it to be a part of the student's natural movement. From there he'd go on to the next biggest flaw and work on that. It would go on that way until the student had a solid swing. That's the kind of teacher I saw in Tommy and that's the kind of instruction I'd suggest players look for if they're searching, because that is how you progress without tearing your whole swing, and yourself, apart.

Setup

Balance is so important in golf, and you can't have balance without a solid setup. And you can't have balance without being comfortable enough to feel natural. So many try to complicate setup when it's really so simple. I tell my students: Stand tall, tilt (from the hips so the butt's out), hang like a monkey, hands together, look from eyes to hands, get a grip. That's it. That's the balance. That's the setup. I repeat it until it gets inside them, like a song: Stand tall, tilt from the hips, hang like a monkey, hands together, look from eyes to hands, get a grip. That's it. It's that simple. Stand tall, tilt, hang like a monkey, hands together, look from eyes to hands, get a grip. It's simple.

Like a Horse

Make no mistake. In golf you need to be strong. I was strong like a horse. But you also need to be strong in gentleness. You need to have a mind and mettle and a wholeness.

Leg-Work

On the tour, in my swing, I was known for my timing and leg-work. I learned from the hula and I got the most out of my legs, that's for sure. Working with Tommy, he introduced me to Gene Sarazen. Whenever I met up with Gene I always watched him closely to learn from his leg-work because he was short and stocky like me. No matter who I watched I was always looking for a further lesson in leg-work. Leg-work, leg-work, leg-work. Until one day I was teaching. It was the mid-sixties. A man with two artificial legs came to me for a lesson and he taught me a bundle. He was a 5-handicapper using only his upper body. He allowed me to see that wherever your will and center is is your real power. You just have to find it and know how to use it.

My Dad's Advice

When I first carried his clubs around the course for him at six, this was my dad's advice; I've used it all through my career: "Just be quiet," he said, "watch, and learn."

The Hat

On my island, we use the ti leaf for many things. We put it on our heads if we're sick in bed, or if we are hot, to keep us cool. The ti leaf breathes. It is many things to us. When I played, I used to put a ti leaf in my golf bag for good luck. When I'd go off on the road, there goes my ti leaf in my golf bag. The cooling effect has a scientific basis, but it was also a charm, and charms are fun. They are all reminders of the breadth of this great world.

Once, I think it was the tournament in Las Vegas, some of my Hawaiian people who followed me when I was there every year were pulling for me so much, they gave me a straw hat, and under it I stuck the ti leaf on my head. I loved to play wearing that gift because inside the hat, on the band, they'd written, "Cool Head Main Thing." And isn't that the truth.

What We Forget

I teach the blind, and this is not hard because there you are totally soul to soul. I bring my intuition with me because that is where they are. I teach people with eyes and often they don't get it as quickly as when I teach the blind. Because the blind trust. I have movements, places where I stand on their backswing and their forward swing so they can find the plane. They can feel where I am. I take them through the movements and then I stand and they can feel me there where I am. I know how tall they are, how long their arms are so I can stand at the angle they have to get to. I guide them through the swing and they feel it—the movements and proper plane—and then I stand so if they break it above or below, they will hit me. They don't break it because they can feel me where I am. There is mutual trust. They trust me for giving them the right information, for standing there. Trust is both ways because I have been teaching soul to soul. They swing and all of a sudden they are hitting it.

You look at people like Fred Couples and I see him very intense. Tom Watson. These people are all playing from their soul. It's a gift given to them. Se Ri Pak. I admire watching her. She sets it up. She's very much within herself. Very much. Same swing, same follow-through, same tempo. An evenness of soul. Feel and soul. That's what it's about. With eyes, we forget that.

Pat Lange

AFTER I ASKED, "Who are the wisest women in the game?" I listened carefully to the names repeated, the ones that kept coming up. Some I'd heard before, a few not at all. Some I could never forget. Others, I had to ask twice, "Who was that?" I'd write the name down, close the page, then forget until it was spoken again. "Who was that? Oh, sure, I've heard of her," but it would be filed once more, tucked away until another mention, then again, and again, until I couldn't help but pay attention. Pat Lange was one of those. In a world of multimillion-dollar high-gloss ads, hype, and promo, I'd never heard her name, but when I entered the land of those who know, nobody would let me forget it.

Pat Lange's domain is unusual as of yet for women—a place of CADS, gram weights, shaft patterns, inertial and modal properties, frequencies, tips, butts, tolerances—she's an expert in golf equipment. She knows equipment through and through, up and down, around, down the way and back, and while up to date, state of the art in her thinking, she trawls the past for what might have been forgotten and holds the old Scotsman who trained her close to her heart.

She owns her own company, Lange Golf, Inc., in Golden, Colorado. She has her own foundry where clubs are crafted to her own design. There are two hundred club fitters for her product, and a manufacturer in St. Andrews, Scotland, for her European market.

Lange grew up in Mount Prospect, Illinois, a suburb of Chicago. Her parents loved the game. "My dad was an avid golfer," says Lange, "he loved to play. My mother had never played but my father was so crazy for it that's what they did on their first date—thirty-six holes. He's very lucky that she could hit the ball or she might not have dated him again."

Though children had to be ten years old to play on Chicago's public courses, Lange would, early on, run along the fairways. "I'd whack the ball around when no one was looking and pull my dad's cart and look for lost balls. I'd get a nickel for every one I found that was decent. As odd as it sounds, to this day I love hunting for golf balls.

"As I got closer to ten, every now and then if it wasn't busy, my dad would give me a ball and a club, and if I lost either one of them the game was over. So I never lost a ball. I'd search and search, I'd stay behind until I found it or another one, and, of course, I held on to the club. Necessity, back then, trained my eye for the highest weeds and dankest pond."

Lange belonged to no country club and grew up without instruction. "There was no junior program. I just imitated my parents and friends. When I got into high school, my friends were taking lessons and I was like secondhand Rose. I got all my information secondhand from them and did the best I could."

She played in college without teammates. Ball State, in Muncie, Indiana, where she majored in physical education, did not have a women's golf team. She was it. "My junior year I wanted to go to the National Intercollegiate Tournament," she says. "I was already working as a lifeguard and I talked the administration into giving me an extra job—janitor of the gym, which brought in enough extra money that I was able to go to the tournament. One of my good friends, Julie Eller, won that year, and Carol Mann and JoAnne Gunderson were there, so I met some people I've known for a long time."

From the beginning, because of her own lack of instruction, Lange was interested in teaching the game. It was never her intent to play on tour, but she had a lot of friends there, and one summer when her teaching load was light in the 106-degree heat over Tucson Country Club, she went out and joined her touring friends. "It was fun, that was the seventies. It wasn't nearly as crowded as it is now; there was no qualifying school. I played respectably enough, but you've heard of the leading money winner? Well, I always said out there that my claim to fame was being the leading money spender. It took a lot to go from stop to stop if you never won."

While working on her master's degree at the University of Arizona, Lange played golf every Sunday with three foursomes of men whose habit it was to play for money. That money, she said, helped get her through school. Also, one of those fellow players happened to own a course and asked her to teach there. She soon became manager, and the following year she moved to Tucson Country Club where she met David Rogers, a club maker from Scotland. There she began what became, for her, an art.

"I was fascinated and used to spend hours watching him, asking as many questions as I could. He was a careful, deliberate craftsman. It was all about quality, feel, and balance. I could see it was an art and a science. It was my new love; that's what I wanted." After a number of years they both moved on, Lange to the Vail Golf Club and, later, a club in Golden, Colorado, where she started manufacturing her own golf equipment.

"Two years ago I was giving a club-fitting seminar down in Arizona. I thought, I'm going to check on David, and I found him. Ironically, he's at the course where I had my first pro shop, a little eighteen-hole par 3 in Tucson. He's still teaching and still tinkering with clubs. He's ninety-four years old now. I said, 'See what you got me into, David?' We went out and rode around in a cart, and, of course, talked clubs.

"I was very fortunate to have had such patient lessons in that art. David had a rare understanding. No one should be held hostage trying to learn the game with improper tools when it's so demanding a game to begin with. Golf is about balance, and that includes both your tools and you as the user. So when it came time to do something about the lack of proper equipment for women I said, 'Okay, I'll take that role.' Who knows more than a woman about what a woman needs, and yet has the technical knowledge to maybe do something about it?"

But Lange didn't just up and decide to have a company. It was trial and error, and twenty-eight years went into research, six to full-time specific field study. The models were zero. The goal was to design equipment for women, equipment that would fit them properly and help them play better. No lavender putters, no pink grips, no turquoise frills. Instead, high-quality, finely honed tools. Even today no one can buy Lange clubs without being properly fitted, and although this practice invariably costs Lange many sales, she remains committed to the goal of women having clubs that are exactly right for them. "If your husband came home with a present, a good-looking dress you liked but hadn't tried on, would you wear it to a party, a size eight when you wear a size twelve or fourteen?"

Lange is an LPGA Master Life Professional. She was 1989 Professional of the Year and is in the Colorado Golf Hall of Fame. Many of golf's finest teachers are trained to club-fit players for her clubs, and many carry Langes in their own bags. She is cofounder and consultant for Denver's Girls in Golf Program, a summer program dedicated to opportunities for underprivileged girls. She travels the country doing teaching clinics and golf seminars and is on the staff of the PGA of America, where she teaches their many male PGA professionals club fitting. Shirley Spork says simply, "Lange knows everything there is to know about golf equipment. She could make clubs for a giraffe or an elephant, she's that good. There's not another like her."

"It's been a steep climb," Lange says, "but we all know that's true any time you're a woman in a man's world. You can't BS. You have to know your subject twice as well. We can't afford to be mediocre. It's the usual fact; we have to be better in order to be accepted."

Could I Help You?

When I had a shop, I had a male counterpart in the shop and one day I was vacuuming. And this was a big shop, eight thousand square feet. We had indoor hitting areas where people could come in and hit balls in the wintertime because we're up here in the snow country. So while I was up in the front of the pro shop area vacuuming, these two guys in business suits came in. They're looking around, and I turned off the vacuum cleaner of course and said, "Can I help you with anything?" And they said, "Well, is there anyone around here who can help us with equipment? We're looking for some new clubs." I said, "Oh, I can help you with that." So I took them over, and I was starting to talk to them about clubheads and shafts when I saw that I didn't have their attention. They're kind of looking over my shoulder, looking around, so I said, "Excuse me just a minute. Let me see if Jack is off the phone." I knew he was in the office reading a magazine, so I went in and I said, "Jack, there are a couple of guys out there who seem to need a guy to fit them with a club." He went out and spent about an hour. I continued my cleaning, and they went in the back. Eventually Jack took them out to the range to fit them. On their way out, I heard the one guy say to Jack, "Man, you certainly know a whole lot about clubs. More than anyone I've ever run into. Where did you learn so much?" Jack said, "Oh, that gal that's up front vacuuming taught me everything I know." And it was true. I thought, Well, there you have it. The old "You can never tell a book by its cover."

$10.98

A couple of weeks ago, I was speaking at a gathering of CEOs and vice-presidents from around the country. All these women were top-notch in some corporation. Very type A personalities, real go-getters. I was on two panels and also did a two-day golf clinic for these women. It was interesting to see how they're very dynamic in their business, but in golf, they were lower end in terms of understanding. I know it's because they didn't have access to clear information. That's what I find in this game—so many women don't have a concept. What they have instead are bits and pieces—little comments scratched on little scraps of paper and then they have to put it together in some kind of order. They never get it together because it has never been presented in a crystal-clear package to them. To say, "Hey, this isn't about strength. It's not about speed. It's about power, which is different than strength. So let's take another look at how you can be powerful and what it takes, because the effort involved in a great shot is not that much." What I find is that most women pay $10.98 for something that costs only $1.25 when it comes to effort because they don't have the right information. They think if you want the ball to go far that means you swing harder and faster when it's not about that at all. It's about leverage and releasing your energy through that leverage in the direction you want to launch the objective, which is the ball to the target.

Think of it. When you make a really great shot, do you grunt? I don't think so, no. But it feels very powerful. Have you exerted a lot of strength? Not necessarily. Certainly not an all-out effort. Getting that perspective, understanding the structure of the swing and how you fit into that picture, that's what needs to be very clear. But women don't get enough clear information to make it easy. Because it should be easy, it's effortless power.

There's not enough said about *target*, either. We're trying to propel an object to a target. We've got a club and the club is the launcher. It's not a beater. We misunderstand that. We think that in order to hit the ball, we've got to club it. That's what you see looking at it, when in reality, what you want to do is launch the ball by swinging. That's why we call it a golf swing rather than a golf swat. It's all a matter of perception. Where do we get our information that causes us to go so wrong?

If you're told right out of the chute by someone who's not qualified to be doing the telling, if you're told to keep your left arm straight and you need to keep your head down—what a hard way to play the game! Instead of selling golf clubs, I should be selling golf casts. "Here, put your left arm in a golf cast and clamp it every time you play and see how far you get." Of course you wouldn't be able to play at all.

Those CEOs, those very bright women's worlds, were clouded by very poor information, and too often that's a common occurrence.

The Ones You Want to Keep

In regard to equipment, I think women need to stand in line in terms of saying, "Take me seriously as a player." Manufacturers have taken us lightly. "Oh, let's give her this. She's a woman. She won't know the difference. Let's paint them in a pretty color and her husband will buy it for her like he buys her a dress or a handbag."

Golf clubs are a very personal item. If you want to play your best, you need to have something that responds to your style of play. It has nothing to do with size or clubhead speed. It has to do with how you play the game.

The best way to find equipment that's right for you is, first of all, never assume. Never assume that you know what you need based on an advertisement. An advertisement knows nothing about you.

I've kept a lot of statistics over the years to determine how I could best help women players play their best. I started out looking at my own players, then other pros would say, "Well, gosh, help me, too. I can't find anything out there to help my players." Because everything out there is manufactured to a single women's standard, it sits there on the shelf, all the same-size clubs, as though we all wear muumuus. God forbid the industry should figure out that women golfers are not all built like geisha girls. We don't all need everything very short, small, and in colors many of us would never choose. Some companies are finally getting with the program in some respects, but the problem, of course, is that it's not profitable for a manufacturer to offer too many choices. The more pieces you have to turn out, the more skilled labor it takes.

I can tell you I cannot put my product on the shelf because I don't know who it's for. I don't know how tall you are, I don't know anything about you, and just because you're a woman doesn't mean I can pack up a set of clubs and send them to you and assume they will fit. So it's not convenient for these manufacturers, and it's not convenient for me, either, but it's the right thing to do. If we want women to stay in the game, we need to give them proper tools. It is a perfect game for women because we can be powerful without exerting a lot of brute strength.

Golf is a David and Goliath story. You can become a powerful player without being big and strong. Take someone like Sandra Palmer. She hits it far and she's a shrimp when it comes to size. It's not because she's stronger, it's because she understands where power comes from and how to use it in her favor.

Here's a fact: 65 percent of women don't hit a driver off the tee. Why? Not because they're terrible golfers, but very often because the driver isn't right for them. So now the problem is to decide what's not right about it. There are only three parts to the club—the head, the grip, and the shaft—how difficult can this be, right? Well, in this day and age, it can be very complicated. We can find a shaft that works, but it's generally the loft that must be considered in relation to style of play. If you don't launch a ball off the tee that gets the ball airborne long enough for it to go anywhere, it will hit the ground too soon. Of course, you'll get more roll off of less loft, but if it hits the ground sooner than a 3-wood, let's say, it's not going to gain that ground. So when I look at that I'm thinking, Here are manufacturers' starter sets for women that come with a 1 and a 3 for woods, and a 3, 5, 7, 9 for irons. Well, what a stupid choice that is. And therein lies a problem— the industry is not paying attention because women are not taken seriously. Do they want you to play your best? They don't care. They want to sell you clubs. "Oh, sure, we fit clubs for women." But what a farce that is. They want a bite of the market, but have they done their homework? No. If I'm going to sell a woman clubs, I want her to play better. I want her to enjoy everything. It's kind of like my dentist says, "You don't have to brush all your teeth, only the ones you want to keep." You don't need to have the right equipment, only if you want to play your best.

In irons, about 95 percent of what I've seen out there for women is an offset head design. All the major companies have an offset design. Well, that's great. It hits the ball higher, and so the industry assumes, Well, poor little woman has trouble getting the ball airborne. Well, I got news for them: Not everybody does. Actually what it boils down to is that 63 percent don't hit the offset well, given the choice. That means 63 percent can do better with something else. What is that something else? Well, it happens to be a traditional straight hosel. So 37.5 percent hit an offset hosel; 37.5 percent hit a straight, traditional hosel, and the other 25 percent, given the opportunity, improve with a bore-through. That means 63 percent do better with what is unavailable on the shelves. With woods, it's the same thing.

In teaching, I find that when I ask people, "Do you prefer hitting woods or do you prefer hitting irons," it generally has to do with their style of play. If they like their irons, their swing is generally relatively upright, and if they love their woods, their swing is usually flat. So knowing that there is an advantage to hitting woods, of course because of the leverage, we have to have a variety of choices available.

One of the best things I feel I've done for women, something that's made a lot of difference, is that I've taken the number off the woods because of the mind-set of having to hit a 3-wood off the fairway when you're a long way out. If you can't hit a driver off the tee, if you're in that 65 percent, what makes you think you can hit the 3-wood off the tee and now turn around and hit it off the ground? It would be like telling everyone that they have to hit their driver off the fairway. Women get hit from both sides. The husbands have advice: "Well, honey, if you hit your driver off the tee, you'll be a lot better player." Now we know women don't do anything in moderation, right? So a woman will think there's something wrong with her because she can't hit her driver. So with my offset clubs, I call the 3-wood the "Tee Club." But what I've done is, when I have it cast at the foundry, it's cast at driver weight because the driver head weight is less than a 3-wood weight. So I have this tee club cast at driver weight so I can make it driver's length, but we make it a 3-wood loft. We've had a great deal of success with that. Then I've taken the 5-wood and we call it "Fairway," and we make it a 3-wood weight and 3-wood length. And then a 7-wood, I call those "911." They are emergency clubs. Owning the company, I can call them whatever I want, and women love it since out there we all occasionally have a use for a 911. Then, for the women who hit a driver well, I have one called the "Big Tee." With the jumbo clubs, my dad used to talk about Long Tall Sally, a woman who was long and tall, so the jumbo clubs are always longer than the traditional size, and I call her "Long Tall Sally." That comes in 9.5 or 11 degrees as a driver. But other women may need a higher loft, a 15-degree loft (3-wood loft) but driver length, and we call her "Sally's Sister." And we sell a good lot of these.

The thing about it is, the husbands don't know what any of them are so they can't advise in the traditional way. Neither does the wife know, but she doesn't need to know. She just needs to know that she's successful. So once again, it's the mind-set. The women love them because they're clubs that are built for them. They have a choice, a choice geared to their individual games because club fitting is about the person being fitted. (And remember, club fitting cannot be done adequately indoors. It can't.)

You should not put yourself through learning and then play the game with inappropriate tools. Golf is about balance. If you can afford only one club, then get one club, but get one that's right for you, and one that's a good one—one that allows you at least the opportunity to experience success consistently. With improper equipment, our games suffer, and not only do we beat ourselves up and think that something is wrong with us, but we say that we're not worthy of custom clubs: "I'm not good enough." Well, without them, you're not giving yourself a chance to get good enough. You can only be your best if you are using equipment that responds to your style of play. That's why it's so important for both men and women to know that clubs cannot be given as a gift without that person participating in the process. It's the same as getting glasses or shoes. If you were going to walk around the world, would you do it in shoes you hadn't tried on?

Debbie Massey

AT ITS BEST, teaching is no different than being a priest or a rabbi, since, day to day, what matters most is carrying on a belief in goodness, the spirit, and the importance of high standards. In central Florida, as I drive inland toward Deland, a seemingly forgotten small, lovely, vine-covered mecca, I wonder what of Ellen Griffin I will find here in Debbie Massey.

No one has mentioned her without bringing up two things: two-time British Open champion; favored student of Griffin. I know she's in her mid-forties, has an easy sense of humor, and absolutely courts adventure. I've also been warned that if I want to get anything done, I should hide my interest in cars so as not to get her started.

I park in the driveway and head toward two shiny Labrador retrievers who are eyeing me from their fully blooming backyard. A low chain-link fence curtails their sloppy kisses, but they nonetheless dance and turn gracefully on tiptoe. Before I appropriately praise them, Massey is there, a smile blazing from her face. For an odd second I flash back to a long-lost aunt I met during my junior year of high school when she traveled through the Midwest on her way from the Southwest to Nova Scotia; we didn't write or phone again, but for my graduation the next year she sent fifty dollars and a seascape card inside which was written, "Anyone who takes the sure road is as good as dead" (Carl Jung).

"Good car," Massey says.

"Thanks," I say, but move quickly on to something else. The dogs are on their hind feet, front paws poised on the fence and noses hanging over as if oh so interested in coming with us. "Great gallery," I say. She laughs and I can tell this is going to be easy.

The house is a grand, old one, redone in such tasteful, vibrant colors that there seem to be cut flowers in every room though I see none. Though it might have been brocade, the sofa where we sit with tea is in my memory cool and supple leather, so large and soft that at a different hour I might have had a leisurely nap there. But this morning the house is full of light and the windows are open.

A few weeks ago, I heard Massey on tape eloquently giving a tribute to Griffin, so her voice is familiar. She says first, "If it hadn't been for an allergy to horses, we would probably not be here." Massey's mother is a horsewoman and Massey would have gone that route if the presence of those wonderful animals hadn't made her eyes swell and her nose run persistently.

She was, I know a child of privilege. She was born in Grosse Point, Michigan, the older sister of two younger brothers. She lived as a child first in Winnetka, Illinois, then Bethlehem, Pennsylvania. Her mother was a member of the Grace family, whose dynasty was Bethlehem Steel. Her father, after college graduation at twenty, started as a trainee there and worked his way up to vice-president of sales.

Though her parents were both fine golfers, she didn't start playing until age fourteen. "Before I picked up a club, I had to learn course etiquette, and we had to learn how to caddie. My father loved the game so much he presented it simply as a terrific opportunity to figure things out. He said it was 'an example of there always being more than one road to go.' Our family rule when we played was, 'No whining.' We learned fast—'Just take your lumps and go on.' "

Already a superb athlete in baseball, football, soccer, and skiing, she picked up the game quickly. "And I got better by playing alone," she says. "In my imagination I met all the great players and they always wanted me to join in—I played a lot with Mickey Wright. I'd hit one for me, then I'd hit one for Mickey. 'Nice shot, Mickey.' We both tried hard but it always happened that I was just a little better than Mickey at age fifteen. And I did what every kid does. 'Here I am at the U.S. Women's Open. This putt is to win it all!' "

Golf at first, however, was not a serious pursuit. Through college at the University of Denver she skied professionally and played golf only in the summers and on family vacations. Yet with startlingly little experience, she found herself qualifying for and tied for the lead after the second round of the 1974 U.S. Open. She faltered on Sunday but finished low amateur, seventh overall. She played on two Curtis Cup teams and World teams before 1977, when she turned pro.

Through her early days she was best friends with the great amateur Carol Semple Thompson. "We played an awful lot of golf together, and Carol, through her parents, was a member of the course in Delray Beach, Florida, where Glenna Collett Vare was a member for years. Carol and I would go out and if Glenna was coming, we'd run and hide in the woods. We always let her play through. She hated slow play more than anything else."

The image of two terrific Curtis Cup–caliber players running for the woods seems so curious that I double-checked their ages with her and later again with Semple Thompson. "That's right. College age," says Semple Thompson, laughing, backing Massey up. "We acted like kids every time. We knew the greatness. We'd head for the woods and just stand and watch it pass through."

But Massey has no reputation for shyness. In fact, it is quite the opposite. She's known for mustering courage and carrying others along. When the 1976 Curtis Cup team went to meet Queen Elizabeth II at Buckingham Palace and petrified team members stood in awkward silence, it was Massey who spoke. "I was scared myself, but I couldn't let the awkwardness go on, so I was the first to open my mouth. I squeaked something at first until I found my voice. I knew the queen was going to see her daughter in Canada, so I asked her whether she got nervous watching her daughter ride horses. I told her my mother got so nervous watching me on the golf course that she hid behind trees. That sort of loosened things up. She said she got nervous, too. She was very gracious and apologized for not knowing much about golf."

Massey is smart. She has been a lot of places, done much, but she is not a tourist. She climbs mountains and scuba dives, pushing the bounds of safety to swim with exotic fish as deep into the ocean as she can go. She skis off cliffs, stands and fishes along quiet streams alone. "My dad taught me many things," she says, "but I took two things in deeply. 'Listen to the old,' and 'Make sure at the end of your life you'll have stories to tell.' "

On tour, when she felt that the country-club lifestyle, fame, and the pedestal that players are on were skewing her perspective, she would leave. In 1984, before a tournament in Japan, she took two weeks off and went mountain climbing, alone with only Sherpas in the Himalayas. "Ellen tried to get me not to go; she thought it was risky. I remember her looking out of her second-story window in an inn in England and me looking up before getting into the taxi; I winked like, 'It'll be okay.' And I was off.

"I went because I felt I needed to remember myself in relation to what is real. To remember, 'I am just a speck.' I'm no more important than this woman threshing grain or grinding corn. Or this fish. I wanted to experience Kathmandu and be on the highest mountain in the world. It took eight days. We walked from dry riverbeds, well after the monsoon, through jungle, pulling leeches off, up and up, where it got very cold. Along the way, I taught some kids to swing my walking stick and launch a rolled-up sock. I still like to think somewhere in that little Himalayan village right now there are at least a few kids playing golf.

"When we reached our highest point, it was so foggy we couldn't see our hands in front of us. The view was zero. But I realized it was the getting there that was important, the journey, and no sooner had I grown happy with that but the fog cleared and there was the most spectacular view. The Sherpas, the kids, solitude, the mountain itself—when I got to the tournament in Japan I played pretty well but I certainly wasn't peaking. I'd peaked ten days before, in Nepal."

Though Massey is at heart a competitor, winning was not always the ultimate goal. "I wanted to win as much as anyone else, but I wanted to win as who I was. I didn't want to have to fit into a mold. I do love chance, and I admit sometimes I created shots just to take them, but as a player, that's who I was."

"And when you missed?" I ask.

"Well, sometimes in life you miss but the miss still takes you somewhere. Any great champion will tell you missing is a large part of being that.

"To be a real player you have to put yourself out there and get banged around a little bit. Now some of the players are so tutored by those around them that it's tough for them to learn some of the bigger lessons—they come, they do a job, they leave. Yet, we're small. Life's big. And vulnerability or openness is so much a part of growing that it's going to catch up with you sometime, inevitably. That's why the Swedish program has done so well. They are really first concerned with developing great people. They know there is a big difference between being a great player and being a great champion. A great player knows and can play the game. A great champion knows life is big.

"Nancy Lopez. People ask, 'Is she really that nice?' I say, 'She's nicer. She's got tons of it. She can give it away forever.' She's had her knocks. You can see the strength of her character after a tough loss. She's not afraid to be interviewed. She knows it's her obligation, tears and all. She's willing to cry in front of everybody. She's not afraid of anything. That's the kind of character I'm talking about, a dedication to your own feelings and values, not to some model, some abstraction. You have to acknowledge that the choices you've made in the past have set you up to make the choices now facing you—that's the heart of a real champion. That's Lopez."

In the entry of her house is an old, faded, wooden placard of Glenna Collett Vare in full swing that Massey coaxed from a resistant pub owner. "I've had it for years, but every once in a while I'll notice it," she says. "Glenna and Joyce Wethered were larger than life to me. Joyce Wethered gave me my first British Open trophy at Wentworth. I got up to receive it and I said, 'I'm not sure right now which I'm more excited about, winning the British Open or meeting you.' And I was totally serious. She was in her eighties by then. She said, 'I'm not really sure why they dragged me out of my garden to come here.' At that point in her life she was a renowned gardener and it was like, 'I'm not worthy of this being here because I'm just a gardener.' That's how it came out. I've never forgotten that, that greatness and humility. She had no use for fame.

As a kid you maybe want to be famous, you want your fifteen minutes, and I'll be the first to say that's terrific, but fame is no good outside yourself. Fame is not intent, it's your job. Like Wethered in that garden, it's day to day, what you do that counts."

For Massey, life is so full she can't get enough. "My father died of cancer. He had such love. He really taught me to live everything. Not long after he died, I dreamed he came and sat on the end of my bed. I said, 'How's heaven?' He said, 'It's really not that great.' " She smiles, remembering. We both smile. "To me it was just another way of him saying, or of me saying to myself, 'Live now.' "

From both her mother and her father she got a true education in the history of the game, its traditions, and a deep sense of appreciation for those who've come before. She played always with a sense of them. Any one of them I mention—Annella Golthwaite, Goldie Bateson, Opal Hill, Cecil Leitch—she has a story. Later I should remind her, she says, and she'll show me "The Girls."

The Girls are her wedges—two sand wedges and a pitching wedge. "The higher-lofted sixty-degree sand wedge Ellen gave me. We've been inseparable. It's about a 1957, made by Spalding, an autographed model Marilynn Smith.

"Then I have a 1971 Wilson Patty Berg sand wedge, and a 1966 Wilson Patty Berg pitching wedge. I refer to them as The Girls, Marilynn and Patty, and every company I've ever been with I've had to say, 'Look, I'll play with your equipment but The Girls [and usually whatever putter I have], they are part of the deal.' The Girls are part of my life. They've been with me through everything, all my professional experience and a lot of my amateur life. I love those clubs.

"There are a lot of classic wedges out on all the tours still. Those older clubs are wonderful and still very playable. Technically, there are a lot of advantages with drivers and irons and I play the most modern equipment available in those clubs, but for me, while Cleveland is superb, no one's been able to do anything better than they did years ago with the wedges.

"The Girls were a comfort. Wedges and the putter, these are your work clubs. When you've missed a green or you need to get yourself out of trouble and into the hole in two shots, if you're in a bunker or rough by the green, you expect them to get you close enough to the hole so you can knock in the putt.

"My caddies got used to The Girls, too. I'd get into a situation and say, 'This is a job for Marilynn' or 'Get me Marilynn.' They knew exactly. 'You want Patty?' 'No, Marilynn.' We talked like that about them and it was always wonderful to have them because playing golf every day with a little Patty Berg and a little Marilynn Smith is very nice."

Mindful of Bobby Jones's Calamity Jane, I tell her my own putter, a cut-down worn black satin Ping Pal 2, is called Friday, as in Robinson Crusoe, and when I had my young high school girls' team name their putters, there was a remarkable drop in putts (though the names chosen were Biscuit, Bananas, Reark (from *The Fountainhead*), Sinker, Winged Foot, Evie, Loretta, etc.). "That would have been right up Ellen's alley," Massey says.

Outside, beside a round glass table, we talk more of her, then of Massey's Opus I, the agency she formed to represent LPGA tour players. She's in her fourth year and runaway successful. From there we go back to Griffin, to music, putting, bungee jumping, back to Griffin in Hershey, Pennsylvania. "Ellen never liked meals. She liked hors d'oeuvres. And she loved chocolate. So on the tour stop in Hershey, Ellen was in heaven. She always came out to that one. Any wind there carried the sweet smell of chocolate and there was this hotel that served the most elaborate spread of hors d'oeuvres. We'd spend hours there. Some of my favorite memories of Ellen are of being in Hershey. We stayed above the clubhouse, and late at night some of the players would gather and we'd putt on the practice green. Ellen would have the night watchman shine his flashlight on the hole and we'd hold large putting contests in the dark. She was a big believer in practicing that way because it forces you to putt totally by feel. And sure enough, the next day at least one of us would putt the eyes out. She was always teaching, by just being."

The bees that have been buzzing around us lose interest, off to the many flowers. Massey rises, taking a moment to inspect the garden where there are lush blossoms and plants all around. Squirrels busy themselves while the two Labradors sit unconcerned, one on each side of us, each with a tennis ball filling its mouth. At one point, a medical helicopter comes and hovers about so we pick up the decibels. "Betsy Rawls, Shirley Englehorn, Mickey Wright," Massey says, raising her voice. "I was always watching them. I'd put myself in position to see every shot. They were such great champions, I wanted to absorb them.

"And I went to Gardner Dickenson to learn about power. I needed to learn about the effortlessness of power. I would never just let it happen, and just letting it happen is a big key. It's not about getting the club back to the ball; it's way beyond that. It's about swinging through and getting out of the way and letting it happen. In everything, I was much more about making it happen. Attacking it. Controlling it. I needed to learn what truly generates distance—where true power comes from.

"I'm talking about something so effortless it can seem like magic. The something that's present when Sandra Palmer, five-one, one hundred and one pounds, stands up and hits it farther than a huge male athlete. Effortlessly. People ask, 'How does she do it?' She's not big. She doesn't look powerful and strong, so watching her you can truly see how effortless true power appears.

"The minute in the golf swing that there is tension and intent to control, you lose true power. That's why fly-fishing is so important to me. I used to fly-fish before big tournaments because you can feel the line load when it's extended behind you, and it's very similar to how you feel the shaft load on the golf club. If you rush the unloading in fly-fishing (the equivalent of rushing back to the ball in the golf swing), you're going to really feel your mistake because it hurts. You're going to catch a hook in the ear and be ridiculous. You must be patient or you're not going to do anything; that's why in fishing that feeling of just letting it happen always really helped my golf."

She received help from many, but Griffin was her teacher, her guide. "I looked for someone after Ellen died, but I knew that would never be. The last days, when she called Dot Germain and me to her bedside to take notes on the future of golf education, that was Ellen's parting shot and for me a real privilege. Even then Ellen had dreams. And she reminded us, 'Make sure you keep having ideas, challenging yourselves; keep dreaming, thinking.' From her I learned that death wasn't an awful, scary thing but that being with someone when the end is so near is instead something to treasure. I was there, too, with my father."

I tell her of something I read of Venezuelan medicine women: their belief that for those who are near as a person takes her last breaths through the closing weeks, days, moments, they must either guard against or welcome taking on the spirit of that person. That person will live inside them.

She smiles and is quiet for a long while. Then she says, "There's a terrible loss when you lose someone who has been your teacher or your mentor. It's a very empty feeling because they're not there anymore for you to call, for you to talk to, for you to work through things with and know.

"I'll never forget looking at Dorothy after Ellen died. I said, 'Now we're going to find out what we learned.' And it was the same way with my father. It's a tremendous sense of duty and responsibility. Both of them left me with the sense that I had to make a contribution no matter what kind of work I did. It was like that wink I gave her when I left for the Himalayas. It was like, 'Now we'll find out.' Ellen's death was a defining moment for me. Dot and I were terrified, but for me there was nothing to do but gather it up and say, 'This is where it begins. Right now . . .' "

She pauses for a second. "But those medicine women may be right, I think. Loss is only physical. When I'm pressed or I have a big dream or a great idea, I can always feel both Ellen and my father in there rattling around."

Commit

My mom told me something years ago. She rode horses a lot, and when we were little kids, she'd pick us up from school and we'd go to watch her ride. One time there was a hole I was playing in a U.S. Open championship at Colonial. The tee shot off this hole was tough, and I was having a hard time figuring it out. So at the end of the day, after the practice round, I went out to that hole with my caddie and just hit practice shots. We stood there until I decided to hit a 3-wood to a certain spot rather than hit a driver. I thought I'd worked it out, but it was still in my mind. I mentioned it to my mother that night on the phone. I said, "There's this one tee shot that's really had me bamboozled, but I was out there all afternoon, and I've decided this is what I'm going to do . . ." When I'd told her my tale, the line was quiet for a minute. Then she said, "Just remember, the first thing that goes over the fence is the rider's heart."

I've never forgotten that. That the first thing to clear the fence is the rider's heart. So if you're not totally committed to the shot, you don't have a chance. So you stand up to those shots that are challenging, you put yourself into that shot, you pour yourself into it confidently, so you're there. I've always remembered that. Stand up and commit yourself completely. If you miss it, you miss it certainly. You've done everything you can.

It's a great feeling to play that way and have it work, and it's terrible when it doesn't, but then it's done, and you haven't sabotaged yourself. So much of this game is about that. So much of this game is self-sabotage. Because at the pro level especially, we all "have it." We all have what it takes to win, it's just, "How do you make it come out at the appropriate time?" Too often we talk ourselves out of it. We second-guess. We play only half there. What my mother said is good. If you feel afraid, or hesitant, don't make the shot. Back off and see something else. You can't play golf with a frightened heart. Back off until your heart's totally there.

Collecting and Firing

Most women I see in Pro-Ams have absolutely no idea how to generate power. None. Many times it has to do with how they were brought up. Older women of my mother's generation, a lot of stuff done as a woman was done where the arms were far away from you, whether it was dancing, hanging up clothes, reaching into a cupboard, painting a wall or a ceiling. There was no feeling of collecting and firing, no sense of a drawing in so that you can extend with power. Lack of a collecting and coiling that can be released as power is why a lot of girls didn't throw particularly well; the elbow isn't in, the arm is out away from their body. It's the same with golf swings. A lot of women weren't taught as boys were. They were taught differently for some reason, or not at all. What I see at the Pro-Ams with women amateurs is often that the right elbow isn't folding and the hips move laterally, so there isn't a sense of coiling and collecting. When that's the case, there's nothing to be released and to just let happen. Women I saw, women I still see whenever I'm out, are really working for every yard they get. Most often it's entirely counterproductive.

Cooked

When I was still playing, there was a tribute to Kathy Whitworth. Those getting the program together said, "We need someone to do something that's out of the ordinary; everyone's so serious here." So I agreed. I knew that golfers have this recurring dream quite a bit and it is: You've hit your ball into a house. My particular version of this was hitting the ball into the kitchen.

Whitworth was always in this dream; she loves this story. I am in the kitchen—which I've never been very comfortable with anyway, in any capacity—and there's my golf ball lying on the floor. There's a window over the sink that is open maybe six inches, and I'm thinking, How the heck am I going to get this up and through that—I've got to get this back out onto the golf course. I've gotta figure out how to do it. I look out the window and there's Whitworth standing there with her arms crossed, looking in at me and saying, "Massey, you've done it again, and you just better get out here. Get back out here and play." It's always Whitworth, because to me she was such a pro, such an example of doing things correctly, and here she is looking at me and saying, "You fool!" That's the way I felt. She was looking at me, just waiting for me to figure this out and get back outside. And every so often I'd hit it. I'd make a swing, and it would end up in the sink, down in that little stopper hole, and I'm thinking, Now what do I do? Now I'm really cooked. In the stopper hole. What club do I have to do this with?

That's usually when I'd wake up. A lot of players have that, stuck in a house, or you can't get to the first tee, you're running and can't get there, or you can't find your caddie, or your clubs.

I didn't have wonderful golf dreams while I was playing, never. I've had marvelous golf dreams since I retired. I haven't had any dreams like the sink since I stopped playing.

I'm starting to play golf well now in my dreams, which is nice.

Courses

Courses are like people when you get to know them. You just know what you bring up, what you approach, and what you don't approach with them. They have their own personalities. The first time I play a course, I use the practice round to get to know it. You first think about where the pin placements are going to be during the tournament; by looking at the greens you can get a feel for where the pins are probably going to be. Then working backward in your mind, where do you need to approach that pin from? Where is the shot that you want to have? How do you want to be looking at the pin when you have the approach shot? That will dictate where you want to hit it off the tee.

Sometimes a hole will be so obvious when you stand up there. But the older courses can be much more subtle. We're very obvious now in many of our designs of where you want to hit it and where you don't. There are obvious good places and bad places. So you just take certain things out of play, especially in major championships. You're silly if you even keep trouble in play. Just take it out of play. This is how you do it: Trouble exists, but you make sure in your thinking and visualization of the shot you want to hit that the shot is *to* some place. It's never *away* from anything. It has got to be positive. You play to something rather than away from something else. And I don't mean to sound like I did it every time; obviously I didn't. I found my share of places to avoid. But I had respect for the courses and tried my best to understand them. It can save you a stroke, maybe two, maybe three, and on tour, a stroke, a half a stroke, is big.

Divot

I had the chance to win the U.S. Open in 1979, a very good chance. I had a three-stroke lead going into the final round, it was mine to win, but I blew it on the front nine, then came around to the back nine and just put on this amazing charge. I had five birdies on the last six holes to draw even with the lead coming to the last hole. I have never felt anything like that exhilaration. The closest thing I can find to describe it is a time when I was skiing and I almost died. I was skiing above the timberline. It was snowing so hard there was a whiteout, and you couldn't tell what was up and what was down. I skied right off the end of the slope into nothing. I ended up in the air. I'll never forget the moment I realized, There's nothing below me, I've gone over the edge. It wasn't terrifying; it was so sudden it was exhilarating. When I hit, I couldn't stop, I couldn't dig my ski in, I was out of control, and I rolled and rolled until I finally drove my arm down into the snow, rolled over it, and stopped about two feet short of this huge boulder. When I managed to sit up, all I could think was, Well, isn't this lucky.

The birdie charge that brought me back to being tied for the lead was that same kind of exhilaration. It was this feeling you get when the adrenaline kicks in, where you're physically as strong as you've ever been and mentally as keen as you've ever been. So you have this combination of extraordinary strength, where your caddie has to know when to start clubbing you down, and this finesse, this touch, this tremendous heightened feel that goes along with this strength, the ability to hear the wind, feel the light, see the grain of the grass, sense all these things so much better. Other athletes have it, too, but I think it takes a sport as quiet as golf for this to happen fully.

So that's where I was when I stepped onto the eighteenth tee. I was that high. I stood up there, and my drive was perfect. The sound—I hit it squarely, purely, far down the left half of the fairway just where I wanted to be. I walked to it completely exhilarated. But when I got there, it was total golf. The ball was in a divot, the biggest fairway divot I'd ever seen.

At that moment, I was still new to the game, and I knew just one way to deal with it, which was to just become the strongest woman who ever lived and dig the thing out and put it on the green. I was going to make it happen somehow because I'd been making things happen all the way around. What I didn't know then was that I didn't have the shot. I didn't know the shot. I took a 4-iron and tried to take up as much ground as I could, and I did, I hurt my hand, it went so deep, but it ended up short of the green. So it was, Ohh, well that didn't happen. Well, now, okay, now we'll have to pitch it. So I pitch. Oooops, well, that wasn't good. Oh, well, I lost the Open. It's over. It's all over now.

So I lost the Open. And that was the defining moment of my career in terms of what I'll remember. I had big highs when I won tournaments, the Amateurs, the British Opens, but I can say honestly, the biggest high I had was one I lost.

I revered the U.S. Open. I still haven't been able to look at the tape of it. I don't think I ever will. As soon as I got home, I got my teacher, who'd taught me when I was growing up, and I said, "You know what happened. This will never happen to me again; let's go to work," and we did. I went out and made the same divot, cut it right out of the ground, and I said, "How do I get out of this?" So I learned how to get out of it, which at that distance is to get a lofted wood. I should have taken a lofted wood. With that much weight at the bottom of the club I had a much better chance of getting the ball airborne than I did by taking an iron and trying to really cut a wider swatch of turf out and pick the ball out. But I didn't understand. I was carrying the club to do it, I just didn't know the shot. So I began again; I hit it out of this divot, this divot, this divot. I learned a variety of shots. I learned to know trouble and embrace trouble.

I became my best in bad weather. Terrible weather. That's when I won. Snowing, so windy you couldn't believe it. That's when I stepped to the fore. I loved trouble because I'd learned to look at those situations: "Okay, I've got four or five different choices, and I'm going to choose this." I practiced shots some players didn't practice. I practiced them until I could pull them out. Up against a bush, a wall, I'd turn the club so it was almost pointing at my left toe. I'd practice it over and over a million times in the backyard with friends. We'd crack each other up. We invented this shot we called the "wall shot." We hit cars, windows. "Hey, watch this hook! I can make it hook fifty yards!" Trouble got to be fun, so in the Dinah Shore, up against it, I just took out the 7-iron, and I said, "I'm going to do the wall shot," and Judy Rankin came over, saying, "How the heck did you do that?" I said, "I practice that shot all the time." She said, "You do?"

That moment in the divot in 1979 changed me for the better because I realized it wasn't the divot that finished me that day, it was knowing I didn't have a shot. I was trying to pull out a miracle when all I needed was a shot.

Sure, golf has its disappointments. I would have loved to have won. But it taught me something about being stuck. Now, myself, my friends—in business, with our families, in our personal lives—we call each other up when we're stuck and we say, "Let's sit down and create some options." And we do. We take pressure and trouble, and where we can, we make it a challenge. Oddly, it becomes fun. Because when I left the eighteenth that day, I took something with me: "This will never happen again." To the end, I am going to do my best to never be without options, to never be without a shot.

One Shot

I asked the great player Gardner Dickenson to teach me about lowering the trajectory of my iron shots and having them be really true. They weren't necessarily full swings, but they were very controlled. He said, "You need to have a shot that you know you can hit. It may be coming down the line when you're so nervous your hands are shaking and your legs feel like they're falling out from under you. Or it may be terribly windy and the weather may be awful. You may not be feeling well. You may have an injury. You need to have a shot that you know you can get on the green." And he gave me that shot. And it was a shot I often played in the wind, which is probably why I always played well in terrible weather. I looked forward to it. I loved that shot, and I practiced it all the time. It's taking a little more club than you might normally hit and gripping down on it a little bit and making a swing that's not a real full swing but it's a real crisp swing, a shot that you stay with, and it's very controlled. It doesn't go terribly high but also it doesn't get affected by the wind. I could do that shot with any iron. The shot is in the shot, not in the club you select.

But Gardner also taught me that it's very important to have a club you know very well. So I did that. For me, it was my 7-iron. I could do anything with that club. "You need one club that you can do everything with. And you need one shot that you can count on." And that's what I loved about working with him. He was a wonderful player. He had such a passion for playing. It wasn't theory; it was all about playing. It was "Does this work? What do you do in this situation? How are you going to correct this on the golf course?" Or I'd come to him and say, "I can't draw the ball. I'm having the worst time." And he'd say, "Well, close your stance, play the ball back, shut the clubface, and release. You know you will draw the ball. If not, well, then stand up and hook it. You know what to do." "Yeah, I know what to do." "Well, do it more." It was "Don't ever not have these options. Don't ever say 'I can't do it.' " Either resign yourself and say you're going to play a fade all day, or stand up and hook it. Commit yourself to something other than what is going on. Don't sabotage yourself. Don't let it get you. Don't let your lack of ability to commit to something other than what's going on back you into a corner.

Extraordinary Experience

The times you play your best, and you'll hear most players say this, you weren't thinking about anything. You just see your target and you hit the shot. When I played my best, all I would hear was the sound of my own breathing. The wind, I could feel the wind, I could sense how hard it was blowing, where it was coming from. You can feel and know whether you're uphill, downhill, sidehill. It's looking at the green, looking at the hole from the tee and knowing how it was designed to be played, knowing what the architect wanted. Being able to see that, to see where the pin is, knowing the subtleties of the green, how you have to approach that pin, it's taking in everything. They say I blocked everything out—I never did. I took it all in, but what I took in was crucial to making the shot. You have to make room for all of those things to come into your decision making; you really do become a part of the golf course.

When people are getting started they have to think, but after a while, thinking disappears into what you do. That's what professionals do. They have a lot of information they're dealing with, but it becomes natural. You're out there, you really are part of nature and you work with it, and that's when the game becomes an art. Hopefully you get to that point in your career, to the point of nontechnical experience. There have been times during a round when I know I have to just look at the target and hit the ball, just try to clear out some of the other things that may have come into my mind. If I'm suddenly, What about my backswing? What about that difficult flight I have to take this afternoon? If something comes in, I don't "block" it, I just let it pass through. I let it go. I start to bring in that information that I really do care so much more about: Is the wind behind me? Is this green receptive? It's taking the proper information in at the time. It's very simple information, but it comes together to create extraordinary performance. And it is extraordinary because golf isn't about who's the greatest athlete. It's about who on this particular day has best blended with the target, with the course, with the weather, with that great whirling arc, and what the game gives up.

A Little Thing

There's this little thing I carry with me, something my father was given by a friend, with a note at the top: "These British are really dedicated to your game!!!" It's a clipping from *The New York World Telegram*, a reprint of the "Temporary Rules—1940—Richmond Golf Club, Sudbrook Park, England." I think it speaks to people's love for and the resilience of the game. It reads:

> Players are asked to collect the bomb and shrapnel splinters to avoid damage to the mowing machines.
>
> In competition, during gunfire or while bombs are falling, players may take shelter without penalty for ceasing play.
>
> The positions of known delayed-action bombs are marked by red flags at a reasonable, but not guaranteed, safe distance therefrom.
>
> Shrapnel and/or bomb splinters on the fairway or in bunkers within a club's length of a ball may be moved without penalty, and no penalty shall be incurred if a ball is thereby caused to move accidentally.
>
> A ball moved by enemy action may be replaced, or if destroyed, a ball may be dropped not nearer the hole without penalty.
>
> A player whose stroke is affected by the simultaneous explosion of a bomb may play another ball. Penalty, one stroke.

Wiffi Smith

In 1959, THE HEADLINE of South Carolina's *Spartanburg Journal* read: "Wonderful Wiffi Wins Again." It was a popular sentiment at the time, as well as one that was long remembered, "Even if," as competitor Betty Jameson recalls, "it put us all further down in the money. Because Wiffi was wonderful. She was marvelous. At every stop, at parties, people didn't just like her, they wanted to adopt her. Everyone felt that magic working."

Born in 1936, Margaret Chamberline Smith spent her first ten years among the orange groves in Southern California. She was nicknamed before she was born when, in the lower regions of Mexico, in a small Zapote Indian village, a witch doctor put her hand to Smith's mother's stomach and said simply, *huifi*. Smith's mother was an engineer, architect, and navigator who loved adventure. She was traveling with Smith's aunt and uncle, who were explorers en route to the jungles of South America. "They were all in this tiny Indian village," says Smith, "and according to my mother, she was walking along the main drag and this witch doctor stopped and looked at her and just smiled, then came over and patted her stomach, *Huifi,* pronounced 'Wiffi,' meant 'Something is coming.' My mother didn't know she was pregnant. At the time, she wasn't even a month along. When she went back to Mexico City, she got checked and found it was true."

Smith's parents divorced when she was eleven, and her mother took her and her younger brother and cousin and moved to Guadalajara, northwest of Mexico City. Though her father was an avid golfer with a 2 handicap and her mother also a fine player, Smith had been more interested in swimming and tennis, but now in Mexico she found herself without companions and turned to golf as a game she could play alone. "Once I started, I really liked it," she says. "Whatever sport it was, I wanted to be up there in the top leagues. I didn't want to do it just to do piddly. Right off, I tried to learn all I could about it—how to work the ball, how to make it do things and go places. I had a pro in Guadalajara, Tom Garis, but I learned shots from anyone I thought was good, and I also made up shots."

By age fourteen, she dominated Mexico's junior ranks. She was also spending several months of the year with her mother and brother in Somerset, England, where she honed her game on a remote nine-hole course mowed by sheep. Later, with Smith still in her mid-teens, her ever venturesome mother moved to Spain; Smith stayed behind in the States, spending much time with Warren and Peggy Kirk Bell at Pine Needles in Southern Pines, North Carolina, where her job was to play golf with the guests.

In her late teens, on a summer trip with the Bells to Michigan she met local businessman Bob Holden and his family at a Country Club in St. Clair. "Bob was a wonderful man. His whole family took me in and helped me financially and encouraged me in all my endeavors. I remember I learned to dance in their kitchen. Like with the Bells, I became family, and they helped me move along in the world."

In 1954, she won the USGA National Junior Championship, and in 1956, the Trans-Mississippi, the British Women's Open Amateur, and the French Women's Open Amateur. She was low amateur at the Jacksonville Open and that year's Titleholders, and won all of her matches for America's Curtis Cup team. When she turned pro at the end of that year, at the age of nineteen, she had a total of twenty-eight amateur victories.

As a pro, six months into her rookie season she ranked first on the LPGA money list and had already won the Dallas Open. The August 1957 issue of *Golf Digest* put her on the cover with another emerging sensation, Arnold Palmer, and said of her, "Smith is nothing less than a natural in the field of women's golf.

If she is not the reigning player within three years, a great many of us will be surprised."

From early on, her mother had encouraged her to court adventure, to live creatively with her imagination engaged, and to seek the spiritual in both the grand and the ordinary. "My mother always told me 'Life is big if you take your chances and stay with it.' " For Smith no shot was impossible, and every bungle a challenge. British golf writer John Stubbs said of her back then, "She stands on a fairway as if she'd grown there."

When she turned pro, she signed a contract with Spalding and bought a green 1928 Model A Ford that she named Susie. While others whizzed by in Cadillacs and Packards, Smith was content to move along at forty-five miles per hour. At local clinics, she'd arrive on her high, dark, chestnut horse, Flashy Mike. She'd hit the shots, entertain as she was asked, then climb back on and ride away. One year at the Peach Blossom Open in Spartanburg, South Carolina, Smith turned her ankle tromping into a gully, accidentally nudged her ball when she dropped her club on it, and so gained a penalty, then was stung by a bee when she backed into a bush in an attempt to straddle a difficult lie. On that par-3 hole she took a triple bogey, but only smiled and laughed at it all. That year the *Spartanburg Journal* wrote of her, "So refreshing was her reaction to adversity, you found yourself hours later, smiling at no one in particular."

Her talent and poise seemed limitless. "She'd have been the greatest ever," says Peggy Kirk Bell. "She had it all. She was longer off the tee than anyone on tour, including Mickey Wright. Her swing was so sound and consistent, and her putting was excellent. At the time Wiffi got hurt, I'd have picked her to be the number one golfer for many, many years."

Mickey Wright, second in all-time tour victories with eighty-two, and who solidly carries the reputation "the greatest ever," told *Senior Golfer* this about Smith: "I have no doubt that if she'd been able to play just ten more years, she'd have had Hall of Fame numbers, easy.

"During my career I played against Louise Suggs, Patty Berg, Kathy Whitworth, and Nancy Lopez. But only one golfer made me feel intimidated on the course, and that was Wiffi Smith. I adored Wiffi's personality and think of her often. It was just her pure ability to strike the ball and her incredible putting, that, well . . . she intimidated me."

"We'd look up," says Betty Jameson, "she'd be walking along on her hands, or there she'd be trotting along on someone's horse, or at a party sliding down a banister. She was everyone's young hope, but in the form of a daring, mischievous angel."

"If only she could have held on long enough," says Polly Riley. "She was something you couldn't imagine. She'd take chances with shots, we'd think, What on earth? But she'd pull them off whether she needed to or not, then think up another one. It was almost as if she wanted to see how many situations she could escape from. Like her name, she was something wonderful."

The accident, seemingly not so serious at first, happened in the parking lot at the 1959 Tittleholders at Augusta, Georgia. "I had finished my third round. I was leading. This caddie I knew was in the parking lot getting ready to leave on his motorbike, and I said, 'Hey, do you mind if I take a little spin around the lot here?' The accelerator on a motorbike, when you want to make it go faster, you push it away from you. On his it was just the opposite, so when I was taking a corner I thought I was slowing it down, but I didn't make it. I ran into the back of a car. It threw me and you know how you land. It kind of gives you a shock. I went to the doctor and my legs were all skinned up, too. But they didn't know how bad it was right away. My hands hurt, and my wrist, but I played. I finished second."

She was a "feel" player. Because her hands were small, she played with clubs wrapped at the top with only the thinnest layer of leather. "She played with the thinnest grips and the stiffest shafts," says Betty Jameson, "Her hands told her everything." What her hands didn't tell her was that she had crushed a small bone in her wrist in the fall. And Smith, not knowing the extent of the damage, played through the pain at the Titleholders and continued to push her injured wrist and hand, with every shot doing further damage to the bone and cartilage. When she knew the seriousness, she tried to do all she could to reverse the harm. She bought a Volkswagen bus and had a piano loaded into the back;

she loved music and figured that playing up and down the keys might help her regain the touch and strength she'd lost with the injury.

But later that same year, driving in a dense fog near Baton Rouge, Louisiana, she hit a mule. "I saw the white one on the side, but I didn't see the dark one in the middle. I hit the windshield and glass was everywhere, all around. And my hand, the other one, took it pretty bad. What was worse, I tried to track the mule because I knew she was hurt, but I couldn't keep up the search." She continued to play, all the while doing further damage. By 1961, her hands were so bad she couldn't pick up a piece of paper.

At age twenty-four, she'd won nine professional tournaments in four years, three of them after her injury, but she could no longer hold a club. "It was tough," she says. "I'd worked to be an artist by watching those I recognized as artists. From early on I'd studied how they used their hands on the club, how it affected the clubhead, how it affected the shot they were hitting, the ball and spins, how the ball reacted on the green after they hit it. I'd watch all those little things and then go to work myself, as if I'd watched a very fine pianist. Jameson, the Babe, Berg—I'd memorized how they used their wrists, their arms, their fingers, how the joints bent, how gently they touched the club. I had a lot of interests— music, horses, cars, my dogs—but I lived for golf. Playing the tour had been my art, my mind, my soul."

Without the injuries she says she probably would have kept going for a lot of years, "Unless I found something that was more interesting. But what better thing, if you love it, than to earn a living playing golf? Still, I'd grown up with my mother and I knew the old 'When one door closes, another opens.' I went on, I had fun. My whole life has been fun."

Her tour days over so young, she headed to college in New Mexico to study music and biology, but before she'd completed a degree she was back in North Carolina where she'd spent so much time as an amateur, at the Bells' Pine Needles. Quickly she was offered a job on a local farm helping raise Thoroughbred horses and foxhounds. She also taught golf part of the year at Pine Needles and part of the year in Florida.

As her hands healed and got stronger, there was talk of her returning to the tour, but she never did. More adventurous friends suggested she travel the country as a "ringer." "I told her," says Kathy Whitworth, " 'you know, what you need to do is get your amateur status back. We'll tour the country and make a million dollars because no one will know who you are and we'll just have a little bet on the side—my player can beat your player. We'd be in the easy money.' I was only half-joking because here she is, one of the best ever, a wonderful player and almost completely anonymous."

By the late seventies, Smith had gotten serious about teaching. She taught more at Pine Needles and later also traveled with Penny Zavichas, working with students at the very fine Craft/Zavichas schools (which she still does at select times throughout the year). "I love it whenever I can get her," says Zavichas. "She's a true master. She knows the game through and through and is so great with people. She's never rigid. For her, it's all about imagination and what's inside you, what you see and feel. She inspires students to be as creative as she is."

In 1987, she headed from North Carolina back to the West Coast, first northern California, then Darrington, Washington, an hour north of Seattle, where she felt immediately at home. She has a house there in the woods by a river, with a view of mountains. She has many friends, and is serious in her study of the great masters—not, as in another day, masters of golf, but now philosophy, art, humanitarianism, astronomy, music. "I study them all," says Smith, "Buddha, Zarathustra, Jesus—all the Zen masters."

Wanting no schedules, never wearing a watch, she's the unofficial pro at Cloverdale Golf Club, a place that is itself somewhat unusual. "If you could expect to find Wiffi anywhere," says Betty Jameson, "it'd be in that sort of lovely place." "Cloverdale," *Smithsonian* magazine recently wrote, "is a course for the next century, if only because nearly everything about it suggests that it's a course straight out of the past." One story has it that an old Scottish caddie who had carried bags for twenty-two years at St. Andrews was asked by a golfer about a bush he had hit into, "Who put this here?" The caddie answered, "God. There's nothing on this course that was made by man. Golfers play on it, but the architect of the land is God."

So it is with Cloverdale. In the foothills of Washington's Cascades, Cynthia and Rick Witscher, with their herd of Holsteins and 150-acre spread, were Snohomish County's Dairy Family of the Year in 1988, but falling milk prices forced them to think again. They decided to sell the herd and grow bent-grass turf for the landscaping and golf industries; soon everyone wanted their grass. A nongolfer, Witscher then began reading all he could on course design, visited many old sites, and soon went to work to raise eighteen holes out of Cloverdale's many fields that were lying fallow. The greens he set on existing mounds that rose in gentle curves above the river's floodplain. He let his mind follow those ancient riverbeds, sandbars, and timeworn paths beaten by cattle, and along those contours he shaped his fairways. Large boulders, deep thickets of brush (home to many tiny creatures and skunks and woodchucks), the windswept patches of sand—all that he left in place as hazards. A shed built onto the side of the classic red barn suffices as a "clubhouse." Six fat, glistening native grasses flourish in the hardy turf, so the course needs no irrigation system or heavy haze of pesticides.

A round of golf there is fifteen dollars for eighteen holes. If players encounter a sign OUT MOWING, they drop their fees into an "honor" box. Business executives, doctors, and judges who make the sixty-mile jaunt from Seattle play alongside loggers, sawmill hands, waitresses, farmers. For a while there was the whimsical sign DRESS CODE: NO RUBBER BOOTS OR OVERALLS, then the Witschers realized someone might show up in boots and overalls, so it was taken down.

"When I first started playing," one golfer reported, "I kept finding hot coffee and doughnuts sitting by the fourth hole. At first I thought someone had left them behind. But it was Rick just bringing treats to the regulars."

Hailed throughout her short but wondrous career as "The Natural" and always having fled the trappings of pretension, Smith and Cloverdale are a perfect match. "Too often," says Smith, "beginners, especially women, are driven away from the game before they start. At Cloverdale, there's no phoniness, no stares, no stern words. There's nothing of intimidation. It's a wonderful place to learn and teach."

From the first I heard of her, I wondered, In a game that holds such history and spirit and quest, what must it be like to carry the artistry Smith has and through the years shoulder all the "might-have-beens"? What was the weight of regret? But when I start talking to those who've played with her and still know her now, the portrait is something else—a woman shimmering, larger than life. "Wait until you see those blue, blue eyes," says Carol Johnson. "You have to see that face, walk beside her," says Penny Zavichas. "It's something you won't forget." "She was one of the ones," was all my own teacher said, and in her refusal of more, was everything. When reporter Jay Stuffer saw her play, he wrote, "Her swing has the rhythm and tempo of a Dave Brubeck composition. Her balance could induce envy in a Buddhist priest."

In keeping with all I've heard, we meet in a most unusual place, a place called "Airlie." Here, too, there is a story. Harry Groome, born in 1860, was an avid golfer credited with bringing the sport to Philadelphia, his birthplace, and later in life he created a home for himself in Virginia, forty minutes outside Washington, D.C. On one of his journeys to St. Andrews, he visited and studied a historic castle in Angus, Scotland, called Airlie. He was so struck by the uncanny resemblance to the home he had built that when he returned to Virginia, he named the estate Airlie. The property was later taken over and developed by the late Dr. Murdock Head in 1959, and today Airlie encompasses nine contiguous estates covering more than two square miles. Lakes and rivers abound. Stone walls trail through the property, separating winding roads and meadows and wildflower gardens planted at the turn of the century. In Head's effort to maintain an environment conducive to contemplation (*Life* magazine once named the three-thousand-acre spread "Isle of Thought"), the land has been planted as if the whole were a great old Scottish estate.

This all comes at me fast and in sketches, in bits and pieces over the phone. The younger Dr. Mark Head, now the owner of the property with his two sisters, had read of the Witschers and Smith in *Smithsonian* magazine, and had then asked them to join his efforts to design the world's most environmentally conscious golf course—the Links at Airlie. No bulldozers. No earth-moving. Nothing artificial. An inland echo of the first wild links formed by the elements along the North Sea. A place where the president and heads of state could golf in total seclusion; at other times, where urban youth could roam and learn. No Jack Nicklaus, no Arnold Palmer, no Pete Dye. This is Mark Head, Rick Witscher, Wiffi Smith, full speed ahead.

As Witscher and Head tell it, I like the idea, even if they're dreaming—but they are not. The Department of Agriculture, former presidents of the USGA, Earth Voice—all have lent initial support and expertise, and I receive an invitation to Airlie to a gathering to launch phase one.

Buried in tapes and papers, I only glance at the dates and toss my invitation aside, but a week later, after a call to Wiffi, I am there. That afternoon, one of the last in summer, it is hot and sultry. The road narrows and wends its way onto the grounds through tall, thick, vine-covered pines. Soon the property opens up onto some of the most enchanted land I've ever seen: bowing willows, rolling prairie grass and wildflowers, boxwood hedges, yarrow, wild orchids, trout lilies, herons, a bald eagle. I open my window—the place is singing.

At the manor house at the crest of a hill I grab my bags from the car that's retrieved me from the airport, and greet Mark. He's six-three, fit at forty-four, good looking with a free, adventuresome air. He leads me through a living room the size of a ballroom, its eastern wall all glass. The doors, also glass, open onto a huge two-level stone terrace that looks out over a deep valley awash in shades of deep emerald sparingly tipped by wildflowers. A sweeping lake where it seems the moon might swim at night glistens at its center.

Before the ledge, at the edge of the bottom tier of the terrace, at a black iron table well away from a small, elegant pool, is Wiffi. Back to us, she sits reading. Mark and I stand for a moment, caught in the quiet until just the precise moment before newness is lost, Mark hollers, "Wiffi! Look who I've brought!"

She puts the book down and comes slowly toward us, squinting to get a better view. I bend to greet her, still looking down from where we stand. But looking down at her is like looking up, and looking into her face you see the brightest light and the rosiest cheeks, and ancient eyes burning blue with eternal questions. She's dressed for the humid weather in light cotton baggy purple pants and oversize shirt. She is built so solidly and without excess, she could be a great stone. Yet she dances, something that at a party two nights ago (I learn), she has left other guests wondering about; as she moved to the band for several hours straight, a full wineglass twirled perfectly in her hand and never once splattered or spilled. Little has changed from the tour: she has dazzled here, too.

Mark leaves us and we talk, first there at the table where deer visit below, then on a large, comfortable couch inside where Mark, propped on a stool near us, practices his upright bass. The instrument, with its low, soulful tones, seems almost alive, so there are four of us now. Wiffi feels this too; though I've asked her about Guadalajara, about Sunningdale, and about the time she was leading the Dallas Open and left across the fairway into the rough to help a dog that'd been hit by a car, it's Mozart and Bach she wants to talk about. Life, like music, is "all frequency," she says, and when musicians hear and play they're in the alpha state, a much higher, open state of consciousness—and that, she says, is where she played when she played her very best golf. "The club, when you play from there," she says, "becomes more of a wand than a club, something to transfer your intention into every shot."

We talk about this, as well as about distance and hands and putting, and a detail she loves—her hero Betty Jameson's scorecards. They were works of art that told a clear physical tale, she says; the numbers and scrolling grew larger and darker and wilder as the heat and pulse of competition rose. By the end they looked like a mad Picasso or van Gogh.

Her steady voice makes the re-created life with those comrades sizzle and spark—Babe, Berg, Whitworth, Jameson, the Bauers, Wright, Riley. It's as clear as if it were yesterday; she holds them all close. Soon the bass that has been accompanying us fades as a group of landscape specialists, three women who use no chemicals, pesticides, or insecticides, arrive to see Mark. They go off just as Mark's assistant comes to drive Wiffi and me a few miles to a quaint old restaurant at the bottom of the hill.

That morning Wiffi's been at a meeting of necessary course supporters, and Witscher, who with Mark has joined us, tells the story. Question after question arose, and after a while Wiffi had interrupted. "In a project such as this," she said, "possibilities need to be limitless, and what is natural is the only guide." She then told them a story: "There was a postman in this remote area of Australia. Every day he would go out carrying his load of letters to the far reaches. He wore overalls and heavy boots, because if they weren't heavy they'd wear out. And he ran his route. He did this every day, then he'd return home. One day someone said, 'As much as you run and as fit as you are, you ought to do the five-day endurance race.' He said, 'Well, maybe.' And they kept at him, and he said, 'Okay.' They offered him shoes and little shorts and all the high-tech gear, and he said no, he just preferred running in what he had on, his overalls and work boots. So off they went. The others, they had all the lightest gear and water stops and all these scheduled breaks to refortify and have people pat them off because it was hot, the race run partly over desert terrain. But the postman, he kept going, as in his work, and he stopped only rarely, even for the night, just as if he were running his letters. Well, he got so far ahead, a whole day ahead of the rest of them, that when he arrived at the finish line it was nighttime and all the newspeople and photographers wanted him to wait to cross so they could take his picture in the light. 'Nope,' he said, he had to be 'back to work tomorrow.' "

Witscher, who has been listening, lets her continue. "What I like about it, why I told the story to the supporters," says Wiffi, "is because that postman wasn't seduced by anything outside himself. He wasn't limited the way the others were. The rest of them had their stops, their water, their scheduled rests. The postman had a goal and he ran to it, the way he was accustomed to. That's the ideal mind in playing golf. It's also the ideal in conceiving of this course at Airlie, staying as close to what the land is accustomed to so it is sustainable not only for itself but as a model. The heavily doctored velvety grass of Augusta National has been the model; now maybe there could also be a hardy, mostly feral, self-sustainable one."

By the time we're back at the manor, it's after ten o'clock and Wiffi is ready for bed. We'll start again early tomorrow on the wrists, the left arm, stillness, distance, power, touch. "You stay up for a while," she tells me, "hear their song." The song she refers to

is the background music for the twelve-minute film presentation
on the fledgling course, a song Rick and Mark have written for
voice, guitar, and bass. They have a special chair for me and for a
half second I'm afraid the composition may be homespun corny.
What if, sitting there, that shows on my face? Everything shows
on my face. I've never been able to hide a thing. But I am amazed.
I ask them to repeat it three times, and might have asked once
more, but Martin, a Russian pianist friend of Mark's, has slipped
in through the side door, and Brian, the filmmaker, and Mark's assistant have arrived, too.

Martin is delightfully short, hair all wild, and charmingly self-
effacing. Mark tells me he is a virtuoso, and in a few minutes
we're in two cars working our way down the hill to the conference
center where there is a grand piano. Though he hasn't practiced in
ten days because he's had a young prodigy visiting from Vienna,
he will play anyway. He begins with Liszt, then Chopin and more
Liszt as he works his way to Schumann. I'm six feet from him and
I've seen nothing like it. His hands hover above, then live in the
keys, fingers moving at the speed of hummingbird wings. It's past
midnight, but I'm wide awake. When he finishes, his face is
flushed, his shirt soaked through with sweat. I finally breathe. He's
pleased, too. Something has come together here. Maybe he will
practice less from now on, he says.

On the way back, when I ask him about the nature and effects
of practice in such an art, what I get is "It's not the physical that
you practice. Practice is for the music of you, inside; not the hands
on the keys." As fog lights help brighten our way home he says,
"An artist, any artist, spends his life trying to find the way to talk
to God. That is practice."

We're quiet for a while in the hum of the car, then as he and
Mark talk the intricacies of Liszt, I wonder what heightened sense
such hands might have on a club, and later, saying good night
under the manor house's dim lamp, shaking his hand I let mine
linger against his, hoping childishly that something may rub off.

In the morning, it's Wiffi again. Martin and the late night
seem much like a dream but the connections remain—the fluttering hands, the piano keys, practice, the alpha state—could it all be
a lesson Wiffi divined? I know better, but when I speak of Martin,

she only nods. We talk a few hours about tournament play, her 3-wood, then putting again before being joined by Rick, Brian, and Mark for lunch by the pool. Below, in that wild valley, is where the links will be, hole one will start amid the pines and wind down along the brook and finally nestle beneath four wide, haunting willows. Hole two will rise to a high ledge of rock, three will roll along a gentle windswept swell. Wiffi and Rick seem to see what the others of us cannot, but we squint to form an outline, a shadow takes form, and we're cheering them on.

"It's no secret there's a lot in the number eighteen," Wiffi says. "It carries the same numerical vibration as the Hebrew word *ch'ai,* meaning 'life.' " There could be eighteen, twenty-seven, thirty-six holes, or what's another meaningful number no one's thought about? And what about a stray hole? After all, those here can do anything they want. Brian has suggested a long par 8. Wiffi takes it further: What about a hole that's a journey? A par, say, 27?

We get increasingly chimerical and go on in this way for a while before someone mentions Marion Hollins's vision for the most photographed hole in the game, the sixteenth at Cypress Point. "I should have known a woman did that," Brian says. At twenty-eight, he's seen nothing like Wiffi and is drawn to her side.

"What about the deer and skunk and geese and herons?" I say. "What will they think of balls flying every which way?"

Rick has the answers. The term is "low impact," and all care will be taken to ease into, not invade, the eco-structure. Maybe there will even be a sign, he jokes—NO STRONG PERFUMES OR AFTERSHAVES. There are already courses endorsed by the Audubon Society, but the care here will far exceed even those standards. Neither will there be a daily fee, nor anything like conventional club membership. It will be something other. The other is yet undetermined, a vision still under way.

"That kind of out-there *Golf in the Kingdom* guy, what's his name, Michael Murphy? He should know about this," a newcomer says. "Seamus McDuff might be camped right now below the cave at Boathouse Lake or wayward beyond the lagoon. He'd go for this."

"Mr. Shivas Irons, meet our Wiffi Smith," Brian says, grinning.

Later on, looking down from high on an opposite ridge, the tone is serious. "If golf courses are to continue," says Wiffi, "they either have to go back and learn from what they were or become completely artificial. The new courses, most are now worlds away from the course I played when I won at Sunningdale. The ideal in most grass is to manipulate it to be all the same shade, when grass is meant to be variegated, our eyes are fed by that difference, but for the sake of someone's cosmetic standard, that's forgotten. Many of the newest courses are little tiny tracks that connect all the surrounding houses. On the tee box it says, 'Please aim away from houses.' How do you do that? It's like going down a narrow street in Manhattan. Then residents get all upset because you're looking in their two-foot space of grass hunting for your ball.

"Airlie is fed by what is natural. And standing here we're fed by all of this: the trees, the sun. We're fed by the birds, their different songs. We're not solid beings. We need this for food, we need the different colors, the wind, not someone's terrace or picture window. It's the elements that feed us. Golfers have always known that deep down."

On the way back, we stop to see the weathered sundial from the days of Harry Groome. It is timeworn, sunk deep into the ground. We sit on the circular stone bench under the wide boughs of a huge sycamore, and Wiffi starts to talk about time, how it is not linear and everything happens in the now. She is the player she was back then. She may be here under this watchful tree but she is also there, walking shoulder to shoulder with Wright, laying a 4-iron close. "All time is now," she says. "That's why we must be in every shot."

The asters and willows are doing better with this than I am, though I believe and bend and try to stretch my mind to take it in. We walk through the butterfly garden, amid the floating monarchs, ringlets, and gatekeepers; pink bleeding hearts, purple columbine, wild orchid. We follow the Trout Lily Trail, cross the bridge to Boatman's Island, then trudge back to the car, stopping to look at the rise where, next month, Rick will begin to guide Airlie's first green to life. On the drive back, among all the white swans, we're lucky enough to spot the lone black one who's lost his mate.

In another half hour, when I must say good-bye, since I'm woefully late for my plane, Wiffi says, "We'll meet someday here for a game." "Sure, the par 27," I reply. "In alpha. Always alpha. I'll work on it from now on." I give her six hugs, five for those of her longtime friends who've asked me to pass one on, one for myself. Then grabbing my bags and rushing for the car, I remember and turn: "Hey, thanks," I say. As everyone has told me with Wiffi, it has been something I could not predict, a small and certain gift. Her message not so much in her words but her wake. As I run, set on getting to my plane, "Do what brings you joy" echoes behind.

Finding the Middle Easily

Part of the wonderful thing about teaching is the give and take of information. Through the years we forget what is "mine" and what is "yours" and no one cares. I've taught often with Carol Johnson; she's a fine one. Carol loves to tell this story, which happened at Pine Needles where Ellen Griffin and Peggy Kirk Bell started that first golf school for women, Golfaris: "This is my favorite golf lesson. There's a wonderful man named Les Bolstad. He taught Patty Berg and all the great ones. Well, one week he came to Pine Needles, he was around seventy-five, eighty, then, and my colleague Ann Casey Johnstone had helped him by laying out clothes that Mrs. Bolstad, Nellie, had sent for him. She told me she laid out shirt day one, pants day one, socks day one, day two, day three, on and on that way. And I said to her, 'The guy's got to be flaky if he can't even decide which clothes to wear. Why is everyone telling me he's so wonderful?' I was just a little skeptical. Then I met him, and he was darling. He was going to teach and I said, 'Mr. Bolstad, can I come along with you?' He had this sweet little hippity-hop walk and he says, 'Come along, dearie.' So I follow Mr. Bolstad to the tee and I'm standing back and I say, 'Do you mind if I watch you?' 'No, come along, dearie.' So dearie's standing back watching him work with this woman, and she's hitting shots. We were on the main range, and Peggy Kirk Bell's teaching shack is down the way on the left. And this woman is bouncing shots off Peggy's wall. Bam, bam, slamming them off the wall, and I'm standing back there covering my mouth watching her destroy Peggy's shack, and Mr. Bolstad says, 'My, that's an interesting shot.' And he said to her, 'Have you ever thought of hitting over there?' and he pointed to the main building well to the right side of the range where these sliding glass doors to the lower rooms were. He said, 'Try the door over there.' She's still aiming downrange and now she swings toward that door and the ball lands in that area and I think, 'Oh, no.' But Les says, 'Try that again, my dear.' And she smacks one over right at the door and I'm thinking, 'There go the windows.' Then he turns to her again and says, 'Try the one over there once more,' and now he's pointing back at Peggy's shack. So she smacks another one off Peggy's shack. He looks at her and says, 'You know, my dear, have you ever considered straight out the middle?' And I'm about to collapse. And she hits two out the middle, and the dear thing looks at him and he looks at her and he says, 'You know, my dear, in all things we do in our life, we must never be afraid of extremes because that's how we find the middle easily.'

"I'll never forget it. In fact, I haven't taught a lesson in my life from that moment on when I haven't pushed people as far as I could using that very way. Right now I have a very serious student with Parkinson's, and I push him until he can hardly stand. When he's so weak that he can hardly go on, we find out how he can play the last three holes, because we discover where he can place the ball and make contact. With all my students I make up games where I have them hit two to the left, two to the right, and two straight. They get six shots off the tee. If I say, 'Straight,' and they hit it right, they still owe me a straight one. If they hit straight when I've said, 'Left,' they owe me one to the left or they're out of the contest. People learn not to be afraid of right and left because I keep telling them, 'It's not right and wrong.' In tennis you say, 'Good shot,' if you hit it in the double-deuce alley. In golf we say, 'Oh, that's too bad, it hooked.' It's important to realize what Mr. Bolstad taught: 'Never fear the extremes. They're your guide to the middle.' "

Action

I've gotten myself into my share of jams out on the golf course, and I can say from all of them that it's important to act rather than react in golf. Golf is an action, not a reaction sport. It's big for a player to learn not to react not only to poor shots and poor luck but to great shots and luck. Reaction is based on a defensive mode. Think of it in your own everyday life. Someone does this and you get excited or upset and you do this without thought when we all know it might have been better to stop a moment, pause, and say, "How can I act consciously here?" Reaction is a form of losing control. It always makes the shot at hand seem huge, while action makes you equal to all that is possible.

Center

In talking about how to live, I know someone once said, "Find your center and stay there." And the same is true for golf. Everyone, especially when he or she is beginning, plays like she's trying to launch both herself and the ball.

The way I try to get a player to feel real power is to call her attention to the triangle formed by the chest and arms and hands as it links her to the club. I have her gather up whatever strength she feels and center that strength in the heart of the triangle, then simply turn around that point, keeping that centered power still and steady.

It's like skaters with crack-the-whip. One skater will start out in the very center of the ring and another joins and holds hands, and then another and another and they keep going, faster and faster. It's the one on the outside who's really moving. The one in the center is moving hardly at all. Yet they are all moving at the same time around that steady center.

Choose Your Magnet

On the course, what is feared is like a magnet. Water, bunkers, trees, ravines, high grass—whatever you fear turns magnetic, whether you're a pro or a beginner. Take a beginner who's setting up to a shot; she's standing up to the ball thinking, Oh, I can't get across this water. Oh, well, maybe I can. Her first thought was, I can't. She's already seen her ball dropping into the water, so everything within her is water. Unless she changes her whole thing around, she's going to go into the water no matter what. In fact, she's already directed the ball there; it's *going* there. In golf, everything's directed by what we think, so the clearer we can be, the better.

We need to know where trouble lies on the course, but then we need to forget it. We need to play the course in our mind in the most ideal way. To do well we need to do that homework so we don't focus anymore on the fear places. You can't be fuzzy about this. If you focus on the places where you don't want to be *and* on the places where you'd like to be, your focus is split. You have duality. You need to be single-visioned. Think about and see where you want to be, and that's all you'll see. You won't see the other places. In checking out the course, you've already seen the hazards, all the pitfalls, and you know the trail you want to take. The best thing you can do for your game is to positively map your trail and clearly and positively choose your magnets. As you play, if you end up where you don't want to be, just identify the next positive magnet and let your ball be drawn there.

The Lessons of Dew

People say that when I was on tour I was a terrific putter, and of course whenever anyone says you're terrific at anything they want to know your secret. In fact, even when the secret is so simple that it's no secret at all, people still think you're keeping a secret. Well, I was a good putter for one reason—because I believed I could putt. Even now, if I'm not putting the ball in the hole I don't believe that I'm a bad putter, I just "misread" the green or wasn't paying attention. No matter what happens, I know I can putt.

There are a few things you can do to help yourself along. I think it helped me seeing golf the way I do—and that's simple, too, because for me it's a game of getting the ball in the hole in the least number of strokes, and putting is just another aspect of it. Golf is like pitching pennies or tossing washers into a soup can. The purpose of playing the whole hole is to get the ball in the hole. You hit drives to put you in a position so you can get it on the green so you can get it in the hole. Putting is not a separate game even though people try to make everything separate nowadays: You have your long game, your approach game, your pitching game, your chipping game, your putting game—to me it's all one hole, it's not separated, and the more intent you are on the hole, the more often the ball is going to go in.

People ask, "How do you putt when the green's this way or that way, or there's dew on the green?" Dew on the green is a great instructor, especially for beginners, because you can see how the green is going to break, you see the path. It's wonderful even for pros as a reminder. It helps etch the path of the ball into your mind so it can be carried over to every putt every day. That is how clearly we must see. We must see that path in the dew even when the dew isn't there. Sometimes when I putt I can see the path in another way; it's like a path of light, a little ion trail. Friends may say, "You're getting way out there, Smith," but just remember, all the great putters will tell you they either see or feel the route to the hole clearly. Like that path of dew, it's inscribed.

Mind and Hands and Club

More than anyone, Betty Jameson could make the ball dance, and it was beautiful. She taught me that it has to do with where you are in your mind, and like a good craftsman, how much you can extend that intent through your hands.

Have you ever watched a good bulldozer driver? He can make that bucket move just so because he can feel that bucket through the controls. The hands are not gripped around for dear life; if they were, he'd lose all feel. Instead, like a pianist, he has his hands set so there's give and take through those controls. That great, huge, massive thing comes alive, becomes the most beautiful instrument. He can set it down within millimeters of where he wants it to go because he's extending his mind out and becoming part of that piece of machinery. The backhoe moves as if he's reaching out there with part of himself, moving that earth. It's beautiful. It says everything about mind and hands and club.

Your Pitchfork

A good golfer can play good golf with crappy equipment because, as we all know, it isn't the equipment that makes the golfer. It's the difference between an oxcart and a Porsche. If you ride in an oxcart for forty-five miles, it will probably take you a couple of days; if you ride in a Porsche, it will probably take you half an hour. But when you arrive, you are still the same person. It will just be a very different ride in the oxcart, not as easy. As with everything, we should aspire for the best, and the equipment these days is wonderful. But remember, you can have a phony getting out of a Porsche and a saint getting out of an oxcart. By today's standards, I played with poor equipment when I won my tournaments; it wasn't inferior for its time, but golfers now would laugh at it. Still, I shot par and birdie. I got there.

Golf is thought. Everything stems from thought and is created by thought. If you believe your equipment is going to make you a good golfer, you're running down the wrong path. Here's a for-instance: If you look at a pitchfork, has it changed much in the past century? There's not a lot of effort to sell us the best pitchfork. There are none with titanium tines and graphite shafts. But if pitching manure became a great sport, there would be a lot of changes in the pitchfork. If we really wanted to get into the game of pitchforks, we'd have a pitchfork for sawdust, a pitchfork for peat moss, a pitchfork for hay, another for straw. Then we'd have to work on the consistency of manure. We'd have to be sure we fed the horses and cows and sheep exactly the right amount of the right feed. But who's to say the new pitchfork and the new manure would be better? The pitchfork might feel better. It might make the job easier; it might be better balanced. It might even have a little more flex in the handle so you wouldn't have to use so much energy. But it would not make you a better farmer.

How you farm, like how you play, comes from within. It's not based on technology. The game of golf is not how well you play. Golf is how many strokes it takes you to get the ball in the hole. And there's a big difference here: If you play with someone who scrapes it along the ground but hits the ball up there and gets it in the hole and birdies, that's golf. If you're playing with someone who has a gorgeous swing and hits it beautifully but can't get it in the hole, they're not playing golf. What are they playing? They may be playing "golf swing," or they may be playing "beautiful shots" or "looking good," but they are not playing the game of golf. Playing golf is different from "Look at my swing." Golf isn't hitting beautiful shots. It's getting the ball in the hole no matter what has happened to it, no matter where it goes, and no matter how old or young your pitchfork.

Polly Riley

*I*F GOLF HAS THE POWER to nurture, then its best argument might well be Polly Riley. When I meet her for lunch at River Crest, though I haven't seen her yet, or even a picture, and many other women come through the clubhouse entrance, I know her immediately. The small, compact body is still tight, fit, and full of energy. Her handshake is firm. Her salt-and-pepper hair is in a sensible cut, her eyes wizened, her smile wide and easy. She is at home at River Crest, knows the table with the best light and the most quiet, and it is she, not the hostess, who leads us to it. The best choice for lunch is not on the menu: shrimp-stuffed avocado with lemon, and following her lead I order it, too.

She's brought no photos, no memorabilia, no magazines, only her stories. She was born in San Antonio, Texas; her father, an oilman, was moved from one project to the next, the family shuffling along behind. Riley was the youngest of five children. Her oldest sister died at an early age, leaving her mother heartbroken, so when Riley's father died of pneumonia when Polly was seven, her mother became even more remote in her grief. Grandmothers joined the household for six months of the year. "One grandmother or the other was always around," says Riley, "and usually a cousin or two. My mother grasped at whatever straws she could to salvage her life."

When Riley was eleven, the family moved from Tulsa to Fort Worth. "By that time I'd been to fourteen different schools, and I'd been allowed to skip one grade," she says. "When we moved, I was already in seventh grade and the Fort Worth school promoted me immediately to tenth grade, so I was four or five years younger than everyone in my class. I was really out in left field, and said, 'Hey, I got to do something here.' "

There was a girl her own age in the new neighborhood who played golf. Her name was Willie Mae Mays. "It occurred to me," says Riley, "that I'd seen people playing golf by themselves and it looked like the kind of game you could play by yourself, so I went to her and said, 'Hey, Mae, I want to play.' I realized I could do that by myself, it would keep me occupied, and I'd have an interest."

Riley was twelve when Willie Mae took her to her junior golf program, where the teaching pros usually gave a twenty-minute clinic on the first tee, then all the kids went out to play. "There were twenty or thirty girls," recalls Riley. "It was unusual. I was really good right away. Behind it all, of course, I was desperate to have something and I knew it. After that day, I didn't have to seem so strange anymore. I could go out alone and nobody thought that was funny. It was a means of recovery."

That first clinic was in June on the number one tee at Colonial Country Club. "The first ball I ever hit in my life was off the first tee at Colonial. Can you imagine? I didn't think about it then, but when I think about it now . . ." Riley trails off with a smile. "By fall, I was only going to school two hours a day. My mother had dragged out my father's old set of clubs and I played with them. I'd race home, get my bike, throw the clubs over my handlebars, and away I'd go until after dark. I learned seven cuss words and I learned to gamble, although not with my own money; other people would put a wager on me, and that really helped my game."

That first fall she played in the Texas Open. The next spring she qualified for the championship of the Texas Southern. "I don't know if I was gutsy or just didn't know any better. At the Texas Open, I'd just turned thirteen and I met up with all the good players: Patty Berg, the Babe, Betty Jameson, Helen Dettweiler, Betty Hicks. Good as they were, and me just three months into the game, I played along and there were no problems. They treated me with respect. I was in awe. Babe called me 'Kid.' She was still calling me 'Kid' ten years later."

What Riley lacked in peers, she found in a teacher: A. G. Mitchell, an Englishman who came to this country in the late 1920s. "All the great players came to him at one time," says Riley. "Hogan, Nelson, Jimmy Demaret, the Babe. When something went wrong, this is where they came. Mitchell was a wonderful diagnostician. When I started that first full summer, I got to talking to him about whether he'd help me. He said, 'Yes, with one reservation—I don't want you to ever ask me for help until you can tell me with an absolutely straight face that you've done everything you know to correct the problem. I want you to be able to analyze and handle it for yourself.'

"I think that is the greatest gift anybody ever gave me in golf. He gave me the knowledge and ability to address the problems on my own."

From her lone rounds at Colonial she went on to a stellar amateur career that included over a hundred tournament wins, a large number of them majors. In addition, she played on six Curtis Cup teams—1948, 1950, '52, '54, '56, '58—and was captain in 1962. The first she played at age twenty-one—"a young twenty-one," she says—and Glenna Collett Vare was the team's captain. On the ship to England, where the matches were played that year, Riley befriended Vare's fifteen-year-old daughter, Glenny. "The two of us became good friends because all the rest were older," says Riley. "Between matches Glenna asked me to join them on a trip to Scotland. She had called ahead to make a starting time at St. Andrews. We were just the two of us going to play a casual round. When we arrived, they had three thousand people out in the gallery just for the two of us. I'll never forget the American flag flying as we drove up.

"The spectators were all out there still dressed for their businesses. They had closed down the shops. I knew they weren't there for me, but I wanted to play well enough so that I didn't embarrass myself. Neither of us expected what we had come into. I was nervous and Glenna could see it. She said, 'This is just golf. Whatever is presented you, just buckle down and play it.'

"I played fairly well; I wasn't embarrassed. There were some double greens and on one of them I was on the far side with a big ridge between, and I asked the caddie for a four-iron. He said,

'You're on the green.' I said, 'I know.' He reluctantly gave it to me. I think he thought I was going to tear up the green. That caused a bit of commotion because they hadn't expected that first, an American, and then, a woman—an American woman—could do that. They knew the shot. A normal run-up shot, hands ahead at address, dead wrists, ball down quickly, with an iron. The green was so large and the hole so far, farther than I could stroke a putter and keep it on-line. To use a putter from that distance I would have had to *hit* it, not stroke it, and the right hand would have taken over. It would have taken me out of my usual rhythm and timing. With an iron I knew I could stay within the stroke better. My caddie just didn't think I was good enough to hit it. Pulling that off, that whole day, was a tremendous experience."

Though Riley had everything it took to win, she never turned pro. Prize money was too low, and Riley, as young as she was, had seen pro life up close and was not lured. The turning point was when Riley was fifteen and Patty Berg (who in addition to her playing greatness was, with Babe, the day's finest ambassador of women's golf) invited her to do exhibitions with her throughout Texas and Arkansas and Oklahoma. "I was to be her 'straight man' at the clinics," says Riley. "We had been out on the road for maybe ten days at this point. You get up in the morning and drive a hundred to a hundred and fifty miles to the next place you're going, check into a hotel or go directly to the club and have lunch with the ladies of the ladies' golf association. Then you go and play nine holes with the club champion or club pro, give the exhibition, and that night have dinner at the club with the club president and his wife. The next day and the next day and the next are the same. You never see anything but the club and different versions of the same people, with different faces in different places. You get so tired you can hardly stand it. I got tired of it after just a few days and Patty had a lifetime of it because in those days there weren't that many tournaments that allowed you to get a break from it. That's essentially what she'd do eight months a year, day in and day out.

"This one day we'd gone through that kind of routine in Oklahoma. Neither of us was a drinker, but we were picked up at the hotel and taken back to the club for a cocktail party and then into the dining room for dinner. As we were having dessert, the president of the club says, 'Now, Patty, it's bingo night. Would you like to go into the ballroom and play bingo?' And this is so unlike Patty, and why it stuck so in my mind, she said, 'I'd rather go down in the basement and read a telephone book.' She was worn to a frazzle. She'd come to the end of her rope and all of us at dinner knew it. No one was offended. We all smiled. It'd just slipped out.

"Being a professional then, it wasn't a bit glamorous. It was a lot of disappointments, a lot of hard work doing what someone else wanted you to do all the time with a smile on your face and the right words on your lips. You washed your clothes out in the bathroom and hung them up to drip in the shower and ironed them on top of a dresser. It wasn't much different for the ones who were winning and the ones who were along for the field."

Though she would never turn pro, Riley won the first Ladies Professional Golf Association tournament ever played. "I just had one of those weeks," she says. "It was the Tampa Open, 1950. I wasn't carrying the pressure of a pro because I was an amateur, I was just playing. The final day, I had total focus. I had received a telegram that morning that my mother had had emergency surgery, and I remember thinking I had to play anyway. I didn't know anything more about what was happening with her until after the tournament. There was no way I could, and I didn't tell anyone. I didn't think of it once on the golf course. I just honed in. I visualized every shot before I played it. I could see the ball going where I wanted it to go. I could see the line of the putts. Anyone who has played and won very much will tell you that you have times you look down and there's something at least the width of the ball that goes from the ball to the hole, like a small canyon, and the ball is in that little rut and can't get out all the way to the hole. It's a marvelous feeling.

"So as an amateur I won the first pro tournament. It was a real mental test because if I'd let 'mother' work its way in, I'd have been finished. I didn't think of any of that, not once during the round. Only afterward when I finished did I go to the phone."

When anyone speaks of Riley, there's always one word or variant thereof tacked on to her name: "fight," "fighter," "the little fighter." "She was just small, but so full of fight," says Barbara Romack, who battled Riley often. "She was a fierce competitor. Don't let her fool you. She loved gamesmanship. She'd arrive on the first tee, all six of her Curtis Cup pins on her hat, all in a row. To make sure you noticed, she'd adjust the brim as often as she possibly could."

"That was Polly having fun," says Jameson. "She was good and she knew it, and everyone else knew it. She didn't need the pins to show it. She could just pull out her four-wood. She was the best there was with that club. If she had really been into gamesmanship, all she'd have had to do was twirl that club around in front of the jittery ones. That would have been enough to put the uncertain ones down."

"I wore those pins because I was proud of them," says Riley. "And I only wore all six of them when I played certain ones—the ones who said I did it to psyche people out. How it started was, I usually wore a beret when I played and I thought the beret looked kind of plain, so the first day I just stuck a pin on it. I might have needled a bit in practice, but not in competition. Gamesmanship, as far as I'm concerned, takes you out of focus. I had enough to focus on just making sure I got the ball to the hole."

In the off season, Riley worked in public relations for General Dynamics, the military aircraft manufacturer. When she didn't have time to get to the range, she took balls to an open field during her lunch breaks and practiced hitting to a cloth she placed on the ground. Golf remained the center of her world, and she kept her game sharp enough for competition on into the early seventies, but in 1974 a misdiagnosed rotator cuff injury ended her playing days. "Golf had been everything. When I couldn't play, it was traumatic, and the only way I could really deal with it was just to remove myself from anything to do with golf. I wouldn't read magazines. I wouldn't watch it on television. I had a hard time going near it. My first real exposure back to golf as I'd known it was more than twenty years later when I went to the Curtis Cup matches. It was a test for me. I think I've gotten over the bad effects of not playing golf. It's gone now from traumatic to just plain missing it. I miss the exercise, the getting outside, the associations."

I understood quickly how she'd bypassed two grades. Her mind is razor sharp and on the fast track still. We talk through the afternoon, and from our table she points out the place by the green, and over there on the range, where, in other years, she and Hogan would practice and talk. At a time when women's career choices were limited, most often going the way of secretary, nurse, teacher, waitress, or clerk, golf drew her into a different world where it was fine to be fierce and strong. There was Babe, Berg, Jameson, Wiffi Smith, Annella Golthwaite, Betty Hicks, Mickey Wright, and on and on. "Golf took me to so many people, so many good friends. There are so many stories," she says. "For that very lone kid on a bike, it's been some way to go."

"So golf can heal," I say. She looks at me the way I imagine she might have looked down a straight-on putt, then smiles and says, "It seems so."

Don't Fight Yourself

Glenna Collett Vare was the epitome of women's golf. Oh, she was a player. She played with a fast tempo and very little patience. She was very short on patience. She had a very fast tempo about everything. Of course your tempo is a natural thing. You either move fast, in which case you play fast, or you move deliberately and take a long time to make decisions, in which case you move slowly. You don't take somebody who makes snap decisions and put them on the golf course and make them swing and play slowly. It won't work. Everyone needs to maintain what her own natural tempo is.

The phonograph and the waltz—I remember watching people with a phonograph on the practice tee trying to get that tempo. Now if you move in 3/4 time, it's wonderful. Then you can do it naturally without the phonograph. If you don't, I don't think that's the way you need to swing the golf club. To me, that's trying to make a tempo for yourself that you don't have, which I think is wrong. You can't do that with great success. You have a natural tempo, and you should stick with it. If you're imposing a tempo, it's much more difficult to repeat, and almost impossible to repeat under pressure. (Now I'm not talking a movement so quick it could track lightning. That's not a swing, that's trouble. If that's the case, you have to learn to feel what a swing is, then find your rhythm.)

Playing golf is no different than anything else in that if you find the path of least resistance, it's going to be easier. I don't care what you're doing, it's true. I always thought of it, "Hey, I'm going to find the path of least resistance." That's certainly true with your tempo: you need to find the path of least resistance. Go with the tempo you're accustomed to, with the way you're used to doing things. We each have a heartbeat, we each have a pulse, we each have a rhythm. Don't fight yourself.

When I think back on the golf matches that I lost—and most players think back on the matches they've lost at least as much as the ones they won—most were ones in which I lost my natural tempo, sometimes for outside reasons, sometimes just because I allowed it to happen. Sometimes I overslept, I got up late, then I had to move things at a faster pace than I was used to moving them. Sometimes I didn't sleep well, I got tired of turning over in bed so I got up too early. So then I had to try to stretch the time out. That affected my tempo for the day.

I believe that the very most important thing you can do in competition is to attempt to keep everything you do, from the time you get up in the morning, keep it moving at your natural pace. In that case, your golf swing has a better chance of moving at its natural pace and you will move at your natural pace on the golf course which will keep you in sync. It's very hard to move fast on the golf course and swing anything but fast. It's very hard to move slowly and swing fast. That's why players like Glenna hated, and I mean hated, a slow pace. It disrupted everything inside her. She then had to take on herself and the course.

"Oh! Oh!"

I met Babe Zaharias when I was thirteen, my first time playing in the Texas Open. She was one of the contenders, and I revered her. She called me "Kid." From that day on, fifteen years later, on to the end, she was still calling me "Kid."

People like to talk a lot about Babe's bravado and gamesmanship, but let me tell you, that was her personality, and at heart, she was very gracious. She never put people down, she built herself up. And that was her way of winning. There's the favorite story of how she'd stop by the locker room at the start of a tournament and say to all of us, "Hey, girls. I just dropped by to see which one of you's going to finish second." If you allowed it to intimidate you, so be it. She had great psychology. A needling gamesmanship. You had to rise to it. People like to think she and I had a big rivalry, but what we had was fun, and we respected each other. Once in a practice round before a tournament in 1949, Babe was standing on a nearby tee and she hollered over, "C'mon, Polly, why don't you hit one for the folks?" I said, "Whadahya mean, Babe? These people have been following you for fourteen holes, and you haven't hit one yet?" She liked that kind of thing. It got her going. The galleries, everyone loved her. They always expected her to win.

In 1948 I beat Babe badly at the Texas Open. 10 and 9 in thirty-six holes. I was eight up after the first eighteen, six under par. I had a house guest who didn't come to the course, and I went home for lunch because I lived close by and she, knowing I was playing Babe, said, "How you doing?" I said, "The margin's eight." She said, "Oh, you can come back, you can come back . . ." "No," I said, "I'm leading." "Oh! Oh!"

It was one of those days I had tremendous focus. The seventh hole across water, 370 yards into a prevailing wind, par 4. Babe hit it to within eight feet on her approach, but I chipped in, and she missed the putt. I remember feeling, with almost every shot, it was preordained. Babe got the message the same time I did. No matter what she did, it was not going to work. I was going to win.

The older I've gotten I see a lot of things in life, in golf, are out of our hands. You've got to love the surprises. I used to think I was in charge of everything. The older I get, the more I realize what little control we have. Babe was very gracious. She saw it. She fought, but there was something in that day, there was nothing she could do to win.

People say I was a fighter. Well, I had stamina, but not sheer physical strength. Babe, she had both and a tremendous ability to concentrate. She was a good pool player, good card player, she was better than most at everything. The background, where she came from, she had to make it for herself, she had to scrabble. What she got, she earned. If you were a good friend to her, she was a generous friend to you. I learned much from her—sheer athleticism, tremendous confidence, searing desire—but two things really improved my game.

One, she had the daring to do whatever looked like it would work. She knew daring, and she didn't cross the line between daring and recklessness. She was not reckless, but if a shot looked like it had some percentage of working, she had the guts to try.

Two, she had a wonderful short game. She was as good a putter as I've ever seen from six feet in. She had incredible feel in her soft, soft hands. Babe would and could play her putts two different ways, which was remarkable. She could play to charge at the hole or die at the hole. In her game, in everything, she was total, incredible feel.

Three in June

When I started to play at age twelve, my mother got out the clubs that had been my father's. "Well, you can play with your daddy's clubs . . ." And I didn't know any better; I thought I had a great deal. She thought that the golf balls that had been in his bag since before he died would do. One of my brothers convinced her that those wouldn't work, that I needed new golf balls, so she took me down to Montgomery Ward and bought me three Denny Shute golf balls for, as I recall, something like seventy-nine cents, and I went off to Colonial to play.

I had very good peripheral vision. I always knew where the golf balls went. I always found a lot of golf balls. I'm not losing mine, I'm finding a whole lot more, so I'm playing all along all summer long and I never had to buy any new ones. Well, I'm playing in the tournament in October—the Texas Open—a big tournament, so I went to Mother and I said, "Mother, I need some golf shoes 'cause I'm playing in tennis shoes, and I need some golf balls." She said, "Well, I understand the shoes. I talked to Willie Mae and she said you needed some golf shoes. She told me some time ago I need to get you some shoes. I'd been planning on getting them for you for Christmas, but I'll get them for you for the tournament. I'll get you the shoes. But," she says, "I don't understand about the golf balls. I bought you three in June."

It tickled my friends, and we all remembered it. When I was inducted into the Texas Sports Hall of Fame, I was with a good friend from childhood when I got the request for clubs, balls, anything of importance in my career for their Hall. And the friend said immediately, "You need to give them the ball you beat Babe with, ten and nine. They'll want that ball." Then she got this funny look on her face. "Unless you're still playing with it."

A New World

I was one of the early ones to play high-lofted woods. I carried a 5 and a 6, but the club I was the most accurate with was the 4-wood. I liked to hit woods better than long irons because I didn't hit good long irons and I worked at hitting fairway woods because I needed to hit them. I knew from the beginning I didn't have the strength long irons take. I couldn't get enough elevation on them to be able to control them well because that's a matter of strength. You have to really hit down on a long iron to get the thing up, and it was apparent, quite early, to me and the pro who taught me, that no matter how much we worked on long irons, I was not going to be a good long-iron player, so we worked on the woods.

At the 1998 Curtis Cup match in Minnesota, I saw Claire Doran Stancik. Claire was runner-up at the U.S. Amateur at Town and Country Golf Club in St. Paul in 1951. We were laughing, remembering I was favored in that tournament because the course was a rather short course and the media had been all excited before the tournament started because, since I was good at getting the ball up and down, when I came to town they all thought I would have this tremendous advantage. The newsmen were all in a fuss about what a great advantage I'd have on that golf course. What they didn't see was that my great advantage was on a longer golf course where *everybody* had to hit woods to the green. That was my strength. Not only would I hit the green when most would miss, I'd hit it close. Even though I was small, relatively long golf courses were the courses I played well.

It wasn't that I had something special. I worked at it. My focus was that I was going to hit it close, when I think most people's focus when they're hitting fairway woods is, "Hey, I want to get it down there somewhere." I don't think enough players think about hitting woods close. I knew I could be dead-on with a wood. I knew I had as good a chance to get it within ten feet as the girl who was hitting the 7-iron because I had to, so that's what I focused on. Not that other people wouldn't have liked to hit it close. I just don't think they had the requirement to hit it close with their woods as many times as I did, so they didn't put the monkey on their own backs quite as hard in that situation. I'd stand there thinking, Close. I practiced exactly that way. I didn't go out on the range and whack away with my woods at a bunch of balls; I hit to a specific target. Specific. Within ten feet was acceptable. Players should try that, women especially now with their high-lofted woods—narrow the focus, play with the necessity and the will to put that wood close. It creates a whole new game, a whole new world.

Easy Does It

There's nothing that upsets me quite as much as seeing a club player, man or woman, whose goal obviously is to hit it a long way. You can tell when they stand up there. All they really want to do is drill it. They're never really going to enjoy the game because they're never going to play enough that they can keep that kind of shot under control. You know the player who plays every day has a hard time keeping that kind of quickness under control. If you're out there once a week, you haven't a chance in this world, so the enjoyment of the game is severely reduced.

Everyone talks about rhythm and I think sometimes people listen and think, Oh, sure, sounds good, and dismiss it with the same speed they like to go after the ball. Rhythm is not just so you can look good, it's what the game is about. Rhythm ensures a higher percentage of solid contact. If you can take any kind of object and hit another object with it, a jerky action is going to more frequently meet with a miscentered contact. It's true in baseball, tennis, pool, whether the object is moving or sitting there still for you. I used to say, "Easy does it," before every stroke, just to remind myself. There's a psychological value to rhythm that's evidenced in everything you do. If you keep your life flowing along on an even keel, it's a whole lot easier. If you keep your golf swing moving at an even pace, everything is a whole lot easier. There's not the wear and tear either physically or emotionally on you.

I know this myself. My friends will tell you I've lost patience in all areas of my life since I stopped playing golf. If you're going to win, you must stay in the rhythm and stay patient. You don't go out and try to make things happen, you wait for things to happen. The best of them all know this and that's what they do.

Batting at the ball up on the tee, trying to belt one after another may bring you a thrill every once in a while, but I promise you, if you play day in and day out without a sense of rhythm, without fluidity, you'll never be a player. It's impossible to keep it up.

Words at River Crest

It was after his accident, when Ben Hogan started back hitting balls, that he came to River Crest to practice. He was still recovering, so he'd go out and chip two or three balls, then go sit down on the bench under the shelter. After I got to realizing what was happening, when I got to know his routine, I started chipping from that side of the green because I knew he'd start talking. He didn't have a reputation as a talkative man, but he was maybe only six months out of the accident, and I was young and green and in the right place at the right time. It was usually just me and him. He'd make a comment, and I'd listen like I never had. We spent a lot of time talking around the green, each in our own practice.

One day I was working on trying to be more aggressive with my putting, and he said, "You really ought to think about the dying putt. The dying putt has got four ways to go in. The aggressive putt has one: center of the hole, back, and it'll go in if it's not too aggressive. The dying putt can hit any corner, any side of the hole, and fall in." I'd heard this before, but from Hogan, the words took on such life. I never once tried to be an aggressive putter after that.

A number of years later, after his third Masters victory, at dinner at Augusta National, I was at his table and I heard him say in that same voice, "I hit two shots today the way I meant to." I thought, Wait a minute, he shot 69. But I knew he was such a perfectionist, what he was saying was, the way he truly meant to. Exactly as he meant to. I knew him enough to know the message was, "Keep it in play, it will work. You can make it work as long as you don't do anything drastically wrong. Don't make any big mistakes." And I think that's the kind of player I was. I didn't make any big mistakes. I kept the ball somewhere around the hole and somewhere around the fairway and tried to take advantage of the rolls and breaks. Ben is the one who really made me understand that. He'd just done it, and he'd done it so dramatically. It takes a lot of pressure off because you don't have to think, I've got to hit this perfect.

You don't have to hit it perfectly. Keep the thing where you can play it. Two shots in 69? Now Ben's standard was much higher—his mistakes might mean he meant to fade it three yards to the right and it faded only two and a half. If you accept his words with that reservation, you can accept what he really said: "Keep the thing where you can play it. Keep it where you can walk and hit the next one. Where you don't have to hunt for it, and you don't have to dig for it when you get there."

Shirley Englehorn

*H*ER FATHER was a superb marksman, so early on, the concept of target filled her life. By the time she was eleven, she could skeet-shoot equally well with either hand and eye. But as she so expertly knocked down the clay birds, one after another, crack, crack, crack, out of the sky, she'd already settled on a different goal: She was going to be a golf professional. No matter that her brothers said she'd have to give up jeans for a skirt, she wasn't going to change her mind.

It was the early fifties, in Caldwell, a little town in Idaho, and hole number three of a small municipal course lay at the edge of her backyard. "People were always chasing me off," she tells me over lunch at the Broadmoor in Colorado Springs. "I was a nuisance. I was there all day, every day, and I'd be out there working on feel way after dark. Even on a starless night I knew where the ball was going. Hit it off the heel, I knew where it would skid. Hit it off the toe, the middle—out alone in that quiet, in that darkness, I didn't have to see the ball to hit it. I could swing and track it by what the club told me."

When it rained, she studied the scrapbook she'd clipped from newspapers and magazines: The Babe, Opal Hill, Sessions, Suggs, Hicks. "It could be the most obscure name, a long shot, I was crazy for all of them. There wasn't a lot of coverage, so I hoarded anything I had. I was about twelve when I wrote Babe Zaharias a letter. She never wrote back. Turns out it was just before she died. I didn't even know she was sick. Years later, her friend Betty

Dodd, who took care of her at the end, remembered she'd gotten it. It stuck out. I was such an eager kid."

Englehorn's father worked for John Deere covering a wide area of country selling and bartering new and used farm equipment. The family never did without, and though far from wealthy, there was enough for young Englehorn's entry fees and travel to a few of the state's better tournaments. Meanwhile, in high school she played on the boys' team. "I didn't care if it was unheard of. My mother, who was unusual, would say, 'The quickest way to failure is giving up yourself to please other people.' So it didn't bother me I had to play with the boys. I played the back tees with them. They didn't like it, but they respected it because I could beat them."

She was as long as any of her teammates and, as the Babe before her, blistered the ball, imparting sizzling backspin. And her aim was deadly. As she went along, she hooked up with teachers Shirley Spork and Johnny Revolta. "Shirley helped me with my left side," she says, "Revolta with my right. Then I worked to refine both."

Fresh out of high school she turned pro, and at her second tour stop met up with Hall of Famer Mickey Wright. "She was a perfectionist. She could hit it so squarely and solidly there was no grass fluttering, the divot came out like a little slice of bread. I marveled at that. I was long and I knew it, but Mickey taught me something right from the beginning. She'd hit a drive, I'd match it. She'd hit another drive, I'd match that, feeling really fine about it. But she was just warming up, seeing how much in me wanted to compete. The next hole she'd hit it a little farther, and on it went, with her inviting me to match her shots, toying with me until suddenly I was seeing her balls flying twenty-five, thirty yards farther than mine and straighter, too. The whole point of the silent exercise was her showing me exactly what it would take."

As with Wiffi Smith before her, Englehorn was a wunderkind. Most older players welcomed her, content to watch how far—to what excellence—she might carry their game.

Her third pro tournament was the Titleholders in Augusta, Georgia. The date was March 16, 1960. It was snowing. After round one was cancelled, Englehorn went horseback riding with friends. "I got the wrong horse at the wrong time," she says. "They called him Swamp Fox. It was slick. I didn't have riding shoes on. We were going along, and he shied, and I went flying out over his head, smashing into a tree. It was bad. I had a concussion, my nose was smashed, and I angle-fractured three dorsal vertebrae. I was given last rites."

Englehorn was immobile, strapped into a foster bed (a bed that's flipped every hour) for six weeks. The prognosis was not only that she would never play again, but more than likely, she would not walk. "Lying there, I tried not to listen. It was snowing when I went in and later I remember looking out, still strung tightly to that bed, and flowers were blooming. I hadn't walked. I hadn't really moved in all those months."

Determination and the will to return to the game kept her going, but as days went on monotony and the morass of painkillers lulled her. The Masters was about to be played and all the best male players were coming to town. Golf chatter buzzed all about, yet she had little interest in it. Then one afternoon, just as she was giving in to sleep, Ben Hogan walked in.

"I'd never met the man, but I idolized him. He didn't say much; he just sat there. He was a remarkable man; you could feel it in his presence. He didn't have to say much, he just looked at me in a way that told me that a lot was going through his mind about his own accident," she says. Hogan's head-on auto crash at the height of his career is as well-known as the man. Seeing the headlights of a bus coming straight over a hill, throwing himself across his wife to lessen the impact on her, he was hurt so badly that he, too, had been told he would not play again. Less than a year later, after a grueling rehabilitation, he was back winning.

"Probably his life went before him," Englehorn resumes. "I hadn't walked; I couldn't. But to me it was like an angel was there. I'll never forget it. I said, 'Mr. Hogan, I'm getting up out of this bed and I'm going to walk to the door with you.' And that's exactly what I did. No doctor or nurse could believe it. I had to get back in bed, but in a few days I went to the Masters in a back brace and a wheelchair. After months and months of work, I returned to golf."

Englehorn came back and won and won. But four years after

her first return she had to make a second comeback when a car accident left her with a shattered left ankle. "When I was little, this very elderly woman baby-sat for me. I remember sitting on the floor listening to her tell stories about how she had come across the country on the Oregon trail. She had to walk most of the way, hot sun, dry dust kicking up in her face from the wagon wheels. I loved those tales, hearing about such hardship, especially for the women in those days, how they kept going, that kind of will was fascinating to me. I know it helped me those years later coming back from the injuries. I'd always wanted to know if I could be that strong. I laugh now; there just might have been better ways to prove it."

In 1962, after the fused ankle, she returned on Pleasant Valley Country Club's course in Worcester, Massachusetts, the hilliest test of the year. "Walking wasn't so bad," she says, "it was having to walk three or four days in a row. But I did it. It was a private test of stamina and will, and that started my four wins in a row."

Though her talent is still talked about today, and talk often turns to the "might-have-beens," Englehorn will have none of it. Though not as she would have scripted it, she had her thirteen tour wins and eighteen seconds, and now she is a teacher—one of the best in the country. Her fall from the horse that snowy day at Augusta, she believes, has left her the better for it. "Bam! Bam! Bam! Sometimes life can do that," she says, "but through the crooks and turns, and in some cases, cliffs and canyons, I believe somehow we end up where we're supposed to be.

"I didn't get to teaching because I couldn't play. I got to teaching because I am a teacher. I probably could have won more, but being out there takes its toll even on a healthy body, and teaching meant a lot to me. I got more out of teaching, personally, than I did out of winning. Winning didn't overwhelm me, didn't inflate my ego. It was wonderful to have done it, but it's very lonely. You move on to the next week and there's another winner. You go to the next week and there's yet another. When I won the four in a row, there was still that same feeling: You're by yourself, you've done it, you know what you've accomplished. There are all the accolades and the hoopla, but you have to keep performing. I found it very lonely. Teaching for me has never been lonely."

As I meet and sit with her a second time, in the living room in her winter house in Temecula, California, I wonder if her students know what they have. How rare to have a player and a teacher in one. At fifty-six she's physically attractive, with deep brown mischievous eyes. The poise she must have gained blasting those clay birds out of the air so easily at eleven is with her, but now is firmly centered. Her voice falls, then recedes, smooth and rhythmic. We sit through the afternoon drinking coffee. She sends me to a large glass case and has me bring out the most beautiful, heavy bronze trophy—the Ben Hogan Award, which she received in 1968 after her second comeback. It is the perfect likeness of Hogan poised at the top of his backswing—wrists cocked, left arm firm, right elbow pointed down, right knee steady, still flexed the same amount as at his famed address, left knee bent in toward the right. I feel the weight of it, all of what it means, as I carry it outside to where it rests between us on the umbrellaed table until night birds and dusk's chill move us back inside.

She tells me how the sculptor had to do several casts of the statue after Hogan insisted the hands be set just right from every angle no matter where you looked at it from across a room. It took five years to perfect. "See here," she says, "here, there, here; they captured it perfectly, finally." And this is how, through it all, I imagine she is with her students: the perfect balance of unbroken excellence. "You've got to spank that ball, spank that ball." "Don't make a teaspoon into a tablespoon and try to help it. This is not the kitchen." "It's a descending blow, a descending blow." "Tie into it, you'll live longer. Give it a ride . . ." She mimics herself, her incantations.

Most will never get close to the realm she knows. With many older women especially, she begins by teaching them to throw. Though she has been to the top, she is willing to go over and over the basics as the whiffer, the caster, the pusher, and the snaker inch their way to launching one airborne. Injury has helped her: "Work, faith, patience. Work, faith, patience."

She received the Ellen Griffin Award in 1991 and has studied all those who've come before. "Griffin, Betty Dodd, Peggy Kirk Bell, Joanne Winter, Shirley Spork, Patty Berg, Goldie Bateson. I've been lucky just to stand in their light as they've walked by," she says. "What do they all have in common? Love and caring. In teaching, it seems you earn the heart for it."

Rookie

Fresh out of high school I signed with Golfcraft (today Titleist). They paid me $250 for that contract, so I had enough money to go to my first pro tournament. The flight, a DC-3 from Idaho to Ardmore, Oklahoma, was bump bump bump all the way, and we had to land on an airstrip that had weeds popping up all over. I hadn't been away from Idaho hardly at all.

When we landed, I thought someone would be there to meet me, but no one was. We were going to Waco and Opie Turner's Lodge to play the tournament, and I saw this woman with the mail who noticed that I had this golf bag with my name all over it. She said, "Where you going?" I told her, explaining that it was my first tournament. I can imagine how green I looked, and she offered me a ride. I said, "Well, someone is supposed to meet me. I don't know where they are." She just took my bag and threw it in back with the mail. I remember distinctly that woman driving along telling me how wealthy the Turners were, and eventually we drive up this big driveway and there are Cadillacs right and left, everywhere. I say, "They sure must have a lot of Cadillacs," and she says, "Yeah, every time one of 'em even has a flat tire, he buys a new one. He's a multi-multi-millionaire." So she drives me up to the entrance of the lodge and here's Betsy Rawls, Mickey Wright, Jackie Pung, Shirley Spork, and I'm just, "Wooaahh." I don't have time for a practice round because I'm late. I've never played the course and I'm paired with the great Betty Jameson and Barbara Romack. I've got this caddie; I'll never forget it. We go to the first tee, and there's a hole going one way and a hole going the other, and I'm up. And my caddie doesn't know. So I say, "Which direction?" Nobody says anything. So I guess, and I guess right, and I'm scared to death. And when I hit the green, you could pick weeds. And no one's talking to me—you know, rookie. So we get on the third hole, I hit it up not too far from the pin and I go up and mark it and Betty Jameson says, "Will you get off the green?" She's going to putt. I think I'm way out of her way and she says, "Will you just move off the green?" I thought, Whooooh. Well, I finished that round and I'll never forget it. Some years later we're paired up again, we're on a par 3 over water, and she gets up and hits this shot, so wonderfully, solidly pure, it soars toward the target. Bursting with enthusiasm, I say, very quickly, "Great shot!" Then I watch, with her whole gallery, as the ball suddenly drops into the water.

Betty turns and in that commanding, wonderfully self-assured way she had says, "Please. Never tell me it's a great shot until it lands on the green!" To this day I can still see that ball drop. And I can tell you, this kid learned, because it was great advice. In this game with its mystery, you've got to wait just a little to offer praise. Wait until the wind and rolls and bumps have played out, until the game's done what it will and the shot has settled. She was fine after that. I learned that her bark, as big as it seemed, was smaller than her heart. But that first day, I was scared to death.

The next morning I went out to practice and everyone's on the practice tee. I pull out my club and start swinging and they leave, everyone leaves. I'm just standing there hitting balls, thinking, Whooh, am I lucky. This is just the greatest thing. Pretty soon Shirley Spork comes out and says, "Get out of there! Come to your room!" I'm thinking, Now what'd I do? I say, "Why?" and she says, "There's a tornado alert." I remember thinking, Boy, they sure do know everything there is to know about tournaments.

The storm cleared and we played. The tournament was just full of prizes for this and that, and I think I ended up winning fifty dollars.

On tour, in those days, Peggy Kirk Bell, Gloria Armstrong, and Betty Hicks all flew planes, and someone had told me I could catch a ride home with Betty Hicks. "Get your luggage and bag together," Shirley Spork told me, "Betty Hicks had a bad day. She'll be in a hurry." Sure enough, Betty comes storming to the plane and she took off with me in it, and she was livid. She was so hot she went from red to purple because she'd played terribly. And there I sat. I thought I was going to die, but not just because Betty was upset. Eventually we were trying to land, and on the ground they kept turning off the landing lights. Finally we got down, and the next day we hit weather. It was terrible. There was just a little hole in the clouds, and she had to put it down and I thought, I am going to die. Betty's an accomplished pilot. In addition to golf, she's taught flying at the top level, commercial pilots. But back then the instruments weren't what they are today, and on that trip home she was mad. But she got us home. Seeing that skill and daring, I've loved that woman ever since. I love her to this day, but I can't hear of her or even see her name without remembering, I'm going to die! hammering in my head. That was some rookie trip; from green to sky, I was scared to death.

Breasts

Men pros, a lot of them come to me to learn to teach women because they've realized physically we're not all built the same way. When they get here I say, "I'll tell you what, I'm going down to get a bra and put two grapefruits in it. To really learn, you guys should get a sense of what it feels like." I do this because it's the best way. I get a bra, and they put it on, and they say, "That's pretty tough." It always opens their eyes, because they begin to feel what it's like to swing when you have breasts, especially large breasts. Suddenly they understand: Large-breasted women have to set up on top of their breasts. Not to the side like the men, but on top—over—because if you're well endowed, how are you going to get around them? Patty Berg used to strap herself down. She'd say, "Nothing's going to get in my way."

If you're flat-chested or small-breasted, of course there's nothing in the way. Then, at address, the arm position is the same for a woman as it is for a man. But if you're ample, at address you have to get those arms set on top, over the breasts, not at the side. This is so important. Only with the proper setup will you really be able to give it a ride.

The Chair

One day I was talking with Jan Stenerud, one of the all-time best placekickers in football. Much of his career he kicked through ice, wind, and snow for cold-weather teams. He told me he'd just been to a kicking seminar, and it was so, so technical. He said, "I had to laugh to myself, and at myself. All I did was, I put the football down, and I kicked it. If I'd had to analyze like they're doing now, I'd have been scared to death."

We talked about how the same is true now in golf. The attention that's paid to technique, everyone's becoming so swing conscious you need to be careful. Attention needs to be brought back to basics. The swing, the swing, the swing—well, it's like a simple piece of furniture. A chair. Nothing more. Is the chair solid? Will it hold you? Will it stand up over time? Good. Then sit in it. Appreciate the wood, the feel. Then do what we most often do with a chair: Forget it's there.

The Trophy

Golf's greatest lesson, I believe, is humility, and I seem to have always had a flair for learning life's lessons in a big way. The day I was presented with the first of a line of Shirley Englehorn golf balls, life was certainly having fun with me.

I'm on the practice tee at a tournament just before a round and here comes the company representative with a whole bag of new Shirley Englehorns, my new "name in lights" so to speak. One might start to think, Hey, I must be getting somewhere. I must kind of be something. But there wasn't time. I'm on the practice tee, and there's a parking lot to the right, a parking lot filled with the cars of many members and spectators. The first Shirley Englehorn I hit was not very straight. In fact, I shanked it, dead right, into the parking lot. I hear the *plunk*. And I know it immediately: I've hit a window.

I go over, and in one of those crank-out, side, triangular vents they used to have in the cars of the sixties, there, lodged perfectly in that little window vent, embedded—just as if I'd put it there—was that shiny new ball with my name as big as day.

I forget warming up, and I go into the pro shop with the license plate number and the make of car. I have the owner paged, thinking, Now what am I going to say? Well, yes, I'm a pro, and yes, my golf ball is lodged in your van. Well, no one answered the page, and my caddie comes after me because I'm due on the first tee. So I play, and after the round, this guy comes up, and he says, "Miss Englehorn?" I said, "Yes." He said, "I'm the one. Your golf ball is in my van window, and I'll probably just keep it there." Just like that.

I apologized and quickly offered to pay, but he said, "No way." He was delighted. He said, "I think I'll just take that window out and save it." I'll never forget it.

I won't forget it because it was a kind of unspoken bonding between people who otherwise were strangers. Golf does that. Over and over, everywhere, everyday. It draws us together—pro, amateur, beginner—because golf has us, we never have it.

Today I still like to think that ball is out there—its own odd little trophy to humility.

The Fish

Golf is nothing but feel. That's why I love fly-fishing. In fly-fishing, you have to feel what you're doing. You feel the line load and you feel the release. There are moments when you are discipline and concentration, nothing else. Go ask three hundred true fly fishermen, "What are you thinking about when you're fishing?" You'll hear three hundred times over, "I'm thinking about the fish." It's not, "How do I do this?" but, "What fish is going to come along?" There's an expression with the old-timers, "Ohhh, they're in there." It's the fish. Feel and fish. It's like that with golf for the lucky ones. Feel and target. That's the complete state of golf.

Nose to Nose

If history is right, this game had its beginnings with good common people biding time, playing in pastures on the sands along the sea. So in the true spirit of the game, no one need put her nose in the air. In fact, I think it's our task as professionals to put people at ease.

There are social rules, of course. Learn what to expect when you join a club. Learn what you can wear, what you can't wear. Can I tote my bag through the clubhouse?

I had one woman who took her bag right through the clubhouse. She didn't know there was an attendant. We hadn't addressed that in lessons. I never thought to, but I learned. There are little things that many might take for granted that newcomers to the game may need pointed out. There are things if you are new that you have to know and probably don't know. You go to a private club, go through the gate, park the car, and take out a pull cart. Well, you can't use a pull cart there. A sleeveless blouse, non-collar shirt, you can't wear it there. But you didn't know. It's our job both as professionals and as people to explain in a non-superior way. It's our job, anyone, nose-to-nose level, not to intimidate but to educate.

Phyllis G. Meekins

SHE HASN'T BEEN LPGA Teacher of the Year, or Professional of the Year, or Coach of the Year. Her name is not likely to be in the running for the Ellen Griffin Award. She hasn't been invited to that New York luncheon, been wrapped in its warm applause, or felt the day-to-day weight and pride of receiving the lovely watch given in Griffin's honor. None of those accolades have wound their way to Phyllis G. Meekins—and now, at age seventy-seven, it's unlikely they will. But it's I, not Phyllis, who ponders this; she's too busy. Her hip is getting iffy, and she's got a lot of ground to cover to keep up with herself.

Much before the LPGA's Urban Youth Program, well before the USGA's First Tee, Meekins taught golf in the basement of Holy Cross Lutheran Church, in her neighborhood in Mount Airy, in northwest Philadelphia. She's retired from her years of various jobs, which included clerking at the Pentagon, a stint in England and France with the army in World War II, and here in Philadelphia, administrating local nursing services to veterans. She taught her golf clinics out of churches, recreation centers, and schools, until two years ago she set up shop in a small, barnlike dwelling on the grounds of a local campus.

There are few trees here, few singing birds, no willow-graced ponds. Cars and large trucks honk and streets pulse with the hum of an everyday city. Still, this early morning as Meekins unlocks the door and I follow her into her small kingdom, I immediately and strangely and happily remember the feel of the small clapboard Tee-House on Griffin's Farm in North Carolina. This place, like that, is open—one main room and a small back one. There are balls here, clubs there, nets in the corners, hitting mats, putting tracks—holes laid out and cut into strips of shiny green indoor/outdoor carpet. Though at the Farm only a shadow remains of its heyday, this place—even in its emptiness at this early hour—is buzzing. I don't find Albert Schweitzer's words that promise love and help and human kindness framed on the wall, but I know they abide in the same spirit they once did there in Carolina.

Meekins is not tall. At least not anymore. At five feet eight, I stretch above her. Her richly lined face is copper-colored—round and radiant; her brown eyes soft; her hair a thick salt-and-pepper halo. The timbre of her voice betrays her age only slightly and when she turns to me with a large smile, eager to lead me through a back room—her incredible bounties of old clubs and discarded shoes she'll refurbish and pass on to her students—there's a hint of a spring in her step and I think how fortunate I am to have found her. By an odd twist of fate, a friend doing work for ABC's *Wide World of Sports,* researching a show, came across Meekins's name, and phoned.

We won't have a lot of time this morning. Despite our best efforts, our schedules won't match. She's got this appointment, that meeting, and is swamped all week and on into the night with golf lessons. Her office, a cubbyhole, with ceiling-high files and papers, calls out with the phone every few minutes. "The machine can get it," she says after she's answered five times.

As I've sat, I've listened—each time someone wanting lessons for herself or her children. Each time Phyllis assures the caller, "Not to worry," arrangements can be made about money. When she comes back she calls no attention to her skill in "making a way out of no way," as the old saying goes. Nor does she spend much time on her countless wins in the East as an amateur during her playing days. Or talk at length of her LPGA professional status, which I know means much to her. As we sit during the next hours her voice doesn't rise or fall to embellish. On a straight-back chair there at a table, amid textbooks and city maps, bulletin boards and rows of snapshots of happy students, she tells her own story in her own way, clear, and simple.

"I wanted golf since I was really young. I couldn't get it. It was impossible. I lived in an area that was affluent, I guess, but not by design. We were just owners of some property in the Virginia woods, and as the years went by share-people moved and the affluent came, and we were still there. The Du Ponts and the like. There was a private school there that had a golf course attached, so you could see it, but you couldn't go to it. My desire for the game of golf—I was just little when it started. You know how you first see something you know you love, how you want it? I longed to be two things then—a jockey and a traveling golf pro. I dreamed and dreamed of it before its time had even come. White men were doing it. But for a small black girl in the South, it was not allowed. Every now and then, I'd get a glimpse of that course from afar. I never stopped wanting it. I went around the world and back in my mind, but I couldn't get it.

"I was born in 1922, and I didn't get to be a pro until 1981, when I was fifty-nine years old. My first set of clubs? An old set of Patty Berg Defenders that my minister divined for me, God knows from where and how. People look at me and ask all the time, "How'd you do it?" I tell them I learned through a lot of disasters. No didn't stop me. I kept after it. I was truly interested, and if there was the slightest hint of an opening, I made it my business to walk through the door. I volunteered here, there. I tried and tried. I got on committees so I could learn more. I'll never forget when I joined an organization here in Philadelphia. I didn't know anything about tournaments, but I said I wanted to be on the tournament committee. To learn. I didn't say I wanted to run it, I didn't ask to chair it, I wanted to work to learn—so I could move on.

"A woman who'd lived in D.C. and had helped Lee Elder helped get me started through Parish Brown. She befriended me when I came here. She'd organized a club and invited me in, which helped get me affiliated. She saw me out on the course rolling the ball, rarely getting it airborne, just snaking it along the ground, and she extended the invitation. I wish more people would remember the power of invitation.

"Golf helps anyone who it touches, and after I got it, I wanted others to help others get involved. Teaching, I started right over there on Anderson Street in the church basement. When I started teaching, none of the kids had stepped on a golf course, or even knew what a golf ball was, for that matter. I started with two kids in my church, from the Sunday school. I went after them. I asked the parents, 'Can I teach them to play golf?' The pastor had given us a room in the basement, so we cleaned it up, put the coffee urns and doughnut platters away, and got started. I knew what golf could do for kids, because I got my daughter Denise started at home, just swinging a club standing between the sofa and chair in the front room.

"I knew then with the game I wasn't only teaching golf, I was teaching the child, and I saw the difference it made in her confidence. She made it into college. I wanted more youngsters to have the opportunity.

"I used to be with those kids at the church from nine A.M. to one in the morning. They paid one dollar a month, just because I didn't think anyone should get anything totally free. That's why my school has always offered Work to Learn. Free, it's too hard to appreciate it. I have some kids in families who can afford it and even they want to be in the Work to Learn program. Here everybody's welcome as long as they learn how to respect each other no matter what.

"For example, one kid had a Burner Bubble, and he said to my granddaughter Jerrel, 'You have cheap clubs.' She said, 'Well, they're mine. You don't have to hit 'em. There're not your clubs.' In a few days, he came back to her and asked, 'Can I try your clubs?' My granddaughter said, "Sure, here, you can hit 'em." So he swung and hit a few, and they got along. On their own, he learned.

"It's just like the men, once I finally got on the golf course, they walked around like they thought they owned it, but when you came down to it, they were respectful. Men, real men, love to see women play well. At the newspaper, the *Tribune* here in Philadelphia, there was a wonderful writer there back then, Claude Anderson was his name, who used to cover me at tournaments, and one day, I'll never forget it, I was playing a big match, and he was so worried, he sent a girl down to the tee with a little plastic bag. In it was a fig bar, milk, and aspirins. That girl came running down out of breath and said, 'He said, "She's getting ner-

vous and she's got to win. Take this down to the tee for her!" '
Mm-hmm. He wrote the most beautiful article. A journalist for
the paper, white.

"So you can see it's not all about color; golf can bring us together person to person.

"The body's like a machine, you got to repeat, repeat, but it's
even more.

"Beyond the machine, the body has to feel. You have to feel,
then see the shot and concentrate. You can't want something too
soon. If you want something too soon you can't concentrate. It
takes time. To be good it takes everything, which is why golf is
such a great game. It doesn't come overnight.

"I know this: To do anything you've got to start with whatever you've got. Even if it means starting awfully small. That's the
key in golf. I tell people to work on their short game the way I
worked on getting myself into this game: Pick a spot. Take X number of balls. See how many you can get there. Maybe you don't get
but one. But keep working. You'll get a few more until you're almost perfect. Then come back tomorrow.

"Like the girls I played with would say about me, 'You're
never satisfied.' Well, I always knew I could do better. Sometimes
you make mistakes, it's hard to concentrate for eighteen holes. Especially when you're playing with amateurs who chit-chat chit-
chat chit-chat. You can't wander; you won't get the job done. I
even went over my scorecards at home. I studied them, the par five
holes, planned where I'd get birdie, scoped out the distance and
imagined my approach. I introduced myself to what I planned to
shoot on the next round and I made myself welcome. It didn't always turn out as I hoped, but that was all right, I kept on.

"That was all those years ago, but now on TV I've been interested to hear that that's sort of what the Swedish do—aim for
what they call a 'fifty-four,' perfect birdie all around. I think that
opens up the possibility to your brain so it can be free to do better.
That's how I did it even back then, because that helped me improve. I thought and planned and worked myself into a lot of situations that I thought had been hopeless. I went through the period
of 'I hope, I hope, I hope,' but that's no way to play golf or live or
do anything else. You have to stand up there, just do it, and know.

"In anything, what I teach the kids here—you can't just be good on paper.

"I tell them about the ones I saw out on the course who dropped another ball, kicked it out from under the tree, threw it over the pond, then wrote 'par' down. They were only fooling themselves, because they knew the truth.

"That's the thing about golf; it has a way of always revealing the truth, always bringing you back to yourself, always showing your true character."

We're interrupted twice that morning by two men in fancy business suits who've come by to see if they could get first dibs on the building once Phyllis has retired. "Sure," she told them, she says, when they've gone and she's come back, "but they'll be waiting till my legs've worn out and my mind has followed. I can't go anyplace. These kids . . ." and with that her voice trails off.

The children she teaches from the surrounding neighborhoods here at PGM Golf Clinics, Inc., not only get instruction in golf but are offered refuge to do their homework. Funded by local business owners, there are three computers that can go full speed, always ready in one corner. The kids, rarely members anywhere, most often without means or transportation, learn the swing here and through six weeks in the summer are bused to cooperating courses where they get the feel of bent grass, put their hands on a flagstick, walk against the wind in the open, and for the first time hear their putts drop into a hole.

As our few hours wind down, a group comes charging in, breathless. They've run all the way from school to do Work to Learn during lunch. There are six of them, two boys and four girls. Each eyes me thoroughly. I shake hands with each one, ages ten to fourteen, I've guessed. Four are bashful and look at the floor, though when Phyllis comes back from another call, all liven up. One bright-eyed girl, has watched me all the while. I delight in her words later as I move on, charmed that this one has told it so straight and true: "Our teacher's the best," she's announced to me there, still looking me up and down. "If she lets you in class, you'll be really lucky."

Why Not

When I played, I went out there to win. Oh yes, I did. I wanted to go pro, but there came a time I saw I was too late. I realized I had to work so in case anything happened to my husband I could still get my daughter to college. But I went after the best I could here in the East. I loved competition. I was not a social golfer. I wanted to learn the game well, work on a good swing, but when I went to tee it up in competition, I wanted to get that ball in the hole and win. Why not? It's nice to win over a field of people. It wasn't a big deal in the whole of life, but it was a big deal at the moment, really, just like getting money. I got so much stuff my husband got sick of it and gave a lot of it away or threw it out. It wasn't the trophies or things—it was the fun. It was fun to win. I won so much around here, as a matter of fact, I said one time, "I wish I would lose to see what my temperament would be." Yes I did. From what I saw, amateur women tend to act a little ugly when someone wins all the time; it could get a little sticky. So I said, "Nah, I wish I would lose." I wanted to see, could I keep the face, because I'd seen so much ugliness. And finally one girl from Connecticut got me. I'll never forget. I said, "I got her on hole number one," that was six hundred and some yards and I was the only person in that area that could get to that green in three. Darn if she didn't come on just like me, we both parred that hole. She was little and she could boom it. It ended up, I lost by one stroke. You know the old "Be careful what you wish for"? There I had it, what I said I hoped for, but that day I had not been hoping—you never want to lose when you're in it. But I was a good sport. Why not? I was happy with myself, how I took it. I was relieved. Because I'd been worried. I'd seen people acting so ugly over a game. I didn't want that to be me. There's a lot that comes with being a winner. If you win one time, it's fine. If you win two times, they're looking at you. Win three times, get out. That's not uncommon. It's worldwide, most people don't realize that the person winning is not winning by the process of osmosis. She's the one who's been working on her game her whole life through. So if you want to be a winner, you've got to be prepared to be one even when it gets sticky. Get ready to handle kindly whatever comes at you.

Create Conditions

You can bet on the first words out of the average child's mouth: "I can't. I can't." But you have to work with them and create conditions for them to succeed. Then you remind them, "I knew you could do it. See?" It's as simple as that.

As a teacher, it's my job to create situations where kids can be successful. You have to. I've gotten to the point with the putting, where I have them putt four inches from the hole. At that distance, they could sneeze and the ball would roll in the hole. But the goal is to give them a taste of success.

Then, building on that success, I move the ball back to eight inches, then twelve. Now I don't have to do that for all children, but for some. And it instills confidence. You have to help them set goals that are achievable.

Last summer I had some kids who said, "I want to be in the seventies after next year." Well, how are you going to be in the 70s, when you're barely 85 now? Just because you shot a low score once doesn't mean you're there. No, you're not, oh no. But there was this one little girl who didn't overreach, because she'd heard me preach so much about achievable goals. I think her low score was 83, so she decided she wanted to come down to 80, a steady 80. She'd heard that message: Be consistent at whatever score you're aiming for. When you've shot it this day and the next and every day again, then you can work on bringing it down another stroke or two.

Yellow and White

I never had any lucky clothes that I thought helped me play better, like some players do. I wasn't a clothes-conscious person. I was appropriately dressed. But I didn't have a thousand outfits, because they weren't necessary. What was necessary to me was learning the game. Now this is a fact, I've said it over and over again: I don't need to go get a dress that's yellow and white and then go and paint my shoes yellow and white. I remember when the girls did that. They had the paint that you could change the color of your shoes, and all the girls went crazy over matching up every little thing they'd see. As if on the golf course dress is the thing.

I had a four-piece outfit. It was whipcord, very nice material, like pinstripe. Whipcord is good. I had Bermuda shorts, a skirt, and two blouses—a collar shirt and another one—adequate clothes. I'd wear the shorts and collar shirt, take my shower, and put my skirt on and the other blouse. That was my outfit, along with my FootJoy shoes, which were black and white. Now my thoughts were, It's not how grand you're looking, it's how well you're scoring. That was my thing. And I still feel that way.

I used to have fun with a lot of the women because they were all so fancy, but they weren't learning, they were not putting the time in they needed to so that they could learn. I had no worries about my clothes. I was practicing. I still say to anyone today: Look good, be well-groomed. You don't need fifteen outfits. What you need in golf is the game. Clothes? The bigger joy is playing well.

Home Improvement

Home practice is great for the short game. Putting, chipping, and pitching, even full swing if you've got the room. You can really improve your technique. You don't need to buy all the fancy equipment and gimmicks. You can pitch balls into a chair, or get a hula hoop, put it on the floor, and pitch it into that circle. You can do it in your living room. Buy a strip of Astro Turf and chip on that if you're afraid of scuffing the floor. You don't need expensive mats.

And for learning, you don't have to put your hands on a club all the time.

You can get the swing motion and the feel sometimes much better without one. Like in putting—putting is just like a clock. If you think of a grandfather clock, the pace is the same every time. Your playing thoughts can be: back and through, back and through. Tick and tock, tick and tock.

With putting, if you let your arms hang down and put your hands together, even without the club, and use a shoulder motion, you've got it. When you do have a putter in hand, for keeping the putter head square, all you have to do is put down two clubs or yardsticks, parallel like railway tracks, and move the club, tick and tock. If you go off-line, those sticks or clubs will remind you, "Keep that clubface square and steady." Back and through.

If you don't, you'll rattle them.

Put a coaster down on the floor for your hole. Line up, visualize your line, close your eyes, and stroke the ball. So many people get ball-bound.

You see the ball and you think you've gotta hit it. When you close your eyes, you don't see it, you can stroke through. So many, beginners especially, every time they see the ball, they stop. Visualize how far back you want to take the club, close your eyes, back and through. Even on the full swing. Go outside where you have enough room. Set up, with or without a club, close your eyes, and practice. Closing your eyes also allows you to really feel. Don't worry that you won't hit the ball. With the best players, even pros, there's times you can bet the club's moving so quickly through the ball, they don't see it. Many have said this. If the swing plane's correct, the club's going to come back to the ball. That's what makes golf so interesting. And so much fun.

To be a good player you've got to learn feel. So get up and practice even at home.

My Jerrel

She's played for two years at the state level at her school. She's not at the top. I think at state she was number nine. But she's at that point of what I call growing. Growing, growing, growing, that's the key.

In her first match at state, round one she three-putted six greens. The next day she had only one three-putt, but she was no good that day off the tee. She had trouble bringing it all together. Who knows why she lost her swing? That's why it's critical to have a well-rounded game. If one part fails, you've got other skills to support you, to keep you going so you can at least stay close. Jerrel understands that. When one part of her game left her, she did not sink down. If she had, she would have been out. She's learning about mental toughness.

How do you get it? Just like my Jerrel. By working through problems. If everything goes well for you all the time, then you don't have the benefit of trial and error. You don't learn what you might from losing. But when you can focus mentally and say, "I know I can do it, even if I didn't do it yesterday," then you're on the sweetest road to success. That's what Jerrel has going for her—a "can do" attitude.

There was another competition she played and she did not perform up to her caliber. She went back the next day and on the next round cut twelve strokes off and won. Now, if she'd had a weak mind, she might have gone straight downhill. Sunk deep into a hole. But she hung in there. And it's the same thing day to day. You have to believe in yourself and your possibilities no matter what. That's mental toughness. Be the same when you're winning or losing, and go on.

Pia Nilsson

ANNIKA SORENSTAM, Liselotte Neumann, Helen Alfredsson. In recent years I've overheard in unusual and varied settings—airports, a garden store in Berkeley, a fish market on Cape Cod—"What is it with the Swedes? What do they have that we don't?" I listened for an answer because I had wondered about this myself. Many have been stumped, and especially so because Sweden in winter is so cold. The game could not possibly be played year-round.

I guess I'm like many people. I have times when I wonder, Now where is the receiver for the portable phone? only to realize just then that I'm talking on it. This is supposedly due to the brain running in too many directions at once. One morning early in the week of the 1998 U.S. Open was like that. I arrive at the crack of dawn hoping to organize the day so I could zing right through. Inside the empty press tent I look at the seating chart to find where in the line of tables the LPGA was set. At that hour the tent is quiet. I sit down and work for a while. A fly, or perhaps the groaning of the huge air fans, makes me look up, and I see someone in the LPGA area; by the time I cover the fifty paces, her back is to me—she is standing alone at the message table—and I speak quietly so as not to startle her. "Excuse me," I say, "are you with the LPGA?"

When her face turns to me I recognize it from tournament clips, and so am perhaps mouthing with her, "I'm Pia Nilsson, coach of the Swedish National Team."

"Pia," I say, and tell her that what I'm doing at that second is trying to find an LPGA representative to help me find her. I'd written to her; does she recall?

"I brought the letter with me," she says. And indeed there she is—brimming, beaming, solid, calm, the picture of health—all of these, with remarkable, clear eyes the color of but much warmer than the sea.

It's said that as humans we can take in up to eleven million bits of information a second, and that we're aware of ten of these. A story many now know shot into my mind, one that was first told quite a while ago on National Public Radio: A young boy who was a fan of the well-known author and artist of children's books Maurice Sendak sent him a wonderful, almost magical drawing. So Sendak sketched one of his own very wild beings (which were his specialty) on a card and mailed it back to the child. A couple of weeks later the young boy's mother wrote back that the child had loved the card so much he had eaten it. "He didn't care that it was an original drawing," Sendak told public radio. "He saw it, he loved it, he ate it."

From the first I heard of it, the story delighted me. The clear passion, joy of life, pure wonder in a moment. While most of us are lucky to mirror the young boy even rarely, I feel it there in Nilsson, not as a collection of moments but as a way of being. We decide to meet the next day and, even with her busy schedule, when the hour arrives she is there exactly on time.

She was born in Malmo, Sweden, in 1958. In the summer her parents lived next to a golf course, and she started to play when she was six. "My parents played and my two brothers, and from early on I never had any limitation because I was a girl. I was raised to believe we can all do anything." She started to compete when she was thirteen, and by fifteen she played on the Swedish National Junior Team, then the amateur team. After high school she and teammate Charlotte Montgomery were the first of the Swedish players to come to the United States, where they attended college at Arizona State University. Summers she played on the Swedish National Team. She was the Swedish Junior Champion, the Swedish Champion, European Junior Team Champion, and the European Team Champion. After graduation, she turned pro, but as a pro, Nilsson's path was not smooth and because it was not, she believes, she arrived where she belonged.

She played one year on the mini tours in the United States and then four years on the LPGA tour. At the time, she didn't have many sponsors. She made enough money to survive but wasn't winning. "I was frustrated because I felt I had the potential to do a lot better and people around me kept saying that, but I was stopping myself by trying to be too much of a perfectionist and I didn't have the tools to know what to do about it."

Nilsson decided to return to Sweden for a while to get a break, play some smaller tournaments there, then come back. But in Sweden, officials of the national team started asking her to come to training camp to help out and play with their young players. Suddenly Nilsson was on one committee after another within the federation and had begun to enjoy it. "So I stayed and played there," she says, "and as I was doing these things outside my own game, my own game got better because I didn't put as much pressure on myself. So the keys that I came home to find, I found, but I also realized in my heart that I really liked to coach. Everything just kind of happened and my whole background suddenly made sense, because I'd given myself the perfect education through coaching and being a leader."

In 1990, she became the head coach of the Swedish National Women's Team. "I used a lot of my experience from having been a player, and I like to read and broaden my education. During what I thought had been my break, I'd become a rules official, a tour official, and a certified PGA teacher—all areas I hadn't covered before." Six years later, in 1996, she became head coach of the Swedish National Team—men and women, professionals, amateurs, and juniors. "Of course, I have many helping me, but I'm the one overall who's responsible for what we do—for the philosophy, the development, and all the ideas. I devise the philosophy and perspective and at the same time get to be on the green grass and work with the players. Since we have so many players in the program, I can't work individually with all of them, but I'm never out of touch. Most of the year I mainly focus on the ten LPGA players we have from Sweden. Those are the ones I've followed since they were juniors." They are the ones who win and win.

That day I'm wearing a round-necked pale pink mesh shirt with the words "Kingdom Golf" embossed so lightly on the left breast that they're barely discernable. But she sees it. "Is that as in *Golf in the Kingdom?*" she asks, and goes on to say how she loves Shivas Irons, as if he's a person, very much alive. "His kind of mind, that's one of the keys to keep on developing the game."

As we sit in this world of celebrity, of private cars and private planes, she is extraordinarily common. "I'm head coach and captain of the European team, but I've tried to get rid of the prestige that many times I have with being 'boss,' because we're all in the same boat. I learned early on that every human being I meet knows something or is doing something better than I am, so I have something to learn from everybody. That's something which has been very useful to me and I really feel that way. If I didn't, I wouldn't say it, because as a coach it's important to me to walk my talk. That's why balance is so important. Though I am traveling a lot and have a busy schedule with the players, I always take time for myself, because if I'm not in balance I couldn't do my job. I can't encourage health and not be so myself. I can't say it's important to be honest and then not be honest. I meditate twice a day and do things that help me to not feel stress, to keep on developing. I read constantly in different areas where I want to improve or get a different balance. Most of all, I stay open. Overall, nothing is hidden."

From one so enmeshed in "sport" you might expect different heroes. Hers are Mother Teresa and Mahatma Gandhi. "I've always liked the integrity of Mother Teresa. From nothing, this little woman without any belongings or money is able—even in memory—to bring the world's attention to dignity and love. It's fascinating."

Our conversation sails from there. Though she has written her own book and a deal is pending on an English translation, she is more than generous with her theory and vision. Through the next days we exchange messages on the message board and even with record crowds on the grounds, we happen upon each other. She is always smiling.

"I write a lot of letters to my players and fellow coaches and I like to include quotes helpful for the game," she tells me, and at my request leaves a few for me on the message board. None are from golfers: "Tomorrow's battle is won during today's training" (Samurai proverb). "If you don't know which port you're bound for, no wind is favorable" (Seneca). "First we create our habits, then the habits create us" (John Dryden).

Birdies All Around

The concept of shooting "54," birdie all around, is one of the aspects of our program everybody catches on to because it's so different. Anything that's discovered or new in the world, you need to start thinking it in order to believe it. I think so many times that par in golf is so limiting. Par is something they came up with many hundreds of years ago. Two putts on a green was figured normal, but it doesn't need to be that. When we compete, the purpose of the game for me is to get the ball in the hole in as few strokes as possible. I believe it's good to have a model that is totally different, and that's what we're striving toward. We know all the players we have on our different teams. On their home courses, they usually make birdie on every single hole at one time or another, so each player can see herself making birdie on all eighteen holes. She just hasn't done it all in a row yet. So instead of having a goal of, "Now I'm going to be the European champion or I'm going to win two U.S. Opens within five years," why not strive for 54—birdie on every hole?

What we ask is, what is necessary for this vision? Who—not in name, but in person, character, style, imagination—will that player be? How will he or she swing? How will she practice? What will she look like?

I'm surprised this approach captures so much attention because to me it's just common sense. Like with 54, what is important today is that I believe it's possible in the future. Like the English word "lunatic"; people think it means crazy and nuts and all that, and how that comes from "lunar," the moon. When people first started saying that they could fly to the moon, people loved to use the word "lunatic" because they seemed so crazy, absurd, stupid to even be thinking about it. Today we know things differently. You might still use the word "lunatic" for someone being nuts, but also for other reasons. So through history, people put on these restrictions, and it's the same with golf. I think our human potential in the game is so much greater than what we're close to today.

Take *Golf in the Kingdom*. One of the reasons that is a classic is because people responded. It dares us. There are many lessons to learn in golf—it's a method for life—and that book leads us to look at the game from another perspective. Way too many of us have a thinking that is restrictive. We want our players to be better than those who today are the best in the world. So it's no good thinking, training, playing, planning, and doing everything else exactly the way others do. I try to get my players, all of them, young or older, to spend a lot more time dreaming and imagining their potential. It's an extremely valuable thing to do. See and dream yourself where you want to be. This is not so often encouraged, because in golf we know we must stay in the present. But dreaming we do off the golf course. Our players are clearly aware that once they're on the course, all that matters is the present moment. Out of that moment, it helps to dream and imagine.

When a lot of people hear this, they object, saying, "But, oh, then you're so disappointed every time you don't shoot fifty-four." They don't understand. It doesn't have to do with that. As a coach, I've chosen to believe that the potential is there. As players, they've chosen to believe that potential is there. It's not a mandate. It's a fun challenge for us to try to discover it and get the most out of each player. What the 54 vision says is: Dare to go beyond the limits. The world is full of perceived limitations that stop us from being as good as we really are; 54 helps us to keep on getting better and keeps reminding us that the purpose of the game is to get the ball in the hole.

The Whole Brain

Sometimes it's easy to become so technical and so mentally focused and physical fitness focused that you forget that those things should always lead to playing better golf. The swing is important because otherwise you can't play the golf ball, but I think swing technique is extremely overemphasized.

The important thing is for each player to find a swing that fits him or her. That has to do with your body and muscles, your build, your temperament, and your personality. There are so many factors to swing. Then, of course, add biomechanics and the laws of force and direction and all of it. Everything needs to come together, but the most important key is to find a swing that you are comfortable with and can repeat in a way that gives you the trajectories that you want. I think, overall, we hear on television and read in magazines that the golf technique is so important. The swing is important to get in place, but it gets totally overemphasized because it's like the whole of society: We're very left-brained. We're very imbalanced. Everything is technical and the whole creative side is not emphasized as much. That is something in our program we work on a lot, because day to day we all basically get a lot of training developing the left side and little developing the right, so of course there is going to be imbalance. To be able to shoot the 54, we definitely will need the whole brain.

Coaching Sense

As coaches we believe that there is a 54 in every player we have among us. I also believe, from all the research that's been done, that how we perceive our students and the fact that we believe in them is one of the more important things we can do for them. If I have a group of ten players right in the beginning, and there are only two I actually believe in, even though I don't say a word that message is going to get across to the players and the other coaches. Even though there are some who perform better right now than others, we still know there are so many who have the potential. They might have a few challenges to work through, but they can get there. We need to be very careful with this. As coaches it is our job to believe in each and every player's potential and to support him or her in getting there.

I can never tell who might be the one. I get the question all the time, "What personalities or what type are the ones who are going to be the champions?" Well, I can tell you, we take them the way they come and work from there. To me, it's kind of scary when you hear people think like that, because we can't know. To me, the idea that we can is so restrictive. I often use Annika as an example. When she was a junior, she was one of a group of maybe six junior girls in Sweden who were very promising, but at the time no one would say that she was the one that a few years later would be dominating the world. I don't single out someone because I never know. No one knows.

So many times, coaches, too early, say, "You know, she doesn't have it. She's not mentally strong" or "She doesn't know enough shots," when it's all there inside them. It's up to us to protect potential and support it.

And there's another thing too: For us as coaches, if our players are going to go toward shooting 54, what does that mean for us? Where do we as coaches need to work within ourselves to be able to support that process? That was something that had to be developed in our coaches' training. I'm always surprised that our approach captures so much attention, because to me it is just common sense.

Who?

In our program, there are no models. I believe all human beings are unique, and all golfers are unique, so that means I can never have a model to do things that work for more than one player. Right now, we have three top women players: Annika, Liselotte, and Helen. They're three totally different personalities with three different ways of playing, of practicing, and of doing things, and that is wonderful. They're all playing golf at about the same level but they go about it in very unique ways that fit them because they're each different. It's up to me as the coach to create a culture where they can discover who they are and what ways work best for them. I provide guidance along the way, but I never do anything; they do things themselves. I'm just a facilitator in the process. Annika is going to figure it out her way, Helen her way, and Lisa her way. It's my job to provide experience for them to experiment with many different ways so they can see what they believe in. For one it could be, let's say, that their thoughts go to the leaderboard when that is not useful, or they start thinking about something in the past; how do we change that? Some of them may just walk and try to be aware more of their feet on the grass, or start thinking about their breathing, or just breaking the pattern and going back to using the senses, all the senses, to be aware more of the present. Some might sing a song between shots because they need to fill their brain with something. They may say, "Okay, today if I have a tendency to start thinking and get off track, between shots I'm going to sing songs or chat with my caddie," or whatever they choose that interests them. There are all different ways of doing what we need to do, and it's up to each player to find "How do I do it?" A couple of seconds before you hit the shot, it's most important to focus on whatever helps you get to the right state. This is not known. I can't give you your answer. It needs to be discovered.

That's why many times we have for students what we call "labs," as in laboratory. We call it laboratory experiments. Let's say a player is normally very visual. Maybe she's been seeing the ball as a line in a red color, and that's been useful. Well, in lab she might take a few hours to try different things just to see what happens. What would happen if she played the golf shot and only focuses on the feeling in her stomach while she's swinging or only hears the putt go in the hole as she putts? What we want is for players to dare to try a variety of things to see if maybe something works even better for them than what they've been doing. Labs provide an opportunity to experience things outside whatever is normal for the player. Is there something she would like to add? Would it work to make things even better?

To get there, we all need to try things that don't work. So many of us are afraid of that, but we must allow ourselves to try things. When you perform at golf, you always get a result. For us, judging that result as a success or a failure is not particularly constructive. The interpretation is of utmost importance. Either the performance tells me that what I am doing is leading me toward my goal, or it is not. If it isn't, then the most important thing is to recognize it and make some sort of change. It's from this process that we learn a lot if we choose to see it that way. It's said that Thomas Edison tried to get a lightbulb to work close to ten thousand times before it did. If we don't try, we're never going to figure out new and different ways of doing things.

I always find it fascinating that if Nancy Lopez is the best player in the world, then everybody wants to be like Nancy Lopez. But maybe the one thing we know is that the next world player is not going to be like Nancy Lopez. Let's say it is Laura Davies. So then everybody wants to be like Laura Davies, but the thing we know is that the next world player is not going to be like Laura. Say it's Annika, or whomever. The same teaching, the same everything, is not going to get you there.

My goal with players is for each one of them to take time to think about who they are and what they want to get out of life, and what they believe in. The essential things. When you are eighty years old and look back at your life, what would you like people to say about you? We always have our own individual golf goals, but we also always look at the golfer's whole picture of life. If I have my own personal belief about something, I never impose it. They must come to things themselves. If I work with twenty people, they're all going to come to different conclusions.

Becoming

I think in the area of swing, in teaching, in coaching, and in thinking, in the future much will happen. Many players work on their technique for many years and it still doesn't make them better golfers because they're led to believe technique is the way to go about improvement. That's very tricky, because let's say with the golf swing, maybe there is something where I can't on that day create the mental state I need to be in, or I have some disturbing phone call and because of that, something happens to my technique. Well, it's so easy to always go to the technique. Technique, technique, technique—instead of going to what it was that caused that change in technique. So many look for a technical answer when maybe the lasting change has to be made at a totally different level. That's why we have so many quick fixes in golf. Get a new putter and it's solved. Quick fixes may work for a short period of time, but it usually is not long-lasting. I'm more for always working for the long-lasting.

I think in golf and golf coaching, sometimes the push for short-term performance is so important that it hinders or stops the long-term learning. Usually the goal is to have the maximum performers at this tournament for this year. There you can get caught as a coach and teacher always telling players what is best to do instead of letting players discover and grow with their own knowledge and experience. The drive is to win and win. I'm more for the approach where maybe they will win this week, maybe not next or the next, but they are growing, so in a few years they are going to be better than they would have been if I were always there telling them. That is very important to me. We want to have very good performers, but who we are as human beings is always going to be more important than performance, otherwise it doesn't make sense to play golf. If, after your career, you realize that your life—you thought just because you made a lot of money or won a lot of trophies you'd be happy—the life you thought was so successful is a total fake. All that success won't change a thing. That's why helping players with perspective early on is important, because there are way too many elite sports where we have world champions who are failures as human beings.

I write to players and coaches regularly and always include quotes in which I find truth. I often say to players, "You need to take responsibility and act to have something happen." There are so many who talk and talk and talk and never do anything. They write all these nice goals and visions, but then they don't do anything differently than they've ever done, and they still think something else is going to happen. I use this quote a lot: "Vision isn't enough as long as you don't begin to act. It isn't enough to look at the ladder as long as we don't start to climb it" (Vance Havner). Usually we look up the ladder to where we want to go, but it doesn't do any good; we have to take one step at a time toward it.

The one quote that's most important to me in my coaching is a Chinese proverb I love: "Give a man a fish and you feed him for a day. Teach him how to fish and you feed him for a lifetime." That's so much what I feel about what I want to do. Always telling the players what to do and how to do things is not my way. I want to work through them so I never teach them anything. They teach themselves. I just can't do things for them and give to them. I need to allow them time to discover things and allow them to sometimes make mistakes so they can learn for the future. I put them in different situations and guide them, but it's for them to be their own best coaches and for me not to be needed. That is my goal.

What You Need to Shoot a 54

In my letter to our present and future golf stars on the Swedish National Team, I make clear what we as coaches believe is necessary to shoot a 54. I say, you need to be able to play every stroke from every lie under every circumstance. It means being able to:

- play with all your clubs
- play a straight shot, slice, hook, draw, fade, high, low, punched . . .
- play different types of chips, pitches, bunker shots suitable for different lies, greens, and flag positions

- read greens and putt on different types of grass, e.g., Bermuda, bent, Japanese korai . . .
- choose the best shot around the greens on different types of grass in different parts of the world
- play when it is hot, cold, wet, windy
- play when the pace of play is fast and slow
- play on different types of courses
- use the right strategy for the course you are playing on
- play together with those you think are pleasant and those you don't think you have much in common with
- play from divots, uphill, downhill, sidehill lies, sand, rough, among pine needles . . .
- play with and without spectators
- be just as sharp on the first round as the last and the first hole as the last
- see, hear, and feel that the ball is going into the hole
- be 100 percent concentrated on your target when you strike the ball
- be motivated regardless of the outward importance of the tournament

As we see it, to be able to do all this you need to:

- have a swing that suits you
- practice in a way that suits you and that results in achieving your goals
- have clubs that match you, your swing, your play
- play a ball that suits you and your game
- play your practice round in such a way that you learn what you need to learn about the course
- have a physique that keeps you healthy and able to play the golf you want
- have a diet that keeps you healthy and gives you the nutrition you need to perform your best
- get the rest you need for mind and body to be able to take in and put into practice what you have learned so that you can perform at your best
- be able to listen to signals within you, and if something doesn't feel right, know what you can do to regain your balance so that the necessary conditions exist for playing your best shot

- be motivated in what you do
- believe in what you do
- use what you can in all situations (not just on the driving range, for instance)
- have clear objectives

Betty Jameson

S<small>HE LIVES ALONE NOW</small> in a small house she named "Morning Glory." Her once fine Cadillac has given way to a tempestuous old blue Ford. "I might be wearing my headband," she says when I phone from the Boynton Beach, Florida, 7-Eleven, but when she rolls in to meet me I see it cast aside on the seat.

She's out of the car quickly, golf's first "glamour girl," and she's a vision even at seventy-nine.

I'm staring and I know it. I start to tell her and then I don't and then I do. "You're beautiful," I say, but my words are poor for what is there. The years are dancing in her eyes—ebullience still caught in her golden-white hair, peering from the sun-rich furrows of her face. My hand finds hers where it waits. "You're so strong and tall," I say, retreating to the ordinary.

"Oh well. . . ," she says, letting it pass like steam. As she opens my door I understand we're moving quickly.

It's been that way for her, I know. She was a master on the links from the beginning, striding the fairways with a command not quite bound by earth. She was the Texas State Public Champion by age thirteen. After a whirlwind amateur career, she turned pro with Spalding, was a founding member of both the WPGA and the LPGA, was the first woman to break 300 by shooting 295 in her 1947 U.S. Open victory, and was one of the original four with Patty Berg, Louise Suggs, and Babe Didrikson Zaharias in the LPGA Hall of Fame. When Lawson Little first saw her play, he told the papers, "She's going so far in golf it will be like trying to reach the moon to beat her."

Young players through the years rushed from their own rounds to follow her, to watch and learn. "She moved as if she had the game in a thimble," one newspaper reporter said back then. "She was an artist with the most delicate finesse," says Wiffi Smith. "When the ball hit the green, it danced. I spent hours just watching, then with all the others I'd go and try to take it to my game. But to watch, you had to know the time. She could be as warm as the tropics one day and as cool as the Arctic the next. Before I went too close, I'd always say to her good friend Mary Lena Faulk, 'How is she today?' She'd laugh. But she'd tell me."

So many of the pioneers relish the stories, and she, too, tells them on herself: "I was always asking people to move this way or that. I had such wide peripheral vision and I guess I wanted everything just right. Once I asked Babe when she was standing too close to me while I was putting, 'Babe, could you please move?' She moved only a step or two, so I said, 'Could you move to the edge of the green?' So she in her great-hearted way waved her arms in the air to the whole gallery, 'Folks,' she said, 'Betty wants us to move so she can putt,' and she herded all of them away onto the next tee!"

She laughs and tells another. "Ask JoAnn Prentice about this," she says. "We were each about 175 yards out from the hole. I don't remember what tournament, but JoAnn hit her approach shot first and it landed on the green and rolled up toward the hole. So there it sat in my line. So I said, 'Could you please mark your ball?' She looked at me like, 'Are you out of your mind?' So I said it again. Well, away she went, club in hand, walking the 170-plus yards on up to the green. Every so often she'd hit the club against the ground as she went. She wasn't real happy, but I thought I could hole it. I was sure I could. Did I hole it? Well, that wasn't the point. I thought I could and her ball was in my way!"

We're both laughing. "But that wasn't quite the end of it," she says. "Somewhere up on this very hilly course in Seattle or Portland, up there in the Northwest, it was a course for mountain goats practically. Up and down the hills, and sometimes we got out of breath. Well, I was really bearing down. I was sure I could win. We had a real climb to this green and Jackie Pung, who I was paired with while I was about ready to putt, she was still puffing, and I needed to hole out, so I said, 'Jackie, would you mind not breathing?'

"As soon as we were finished, Jackie went in the locker room and they all had a laugh on me. Jackie announced, 'Well, now she's finally said it: "Would you please stop breathing!" ' "

We sail across the bridge from Boynton Beach to Delray. As if tuned to her, that Ford hums and it's clear she has lost nothing in speed to Andretti. We head to a tiny breakfast café where we sit by the window with our tea and coffee and share a fresh scone. "We're not going to have a plan," she says. "We're just going to tarry with life today." I hear the self-assurance, the legendary command. Our conversation darts, lingers, then darts again excitedly. Another half hour and then we're back outside.

"This is a great car," I say, waiting for her to unlock the door, along the busy main street. "Perfectly yours."

"It is, isn't it, dear? It's marvelous. Check in the glove box."

I reach in and find what at first seems to be a handful of metal—a snail, tarnished in spots, a large, lifelike replica. "I had it made into a hood ornament. See? Now I just need to get it mounted. But not on the front. What do you think if I put it in the middle, running along on its way to where it might otherwise be? Running, but inching its way. 'I'm getting there,' it will say. 'I'm getting there.' "

She's smiling in such a way that something shines from her, a rare thing I can't place. We chatter, and as we cross the bridge with the windows down, we shout. A copy of T. S. Eliot's *Four Quartets* slides out from beneath the seat as we take a corner. Books— the backseat is covered. I notice them now, turned and tumbled. Large illustrated volumes on Bonnard and Matisse, Cezanne, and in among them, *The Kingdom of Shivas Irons, The Mystery of Golf*. Most well-traveled. Suddenly I remember my bag; it's nowhere. Two weeks' worth of interviews, a dozen and a half tapes. Gone. A catastrophe. She hits the brakes.

As I try to remain calm, I worry. I realize, so eager back there to look in the glove compartment, I might have left it on the street. "Be still," she says, "and know."

"Still?" I say.

"Don't forget, in anything it is the stillness that's important. 'Stand still and hit it,' Tommy Armour used to say. We don't need to fall all over ourselves in anything."

She's right, and mercifully for me, the bag sits undisturbed not on the curb but in the café where it had rested at our feet. "My first car was 'Esse,' Esse—'To Be,' " Jameson says as if we're just starting off from the café for the first time, as if we have all the time we need and have not been set back. "And my putter was Art, like my favorite beau once, Arthur. B STILL is what I'm going to have on my license plate. I love all these plates," she says as we retrace our path.

She takes me by the old house, a house she shared for years with fellow golfer and friend Mary Lena Faulk, until Faulk's death in 1995. An oversight in the will has put her out of her house. She must start over now in a small place back across the bridge. I wait outside as she brings out a tiny Dachshund and a small, shaggy shih tzu—Sam and Willie. "Glenna's dogs," she says, referring to Collett Vare; "we've had them since before she died. They love their little jaunt." The neighborhood is bright and quiet, with high palms and low stucco houses, just right for the Florida heat. We walk up and down the street.

She has a few more months to clear totally out and the change of residence will be momentous, reducing fifty years to a smaller dwelling, casting off this skin in order to make a new one. She says she is leaving much behind. Not for nothing did she once name the house "Cynghanedd," Welsh for harmony, and I gather it has been just that. I wait as she puts the little dogs inside, and I realize that nothing here speaks of order or formality but of a dailyness, of home, of lives lived. Crooked chimes, a pitted birdbath, a few clubs here and there, a rake, the most beautiful old iron lamb lying, as lambs do, on its knees. "You're taking the lamb with you when you finally go, aren't you?" I say when she's back.

"Oh yes! Of course! The lamb. I'm so glad you noticed the lamb. It needs to be scrubbed or refurbished. Or does it? Maybe it's just right."

When we get there, the new house is empty except for two chairs, one straight-backed, the other overstuffed and old-fashioned. There are two boxes of photos she has brought over for us the day before, a hassock, and in a corner a Betty Jameson 5-wood she found at a yard sale a few weeks back. That's all except the paintings, a number of which are her own and are lined up in a row, three facing outward, two turned to the wall. Subtle hues, delicate of form, remarkable. But how could I have expected less? "See all that green?" she says. "That is as deep as the golf course got into me."

The house is airy, open, and we sit, the box and her rhapsody taking us fully back—Vare, Golthwaite, Hollins, Seignous, Wethered, Hicks, and all the later women of the early tour—Babe, Bell, the Bauers, Smith, the men—Hogan, Hagen, Snead, Ouimet, Armour, Jones. And here is her grandmother, a tall, well-boned figure. "She would always ask, 'Are you still playing golf?'" recalls Jameson. " 'Your mother says you should be a world beater and you're playing golf!'" She laughs. Here's her first teacher, Frances Scheider, and she tells me how she'd go to him with fifty cents, on the trolley. "I'll never forget, years later when I saw his swing, we were at Palm Beach. I said, 'That's my swing!' I had so exactly absorbed his swing, I couldn't believe it." And this, here, a five-by-seven of her in full swing, the original of the one she says Harvey Penick kept for years in the Austin Country Club, taped beside the cash register. Here, Mary Lena Faulk, the two of them, young and strong and smiling, striding in perfect sync toward the camera, putters in hand. "She was a great putter," she says, "she always saw the ball going into the hole—I was always coaxing, coaxing. When I got older, I learned to putt." And here's an eight-by-ten of a young woman up to her neck in water, arms raised, club hailed to the sky, wild glee, abandon in her face. "That's Peggy Chandler. Oh, what a one. Jumped into the flood when we played the Trans-Mississippi, 1937, in San Antonio. She'd say of herself, 'She never made a putt, but she never missed a party.' She taught me to really love golf and life. It could be way after dark, hitting balls, 'Just one more, just one more.' It could even be two in the morning. But she always said, 'Don't just be a golfer.' That kept ringing all my life."

There are clippings, Herbert Warren Wind, a thin pencil line marking an old *Sports Illustrated* and what he said of her there: "I never saw anyone hit the ball straighter—other than, well, perhaps maybe Ben Hogan." I look at her, thinking that she'll want to dwell on this, but she's moved on to something that makes her say, "I sold my soul to Spalding, that's what it feels like. I shouldn't have at the time because I wanted to play those match-play tournaments. I wanted to play in the British. I wanted to win it. I wanted to be the first American to win it, but instead Babe went over and won it. She did what she said, she loosened her girdle and let it fly. That's what made her—she won seventeen straight tournaments. But you don't think that if she was competing against me she could have won seventeen? No way. I'd turned pro. I couldn't play in any of those tournaments. Oh, well . . ." She's quickly on to an old program from a museum promoting a Picasso show. But I am looking now at her hands. "Wait until you see those hands," Debbie Massey has said to me. "Have her put them on a club. It's something you won't forget."

And there are her hands, indeed traveled, large and graceful. No rings, no manicure. There is pain in them now when she closes the fingers. On a club they too often produce a shank, so she no longer plays. "I liked to get out there and compete. For me, the game was never social," she says. "I was intent on getting the ball in the hole, that's all." It is hard now for her even to paint.

"My hands. They were my intelligence, far beyond the brain. It took years for my calluses to wear away. My game lived in these"—she holds them out—"the hands; I put them to good use. Now they tell me often, they are tired. But I heard of a doctor and I might get an incision so I can paint."

With them now she is digging deeper into this pile and the past—cards, artists' exhibition announcements, more clippings. The hours slip by. We forget lunch, open another window. We rehearse her new house as it might be, the books here, the paintings, here, here, there. "What about using this whole area as a studio?" she asks, and in the kitchen, should she maybe take off the cupboard doors so she can easily see what is there?

We settle again, go on between golf and art and the neighbors and books and places and my loves and wishes and hers. She reads to me, I read to her. We sift through more photos, letters. There are more stories.

"The first thing I heard of the game was: 'That's a game for old men.' And I thought it was true because the first I saw of it, a friend's dad had a big carpet hung from a clothesline and was hitting balls against it, and he did seem old to me, so I wasn't much interested in that. But when I was eleven I saw Glenna playing Helen Hicks in the finals in the movie shorts, and that's what did it. I went home and said, 'I want to play.' Later, when I met Glenna, she invited me and my friend Caroline Brown up to a major amateur tournament in Huntington, Pennsylvania. Caroline had been there before, so she wasn't as excited as me. She said, 'Betty, you go, it's just another dress for me.' I went, and I remember I picked up a couple of the balls Glenna had been using on the practice range and I played the tournament with them because they were much better than what I'd been using. I won that tournament, and as it turned out through the years, Mary Lena, Glenna, and I, we were friends our whole lives."

"Betty could travel with any crowd," Polly Riley would tell me later, "because it wasn't the people she was after, but life. She never changed, no matter who she was with. I remember at the Trans-Mississippi at River Oaks in Houston, a very wealthy couple who had been great backers of Betty had a party in her honor. They invited everyone in their circle to meet her and a lot of players were there. I saw Betty when we came in, but it wasn't long before somebody said, 'Where's Betty?' No one could find her. Then, after a while, someone came in and announced, 'She's out in the dog run with the bird dogs. She's out there with a flashlight reading a book.' "

Just past dusk now, barely light enough to see, on the way to the restaurant she has me read from the art critic John Summerson a passage quoting painter Ben Nicholson on his visit to Piet Mondrian's studio in Paris. I raise my voice over the hum of the car, " 'I remember after this first visit sitting at a café table on the edge of the pavement almost touching all the traffic . . . sitting there for a very long time with an astonishing feeling of quiet and repose. The thing I remember most was the feeling of light in this room and the pauses, the silence during and after he'd been talking. The feeling of the studio must have been not unlike the feeling in the hermit caves where lions used to go to have thorns taken out of their paws.' "

"That's it!" Jameson says. "Real players need to imagine that. That's where the true power is, in that stillness-of-being at address. People get so caught up in the swing, they forget." But then quickly we're on to adventure. "Life," she says, "is meant for adventure." She mentions the snail again—"I'm getting there . . ." But for her it's clear the goal now is further. This one who so fully eyed her target on the course, making perfectly sure her way was clear, rattling the flagstick from afar, her aim now is different. "One mind. One world. Love. It's love we're here for," she says, "everything we need is within us. We're divine ourselves, but we all forget that." She's not smug, or dreamy, or self-righteous. Nor silly, either. Just sure. Yesterday, today, tomorrow her map is dotted with the pleasure of small moments, and in this one, even as brief witness, I feel incredibly rich.

We eat like fiends when our food comes, both of us, and only slow through dessert. Just before the restaurant she's dropped me to retrieve my car, so she leads me after to a Kinko's and a bookstore. When that closes, I weave my way back alone through the maze she had earlier made seem easy and straight. It's near ten when I get to the small bungalow where I'm staying and the separate office is closed—too late to pay the phone deposit, so I have none. When I find a gas station where I can call and tell her I have no phone for her to give me notice in the morning—that she should just come by—the pay phone only sizzles and cracks. I'm forced to use my cell phone far from its home territory, and when she answers I'm still dwelling on the likely $8.00 per minute charge. I rush with the information—rote—"No phone—no need to call, just come by—six-thirty, that's fine"—but hearing her voice, I forget everything—$16.00, $24.00, $32.00, who cares— there she is, asking softly as a way of saying good night, "We had heaven today, didn't we?"

I'm wide awake at 4:00 A.M. I shower and dress, go over my notes, and by 6:00 I wait. She knocks at 6:15, back in full force, bright. I open the door wide and she hurries in. "I want to see these digs.

Oh, how glorious! Perfect." It is, in fact, merely simple and clean. The walls are cinder block and the soap in the bathroom sliver thin.

"Ah, but hey, you're the one who's glorious. I love that jacket," I say. It's bright fuchsia, long and so good on her over the light denim dress falling past her knees. "Well, it's a smudge here on the pocket, a little dirty, but let's never mind that . . ."

It's McDonald's for breakfast, one of her morning rituals. She's made daily friends there but today we're too early. When we get our food, I'm busy with my juice, then I notice. She has a small scissors and is cutting a perfect ring around the outside edge of the sausage she's taken from her biscuit. "For Sam and Willie. They've come to count on it," she says, and with the greatest ease wraps it between a doubled napkin and puts it safely into her bag. "They'd be downhearted if I didn't bring it."

Later Wiffi Smith tells me, "To me, Jameson's one of those souls you meet in a lifetime who resonates in your being as a great entity who's walked before." It's not the breadth with which Jameson tells her tales, not her ability to make obscure philosophers, dead players, artists, and writers come alive, nor the span of her vast mind, her quest for the All-in-All, nor her success in seizing eternity now and here, or even the swift grace of her vivid form. It's this moment I think of, this small act of snipping the sausage, that stretches so free and so far.

"I think you're swell," I say, "but you know that."

We finish and we're on to Delray Beach Golf Club where she learned from Tommy Armour. The pro, excited she's there, gives us the tour. Then it's back to the new house where the hours again slip away, and I take a lesson pitching balls into the overstuffed chair.

"Thank you for saying you like the blue in the shutters," she says when we get back in the car. We remember lunch today, but I had planned to leave by two and now it is four but still we do nothing to hurry.

Back at my car, I put my bags in the trunk. She sees my clubs so I hand her one, then several. She fixes on the nickel wedge. "Oh, I could fall for that," she says. "I was always wedge-happy." My eyes strain to fix the image of that perfect grip, and when we've stood there for some time, I say, "I've got to go or it'll be Alligator Alley cross state by dark." She hands the club back to me and I put it in its space, strangely comforted that those hands have rested there. We don't promise to write or call. Instead she says, "Wait a minute, Lamb." (Since I told her she must take the lamb with her, she's named me that.) She's already given me Joyce Wethered's book *Memories and Methods* and a copy of *Civilization,* but now she goes off to the Ford and comes back with a small roll of clear tape. "Here, take this, you might need it as you go along," she says.

"But you'll need it," I say, "you're the one who's moving."

"Take it. It'll come in handy." I do and walk to my car as she walks to hers. When I pull out, she's standing with one arm raised. "Walk in love," she calls out as I pass. I drive on, still seeing her there.

Golf

Golf is like a love affair. If you take it seriously, it breaks your heart. If you don't, it isn't any fun.

Da Vinci

Golf is finally about hitting the ball where you're looking. It's one of the reasons I hit the ball so straight, because when you've felt centrifugal force, it's trusting, not thinking. You know it and do it. It's, like, if you're in the kitchen and you throw something in a bucket, you just know you're going to hit it where you're looking. No use to get all fussed up about it. In golf, here's the thing: Get to feel centrifugal force and how it works in your swing, then practice and practice and feel it and trust. After that, get up and hit it where you're looking—trust it. You wouldn't get fussed up tossing a potato skin to the bucket.

When you're out on the course, in a game, what's the use of, "What did I do wrong?" when there's so many things that might have gone wrong in a swing, especially if you're just beginning. Da Vinci said it best: "The supreme misfortune is when theory outstrips performance." That's a saying I've applied to golf over and over. We must forget ourselves, give ourselves to the task by forgetting. That's what you do tossing that skin to the bucket.

Edna and Lucy

Edna Chapin Lapham was a terrific part of the spirit of this game, a great lady who loved life's adventure. She learned to fly her own plane at age seventy-five. She was a great golfer, a brisk New Englander whose husband was one of the originators of Texaco. So she played the game in Texas and won many Texas State championships. Her best friend was Lucy Roe. Well, in those days, for underwear we used to wear what were called "step-ins." They had this little button right up at the top, on the side. One day on the most public course in Texas—Brackenridge, at the tenth tee—Edna was out there teeing it up with Lucy. She took one of her vigorous swings and down went her step-ins; they dropped straight to the ground. Lucy, a great sport herself and ever the fast thinker said, "Edna, pick 'em up! Don't put 'em back on!" So Edna walked right out of her step-ins and on down the fairway—thinking nothing, she said, but her next shot.

Einstein

Never straying from the moment is so important in golf. Being alive to the task at hand is the thing. Dwelling in the now. I like to think of Einstein: "For us believing physicists, the distinction between past, present and future is only an illusion, even if a stubborn one."

Be

These young buds coming up, I'd like to tell them what I learned about golf and tournaments. We've all heard the old thing, "When you get to a tournament, you better have brought it, because now is not the time to get it." And it's true. Because at our best, we're not get-ers, we're be-ers. Golf is mostly feel anyway, and so is life. In the world we are the effect, not the cause. Before the tournament, you do what you do. You do the work, hit the balls, the putts, do the tinkering, you practice and practice, and maybe pray. But when you get to the tee, remember the old creation story: God did all the work—six straight days—then rested. That's the lesson. When you're on the tee, the work is done. Be like God. Be alert and let it be. Have even your praying done. Be alert and rest, and let God rest and just be.

The Earth

One of the marvelous things about the game is the unknown adventure, all the wonderful things at work. All the working elements—the air, the grass, the trees, the wind, the water—all that life has out there to work with. We can be surprised at any moment.

I was going along at Tam O'Shanter, and this is a wonderful illustration because it was the year that I won. It made the shot ever so important. It came about on the last two or three holes, a fairway shot that I hit a good distance and it hit *smack,* careened off this tree straight out into the fairway. Perfect lie. I was able to come in and win, and if it hadn't shot out like that—it's like Bobby Jones hitting the lily pad in the amateur at Interlochen—the ball skipped across the water and hit a lily pad and on up onto the green. Or Couples's ball balancing on the bank at the Masters. Those kind of things thrill us, bringing destiny to the fore; however you are going along, that's what you can expect. I had a great friend who lived nearby, and she said after I won, "Well, there is that Bible line, 'And the Earth shall help the woman.' " We laughed, and I used it ever after, every time a playing partner remarked on my luck, I'd say, "Well, the earth's there to help the woman."

After Tam O'Shanter somebody said, "Getting through all those trees, you sure were lucky." Well, trees are made mostly of air. Just a trunk and a few twigs and leaves. You can get through them. That's what's supposed to happen out there on that golf course. Adventure. Thrills and quirks and surprises. If you believe in an All-That-Is-in-All, that and luck, it's the same thing. We can practice and practice and practice. But we all need that little presence of wonder.

The Garden

Golf. Everybody is seeing it as an allegory of life. Anybody who's ever played knows it's like being solo in the marketplace. They know the person who wins is the one who gets in the rough. She uses her imagination and gets out. She doesn't go down into horrible thinking. She doesn't throw her clubs. She's not distracted from the goal.

Everyone knows golf is a game you play within yourself, whether you're playing match play or medal play. It's all in your own consciousness and what you accept. You are not fighting anything. Golf is not a battle; it is accepting. It is like the wilderness. There can be loneliness, doubt, darkness, and then suddenly spontaneity of thought, a knowing in which a material sense of things disappears and a spiritual sense unfolds. Golf is a game. You either play it that way or you don't play it that way. If you do, there's a fascination, a simmering, a creativity, a waiting patiently for things to sprout, for fear to disappear, for your whole being to suddenly see the shot, to feel the course, the day, and all that is acting on you, reflecting within you, for your body to take on that verve and feeling and believing in yourself and everything around you. It is the reflection of the things not seen that makes a winner.

There's a wonderful thing that comes to mind that I wrote down in relation to golf. I wrote it in this same little book where I write everything. I think it was Picasso who said: "Everyone knows that art is a lie about the truth." The artist Monet planted these marvelous gardens around his house, on canvas he painted the gardens, the flowers; however wonderful, a lie about the truth. It's the same in golf. We're reaching for the right club, the right swing, we're reaching for how to get that ball in the sweet spot and our eyes concentrating on seeing where it's going, but until we've felt that spot, that shot within ourselves, it's not going to come about.

What is that line from Philippians? "He who has begun a good work in you will perform it." It's something beyond, within. We think this teacher did this for us, this teacher did that for us. I didn't wake up to the fact that my golf swing was like being born with beautiful bone structure. As a child I had copied, I had absorbed my teacher's swing, and no one was hardly tempted to come up and say, "Well, I think you're doing this or that, or do this . . ." People just besieged people on the practice tee, but never me. Even my grandmother talked, she'd say even to players I knew on tour, "Well, hit a lot of balls like Babe does," or something like that. She didn't know anything, and even she was advising. The physical, the physical—when the truth is, the player as artist, each is alone with her own being, her own reality. And no two are the same. No one is repeated. Ever.

When I was at the new World Golf Village to be inducted into the World Golf Hall of Fame, there we were. Patty Berg, Louise Suggs, Kathy Whitworth, Arnie Palmer—you know all the names. So many of us. All winners. And I looked around and I thought, There's room. We all have our charm. Each one of us there could recognize the other because we all won, and we all knew well that fragile thread of winning. We knew we could be going along, and if some little thing came up, if we strayed, it would make all the difference. The Hall of Fame, we were there for the days we had not strayed, yet the days we had were many. We're all winners if we know this. There aren't just eighteen holes in life as long as we keep putting the flagstick in. There was a feeling there with all the varied champions: Nobody can be everybody, yet everybody is everybody.

For those just starting, for those working and working, for those already on tour and winning and then not winning, I want to say, "Remember there is a simmering, there is a waiting, remember the garden." What do they call it when the garden is quiet? When it is resting? Dormant. But those days there are things going on under there that we don't know about. That's the way it is with improvement. With movement. Remember the love for the game, the fascination and reason for doing this. The long tenure for the wonderful thing that is coming forth, don't doubt it. Just relax somewhat. Anxiety never hit a straight golf shot. And don't worry about being lucky. Pure luck is not so much luck as it is being care-full, caring and full of all that is around you; and yet there's the other old command, "Be careful of nothing," and that's really something to remember.

Epilogue

IT WAS EARLY MORNING when I saw her. Her spindly legs were dotted with summer's bites; the day's heavy dew had soaked through her shoes. She was sitting on a bench on the tee to Thistledown's number four water hole, a wet plastic bag of balls to her side and one lone club.

The sun was just barely up. I wasn't playing, only carrying my bag for conditioning's sake, round and round the same nine holes, as I did almost every morning I was in town. I'd walk until full light took hold and the regulars showed up. Then I'd be back at my desk, tucked into work's netherworld, never having swung a club.

The kids missed me, I knew. They'd miss anyone who took the time, as I had missed my first teacher, Doc, and so had imagined Owen Lux. There was Shane and Tyler, Kyli, Anna, Addy; Jason, Joey, Torie, and Ben; young Hogan, Ashley, Ashton, Matt, Danika, Kelsi, Alex, Bradley, Jordan, and Kim. More than eighty with their dreams, desire, and knack. For lack of time, instead of individual guidance that summer I held a clinic and then checked on them once a week when I was around. The one here now on the bench had been at the two-day gathering.

In Thistledown's small world she had a secondhand claim to fame, and I'm not sure it pleased her. She was Junior Champion Torie Ives's little sister. Because her effort was so ardent and free, I'd named her "Slingshot" at the clinic, and, grinning from ear to ear, she took to it well. She'd gone after the ball with no restraint, as if she, with only her eight-year-old willow-branch frame, could rap it into tomorrow like her sister. She missed one out of four, but when she connected it most often sailed high and pure and true. She had come early and lingered well beyond the end, but I hadn't seen her since.

"Slingshot," I say.

She scratches one ear.

"How you been?"

She grins.

The very first time I saw her was at a grade-school Christmas program I'd been dragged to two winters before. She'd stepped forward out of the group and perfectly on cue had let out the most celestial, melodic song. Her small voice was high, golden, price-less—an unexpected delight that remained with me in the weeks that followed. "Who's that?" I'd whispered to my mother. "Who's that?" I'd asked the person next to me when my mother didn't know.

"Been playing much?" I ask her now, setting my bag down.

"Torie tried to call you," she says.

"Did she?" I ask.

"You were gone." She scratches at one of the bites on her legs. Closer now, I see her shoes are dripping with mud.

"Been ball hunting?" I say.

"Mmmhmm," she says. "I found this, too." She holds up a junior-length club, a battered metal wood. The word "Pinseeker" on its head is barely readable.

"Pinseeker," I say.

"It got burned with the brush," she says, "down by hole five; I pulled it outta the weeds and some mud. I wanted it 'cause I don't want Torie's old one, but it's burned most a the way up."

"No," I say, "that's just warrior marks. Do you know about warrior marks?"

She shakes her head no.

"A warrior mark is a wound we get that heals over and makes us strong. It shows we've lived, been around. Just think, that club's been through a grass fire. Think how strong it is. It's probably stronger than any club around. It just needs a new grip. I can do that for you. This club will do a terrific job. It's a great find. You're a lucky girl."

She looks at the club more closely, raises one eyebrow, asks curiously, suddenly, "Wha'd all those ladies teach you?"

I smile and my mind rushes with it all. This small town, this course, this club, where everyone knows everything about everyone, anyone. Even the young ones. All those far different grand clubs. The great courses. Fine players. Grand teachers. Doc. Owen Lux. The vast distance. The vast difference. Yet the commonness. The hopes. The connections. No distance. No difference at all.

"Wha'd all those ladies teach you?" How should I answer this one and keep it simple? She's looking at me, dead serious—sun-baked nose, jack-o'-lantern-toothed. "Wha'd they teach?" I say, still buying time. I scratch my own ear. "If we talk about that, we might be here until the stars come out. You'd be tired and we'd both be hungry and you wouldn't like that, would you? Would that be fun?"

"Mmmhmm," she says. "I love golf."

I look at her, surprised. Last summer whenever I saw her with Torie and her brother she was always walking along, never with club in hand, always watching, waiting, turning a cartwheel here, doing a pirouette there, doing her best to entertain herself while the others golfed. "I'll tell you what," I say, "next spring, before school's even out, the first warm day, maybe even as early as March, we'll get you swinging."

"You'll be gone."

"Not then," I say.

"Promise?"

"Count on it," I say.

I pick up her plastic bag of balls and she takes it as her cue to go. As I watch her walk away, her soaked shoes kicking gravel absently from the cart path as she goes along, I realize my mistake. "Hey," I call to her, "Slingshot." I wave her back.

"What do you say you take a few swings right now?"

"I can't," she says. "I forgot."

"You forgot?"

She nods emphatically.

"Well, then, you're right on your way," I say. " 'Learn and forget,' have you ever heard that?" She shakes her head. "I got a letter just a couple of days ago from my own teacher, and that's what she said. No kidding." But with her, though true, that's as far as I go. A letter had, in fact, come from Michigan in the now familiar nearly illegible script: "The golfer, like the musician, must always learn and forget. Because only in forgetting can we feel the music, can we feel the swing, can we feel the song—the place where the harmony and the rhythm of the body equals that of the soul."

I save this and instead say, "Come on. Tee it up!"

I go to my bag and find some tees and, sparing hers, a few balls. With Pinseeker she steps up and without a word I readjust her hold on the club. "You're set," I say.

"But I forgot," she says and fidgets.

"Ah, be one of those who's not afraid to draw it back," I say, echoing Gloria Armstrong. "You know golf. Golf at its best is like singing." And then much more to my surprise I hear myself say, "Just reach for the stars, shoot for the moon, it's easy." And in that moment, with a greased, charmed, effortless might, she gathers all of her spare self and slings the ball heavenward—up, up, out over Thistledown; up, on, out into tomorrow.

Index